Rattlesnakes and Rainbows

Daily Devotions Along the Trail of Life

by

Theodore E. Allwardt

May these devotions help you daily look to Jesus Who goes with us on the trail of life.

Theodore E. Allwardt

Published by
Rattlesnakes and Rainbows
Monticello, New Mexico

Library of Congress Control Number: 2003093852

ISBN 0-9741630-0-7

First Printing: June 2003

Additional copies of this book are available by mail from the publisher:
Rattlesnakes and Rainbows
c/o Theodore E. Allwardt
P. O. Box 12
Monticello, NM 87939
505/743-0121
One copy: $12.00 – two or more copies: $10.00 each
(U.S.A. taxes, postage included; Canada – contact publisher)
Additional discounts available for congregations and church organizations.

Printed in the U.S.A. by

Morris Publishing
3212 East Highway 30
Kearney, NE 68847
1-800-650-7888

With thanks to Him
Who has given me

Marian

as my helper and trail companion
for more than forty years

Acknowledgments

Except for a few quotations from the King James Version the translation of the Bible used for this book is:

The Holy Bible, *An American Translation*
by William F. Beck,
Leader Publishing Company
New Haven, Missouri
Fourth Edition, 2000
Used by permission of the publisher,
Lutheran News, Inc.

The devotions for February, June, and July were originally published in edited form (February – October 1993, June – August 1987, July – August 1990) in *Portals of Prayer,* copyright © Concordia Publishing House. Used by permission.

Front Cover: painting by Lara Nock, Monticello, New Mexico

At The Trail Head

I am honored that you have chosen me to be your companion and guide as you travel your trail of life during this coming year. Perhaps you will even continue with me in future years, since I have written this book of devotions for possible repeated use (this is why the Holy Week devotions and other special days are listed separately – see "Trails Map" – so they can be used at the appropriate time of any year).

Before we begin, I want to explain the ideas which guided my writing of these devotions. First of all is the name, "Rattlesnakes and Rainbows". The day after purchasing land outside the almost "ghost town" (some perhaps call it that because it has no businesses in it, not even a bar) of Monticello, New Mexico, we saw a five-foot western diamonback rattlesnake and then a little later the brilliant arc of a rainbow just above the mountain ridge across our arroyo valley. That made it easy to name the place, which has become our retirement home: "Rattlesnakes and Rainbows" (or, "RnR" for short), especially when we thought of the symbolism involved. The rattlesnake reminded us of the Garden of Eden with its temptation snake, which has brought sin and trouble for us all ever since. The rainbow reminded us of God's mercy and promise to Noah after the Flood, and so it serves as a symbol for all of His help and blessing.

We all face so many "rattlesnakes" along the trail of life: temptations and troubles. But we also have so many "rainbow" blessings from our God: help, guidance, protection, and especially His forgiveness through His Son, Jesus, the Savior. I have written these devotions to help us guard against the "rattlesnakes" and be thankfully aware of the "rainbows" the Lord gives us.

These devotions are written primarily as though we are talking as companions on a trail and to make them easier to read aloud with family or other group. Every devotion is based on an actual experience for my wife and myself or it is my personal reflection on some common event, which very likely you also may have experienced.

Just as one usually begins a hike in the morning hours, so I encourage you to use these devotions in the morning as you begin your day's "hike" so that the thoughts from God's Word might perhaps be of special help or guidance for you that day.

Our hike along life's trail this year will take us through much of the Bible. I've used a different theme verse for each devotion. Also, the suggested Bible readings are not related to each day's devotion, but will have us read all of the New Testament as well as many selected chapters of the Old Testament. Please note: we read the Gospel of Matthew in December, as Advent begins, which then makes the first words of the Gospel of Mark quite fitting for January 1: *"Beginning the good news about Jesus Christ, God's Son"*. I have not suggested a daily psalm reading for two reasons: first, there are not enough psalms to fill the entire year, and, second, many psalms have thoughts that do not easily relate to our daily lives (every psalm is God's Word and has meaning for us, but if it takes too much time or effort to figure out how some verses can apply to us personally, it can become merely "a duty to read" instead of spiritual help).

This book began with three months of devotions which I wrote for the daily devotional booklet, *Portals of Prayer*. So many people (some even from other countries) wrote to me in response, urging me to continue writing devotions, that I decided this was perhaps a special way I could serve the Lord and His people, when I finally retired. I thank Concordia Publishing House for allowing me to use those devotions in this book.

My thanks especially to my wife, Marian, for her proofreading and suggestions and also to other members of our family, who gave me ideas for various devotions.

I pray that the Lord will bless you, as you use these devotions on your trail of life this year, so that each day you will be helped against the "rattlesnakes" and encouraged by the "rainbows", most of all by that best "rainbow" of all, the assurance of your being on the trail that finally reaches eternal life because of Jesus, the Savior.

Theodore E. Allwardt
Monticello, New Mexico

P.S.

As you will notice, these devotions are rather autobiographical in nature: I happened to see a relationship between what happened in my life and the comfort and guidance God gives us in His Word. I encourage you to look at your life experiences in the same way. The trail of life is so much more enjoyable when the events on it remind us of His constant caring, forgiving presence.

Trails Map

At The Trailhead

Beginning the good news about Jesus Christ, God's Son.
Mark 1:1

Unless you have already hiked a trail, at the trailhead you don't really know what that trail will be like. You have an idea from what the trail description says, but you don't know the exact details.

New Year's Day in any culture is like a trailhead. We've completed one trail, and another is waiting for us. None of us knows for sure what this year's trail will hold. We may have some ideas: for some the trail may continue the pressure of burdensome responsibility or crushing heartache or unrelenting illness; for some of us this might be the final trail we take in this life as it turns into the trail of eternal life because of Jesus; for all of us there will be "rattlesnakes": temptations and troubles, sin and problems.

But no matter the "rattlesnakes" we can be sure there will also be "rainbows", blessings: at least some times of joy and peace and contentment with the best "rainbow" being "the good news of Jesus Christ, God's Son".

That good news, which we will need each day on the trail, is that, because we sin each day, we have His forgiveness each day. That's why He also walked the trail of life, which led to His cross: so that we might be in His care and protection and forgiveness daily.

Thank You, Lord Jesus, that on this year's trail You will protect me from the "rattlesnakes" and give me many "rainbows", especially the "rainbow" of Your forgiveness. Amen.

"It's Snowing!"

"Absolutely pointless!" says the preacher. "Absolutely pointless! Everything is pointless!" *Ecclesiastes 1:2*

Perhaps you know someone who is absolutely thrilled when it snows, especially the first snow of the season. "It's snowing!" is her excited exclamation. Snow! How appealing it is as we see it almost magically transforming the landscape.

Soon, however, our feelings change, especially after shoveling that white stuff off sidewalks and driveway a number of times. The thrill just doesn't last.

Nor does the thrill of anything in this life "last". Usually sooner rather than later we begin to take even the most exciting events for granted. Why else do children and even adults gather so many "toys" to play with? Why, also, does "first love" in marriage change so that "the honeymoon is over"?

Especially is this so when we realize that all the things of life, all the relationships, all the accomplishments make no real difference in our lives. They may make us forget aches and pains or distract us from problems for a while. But they do not solve those problems or heal those wounds; and they do not keep us from dying. Truly, the prophet in Ecclesiastes has it absolutely right in saying that everything in life is "pointless!"

Except for one thing in life, rather, one Person: Jesus. He gives life meaning and makes life purposeful, because, by His suffering and death for our sins, He gives us eternal life after this life and the desire now to be helpful to others, which gives us meaning and purpose and satisfaction, as we live day by day.

Jesus, thank You for being my daily companion. Amen.

Each One Unique

The Lord told me: "Before I formed you in the womb, I chose you, and before you were born, I set you aside for My holy purpose." *Jeremiah 1:4-5*

All that snow! How many millions or billions of snowflakes in just one snowstorm? It seems impossible, yet scientists say that each one is unique, different.

All those people! How many billions are on this earth right now? Yet each one is different, unique; even identical twins are not "identical", for each knows: "I am me, not you."

Only God can know each person, for He knows everything. What is more, He has given each person a unique role in life. Jeremiah was to be His prophet. Jesus, of course, was the only One Who could be the Savior, which He is by His perfect life and His paying for the sins of everyone else.

Now God has a role in life for each of us, especially for us who trust in Jesus as our Savior. Although the trail of life right now may seem to be just continuing what we have always been doing, still the Lord will use us in unique ways this year, if we keep our spiritual eyes open to opportunities He places along our trail. No one else will be able to give the specific help we can give to someone whose need we see. No one else will be able to speak of Jesus to someone, as we might be able to do.

Each of us is unique, and each of us has a unique purpose in life according to God's guidance also on this year's trail.

Lord, help me to recognize the special deeds You want me to do this year and to do them as best I can for You. Amen.

Winter Wonderland

Cleanse me from sin with hyssop and I'll be clean; wash me and I'll be whiter than snow. *Psalm 51:7*

The day before was bleak and barren. Then an overnight snow, especially if it came down fluffy and windless, clinging beautifully to the tall pines as it does in north Idaho, turned everything into a winter wonderland. Even mounds of trash don't look so bad with that white stuff camouflaging them: still trash underneath, but effectively hidden.

The sinfulness of our lives is like trash in God's sight, and sin makes the trail of life bleak and barren, too, when left on our consciences and piled as a barrier between us and others.

That's why we need the good message from God that He has washed away our sins through the only One Who actually was "whiter than snow" in His life and then took the dirt of all sin to the cross where God punished Him to forgive us. Now by His forgiveness our individual sins are covered, not with snow, but with the shed blood of Jesus so that in God's sight we, though still sinners, are "whiter than snow".

What is more, by forgiving us, God helps us go to those we've sinned against to ask their forgiveness as well as also to forgive them so these sins don't have to remain like boulders or rocks as we walk life's trail with them. The power of God's "Jesus snow" also guides us in our struggle to do good instead of wrong so that at times we even might seem like a "wonderland" to those we live with and help.

Lord, guide me so that those I live with today will see more of Your "wonderland" than my dirt. Amen.

Get Out The Shovel Again!

In God I trust – I'm not afraid; what can man do to me? I'm under vows to You, O God: I will carry them out by praising You. *Psalm 56:11-12*

After a while all that snow gets to wear out, especially when you have to get out the shovel day after day to clear the way for walking or driving. A necessary routine, but more job than joy!

So much along the trail of life is similar. Daily responsibilities continue no matter how inconvenient or unpleasant: diapers to change, obnoxious people to endure, traffic lights to wait out, bills to pay, health pains to suffer, daily job to go to, or perhaps just time to fill (if you are jobless or retired). Life's trail has moments of beauty and excitement, but it also has just plodding. At times it also can feel more rut than path.

Yet our life's trail has been laid out by our Lord God, and He has included routine ruts of responsibility, as well times of joy, steep climbs as well as gentle slopes.

We could look at our individual trails fatalistically: nothing I can do about it, just have to trudge on. But the Holy Spirit has brought us to see Jesus as our trail companion, and we are committed to following Him. As we remind ourselves that He lived and died so our trail leads to our eternal home, then we can more easily accept also the routine, the unpleasant, even the boring parts of our trail and praise Him by living through these as willingly as possible. In fact, when we choose to see them as part of our following Him, we might even realize more joy than job in doing them.

Jesus, may all I do today be thankful praise to You. Amen.

A Message from the Stars?

I see Him Who is not here now; I behold Him Who will come later. A star will come from Jacob, a Scepter will rise from Israel. *Numbers 24:17*

How impressive the stars are on crisp, clear winter nights, especially from the high desert country of New Mexico: so many, so distant, so bright!

Is there any message in the stars for us on earth? The men we call the "wise men", who came "from the east" to worship the Christ Child, thought so, for they were the astrologers of their culture.

Surely not! Astrology has no truth in it! God controls our lives, not the stars!

Yet sometimes God uses sinful things to work His plans. He uses us sinners to do His will, doesn't He? So, in that year when Jesus was born, He used those astrologers. Somehow they saw "His star", perhaps thinking of the above Bible verse, which probably Jewish descendants of various captivities had talked about.

Still, only God's Word gave them clear guidance: "In Bethlehem (as) the prophet has written," said Herod's priests.

On this Epiphany Day, as January 6th is called, God's Word tells us that Jesus lived and died to be Savior for not only some people, but for all people.

Help me, Lord, to follow only Your Word for guidance in faith and living on the trail of life ahead of me. Amen.

No School! Yippee!

The apostles gathered around Jesus and reported to Him everything they had done and taught. "Now you come away to some deserted place," He told them, "where you can be alone and rest a little." *Mark 6:30-31*

"Due to heavy snow and strong winds all area schools have been canceled today!" said the announcer. "Yippee!" said the kids! They might be bored by mid-day, but now they were excited about an unexpected free day.

What do you do with free time, when you have some? It's easy to waste time: watching "the tube", playing meaningless video games, gossiping. We need time for relaxation and recreation, but just "killing time" is neither fulfilling nor good for us. Instead, if we use time constructively: family talking or playing together, completing a needed project, enjoying a refreshing walk, perhaps briefly visiting a shut-in, probably we will feel better as well as be more energized for what we are required to do.

Jesus also at times went with His disciples to "be alone and rest", as He walked His path of life to the requirement of the cross for us sinners.

Lord, help me use time wisely and helpfully today. Amen.

No School! Oh, No!

I am always looking to the Lord, because He can get my feet out of the trap. *Psalm 25:15*

"Due to heavy snow and strong winds all area schools have been canceled today!" said the announcer. "Oh, no!" said the parents, especially in two-income families. "What will we do with the kids?"

How can we handle suddenly upset schedules or added chores, when there hardly seemed to be enough time to get everything done before? Stress! Yet, getting too worked up about it only increases life's tensions.

The better response to unexpected stress is to remind yourself: "The Lord and I can work it out – somehow!" For with every time-trap "rattlesnake" He allows, the Lord always also provides a way through it. We may have to forego something we wanted to do in order to take care of what we now have to do, but He helps us be willing to make that decision.

As also Jesus was willing to do what had to be done (obey and suffer and die) so we sinners could have not just time, but eternity with Him.

Calm me down, Lord, when stresses come so You and I will find good solutions. Amen.

Fun In the Snow

Peter said to the others, "I'm going fishing." "We're going with you," they told him. *John 21:3*

Beautiful, packable snow! Just right for making snowmen and snow sculptures, snow balls and angel forms! It's amazing how relaxing and enjoyable such inexpensive fun can be, even for adults.

So often in our money-obsessed culture, adults as well as children distain simple things in preference for expensive "toys" which insulate the "players" from each other. Television also is usually isolating entertainment.

There is nothing wrong in such recreation as such. More contentment and satisfaction comes, however, from activities which require imagination, creativity, and personal interaction.

He Who sent His Son to save us made us also to play with each other more than just be by ourselves so that even our "fun" will be mutually helpful.

Thank You, Lord, for people I can share relaxing times with. Amen.

Fun On the Snow and Ice

I am the Lord your God, Who took you out of Egypt, where you were slaves. Do not have any other gods before Me. *Deuteronomy 5:6-7*

Get to those ski slopes! Dig that ice fishing hole! Roar that snowmobile! Ahh, exciting winter fun! On the beautiful snow in the icy crisp air! Healthful exercise!

Unless it begins to enslave us, demanding too much of our time and finances! Even good activities can become "rattlesnakes", if they compete with God for our allegiance so that we neglect His guidance received in public worship for our daily living.

We can enjoy anything in life that isn't sinful as long as we keep Him ahead of everything else.

For He is most important by not only having made us, but especially by having taken our sins off our record before Him by His Son having absorbed His cold judgment into the warmth of His shed blood.

Lord, help me so that nothing today or any day becomes more important to me than You. Amen.

Bundled Up for 40° Below

You are all God's children through faith in Christ Jesus, because all of you who were baptized into Christ have put on Christ. *Galatians 3:26-27*

One winter in North Dakota the sweatshirts said: "40° below keeps the riffraff out!" Truly, to survive such bone-freezing cold temperatures you have to be bundled up sufficiently against frostbite – and worse!

Objectively it seems that nothing can protect us from the devil's threats since we are totally exposed to his claims on us by our daily sinning. Truly we should belong to him in hell forever.

But God's message says: Jesus has paid for our sins by His death on the cross and His "parka" of righteousness, specifically applied to us when He had us baptized, completely covers and protects us. The devil may howl, but we are safe – as long as we remain inside His forgiveness through faith.

Lord, keep me in faith in Jesus today and each day as it comes. Amen.

Got to Stay Awake

Some refused to listen to their conscience and suffered shipwreck in their faith. *1 Timothy 1:19*

When marooned out in 40° below because of a car breakdown, no matter how bundled up you've got to stay awake and keep moving. Just to go to sleep invites death, because eventually the cold can get to you and through you.

We are "bundled up" in the protecting warmth of God's love for us in Jesus. But we also can "go to sleep" spiritually by taking our faith for granted. Although it can happen to anyone, especially is this a temptation if we've been in faith since childhood and never have known the hopelessness of unbelief. We can fall into the rut of just being a "church member", attending worship without much attention, praying the same prayers day after day without much thinking, going through the motions of mere dutiful living. That's when faith can easily become mere words we say, but without actual commitment.

So we need to "keep awake" in our faith by daily admitting to ourselves as well as to God specific sins we've done that day and humbly thanking Jesus that He took care of also those specific sins along with all our sins by His cross death. Then we ask His help to "keep moving" on the trail of life He has given us by trying to be faithful to His guidance day by day.

Lord, I admit now and to You these specific sins from this day and yesterday: _____. Thank You that You have forgiven me because of Jesus; help me follow You more faithfully today. Amen.

Meaning What You Pray

When you pray, don't babble like pagans, who think they'll be heard if they talk a lot. Don't be like them.
Matthew 6:7-8

Given how often we use the Lord's Prayer, we usually say it as ritual rather than pray it with meaning. Perhaps the following thoughts to think about will help you mean the words you say of the Lord's Prayer.

Our Father, Who art in heaven
Lord, I know You can and want to help me.
Hallowed be Thy Name
Help me believe Your teachings.
Thy kingdom come
Help me obey Your commands.
Thy will be done on earth as it is in heaven
Help me accept Your plan for my life.
Give us this day our daily bread
Thank You for all Your blessings to me.
And forgive us our trespasses as we forgive those who trespass against us
Thank You for forgiving me and help me not to hold grudges.
And lead us not into temptation
Help me fight the temptations that attack.
But deliver us from evil
Help me endure the troubles that come.
For Thine is the kingdom and the power and the glory forever and ever.
You are in control and so I praise You.
Amen.
Yes, I know You will help me.

Lord, help me truly "pray" all my prayers. Amen.

Preventing Frozen Water Pipes

Make my steps firm by Your Word, and don't let wrong have control over me. *Psalm 119:133*

When the temperatures get low enough for long enough, the frost line can get down far enough to freeze a house's water lines. Even the slight warmth of a steady dribble of water, however, will prevent this inconvenience, which can be quite costly to remedy.

Receiving a steady daily dose of the warmth of God's love helps to prevent our faith in Jesus from "freezing". We receive a "dribble" of that warmth as we admit our sinfulness and thank Jesus for having paid the penalty for all of our sins.

But He wants us to have more than just a "dribble", so He can better "make our steps firm" for doing good instead of wrong. He gives this as we read His Word and a devotion, such as this one, based on a part of His Word.

Of course, His power will not affect us much if we only read words without trying to follow them. Instead, His power works when throughout the day we try to remember what His Word has said, not just about living, but especially that, no matter how well we might follow His guidance, our only hope and our assurance is in Jesus Who walked His path firmly without the slightest misstep in order to save us from our sin stumbles.

Lord, help me keep You and Your love in Jesus in my thoughts all during this day so that I will follow Your guidance better. Amen.

A Night of Dead Batteries

"Father," the son told him, "I've sinned against heaven and against you. I don't deserve to be called your son anymore." *Luke 16:21*

That night was so cold that few cars at the Fargo airport parking lot would start – batteries were dead! But powerful charges from the AAA trucks got them started and on the way home.

Sometimes for some people faith goes dead – perhaps someone you know or even you yourself have experienced that. For whatever reason – neglecting to use God's Word, hurt deeply by the loveless actions of a "Christian" who did not live according to faith at all, accepting the intellectual arguments of unbelievers, living in evil – faith can die.

How was your faith brought back to life (if you once lost it)? What can you do to help a former follower of Jesus return to Him? Nothing! You can't! Only the outside power of God's Holy Spirit can re-ignite a dead faith.

Yet He has to use His people to reach someone now lost. So He wants us, gently but clearly, to tell people that unbelief means eternal separation from God, but He has provided the connection back to Himself through the outstretched arms of Jesus on the cross. By means of such words the Holy Spirit just might be able to bring that person's "faith battery" to life again.

Make me aware, Lord, of someone who has lost faith and give me courage to speak words which You can use to bring that person back to You for eternal life. Amen.

The Silent Killer

His master was so angry he handed him over to the torturers until he would pay all he owed him. That is how My Father in heaven will do to you if each of you will not heartily forgive his brother. *Matthew 18:34-35*

"Be sure your gas chimney and other vents are not blocked," warned the announcement. Frost buildup on them from the blustery North Dakota winter winds can send carbon monoxide, the silent killer, down into the house to kill sleeping people without warning.

Refusing to forgive someone who has sinned against you is a silent spiritual killer. The *sinn-ee* has good reason to be hurt and angry at what the *sinn-er* has done. One cannot just automatically forget the pain that still throbs, whether from a broken nose, a shattered heart, or a depleted checkbook. And so the thoughts of "pay back" swirl and intensify until a real grudge is born. One might say, "I forgive", but lurking still is the "I'm going to get you someday" determination.

Which kills faith without the person realizing it! One still says: "I believe"; but Jesus warns that anyone who refuses to forgive cannot be forgiven. Hopeless? Not when we keep reminding ourselves how God forgives us for Jesus' sake. His forgiving us *all* our sins then gives us the power also, no matter how hurt we still feel, to forgive – for Jesus' sake.

To forgive doesn't mean we immediately forget. Instead, forgiving is to be kind and helpful in spite of remembering – which we can do only "for Jesus' sake".

Help me, Lord, to forgive others – for Jesus' sake. Amen.

Need Another Blanket?

Then He told Thomas, "Put your finger here, and look at My hands – and take your hand and put it in My side. And don't doubt but believe." *John 20:27*

As temperatures plummet, before going to bed one might wonder: Do I need another blanket to keep warm enough tonight?

In a sense the apostle Thomas needed more than just what the other apostles had told him about Jesus having risen from the dead. However, Jesus, instead of condemning him for his weakness (although He did scold him a little: "Do you believe because you've seen Me? Blessed are those who have not seen and yet have believed." *John 20:29*), Jesus came especially to have Thomas touch Him so his doubts would vanish.

Words from God's Word should be enough – and they really are. But at times in our human weakness we feel that we need "something extra" spiritually. So Jesus comes to touch us with His very Body and Blood in Holy Communion. This touch assures us: I know you and all your sins, which is why I gave Myself, this Body, this Blood, for you – so, yes, you *have* My forgiveness; also, I will be with you always to strengthen you in your life for Me.

What a "rainbow" Holy Communion is for us! Which Jesus wants us to receive regularly so we always have the "extra" which we need.

Thank You, Jesus, that the touch of Your very Body and Blood does comfort and strengthen me and give me peace. Amen.

January 18   Read: Luke 1

A Path Through the Snow

This is what you were called for, seeing that Christ also suffered for you and left you an example for you to follow in His steps. *1 Peter 2:21*

When snow has piled up on an unshoveled sidewalk, it's tough going to walk through it – unless someone has already come that way, leaving steps to follow (and the bigger the easier).

The path of life often gets difficult as temptations and troubles, suffering and stress pile up. The "rainbow" for us is that Jesus has experienced even more of such "snow" than we ever could, and He has left us His "steps" to walk in.

When suffering, His example teaches: leave it in the hands of God and trust He knows His good plan for you. When tempted, His example says: use a specific Bible verse to guide and strengthen you. When stressed out, His example assures: you can relax in My protection and care. When facing great challenge, His example reminds: pray. When despairing over failure, His example comforts: trust Me to help you recover.

In our human weakness we never can follow His example completely. Being our loving Shepherd, however, Jesus does not leave us "stuck in the snow bank", but pulls us out with His loving assurance of daily forgiveness and ever-present aid.

Help me to better follow in Your steps, Lord, no matter what I must face this day. Amen.

Feeding the Birds

The eyes of all look to You, and You give them their food at the right time; You open Your hand to satisfy every living thing with what it wants. *Psalm 145:15-16*

Wintertime bird feeding really helps the birds, whose food sources are limited because of snow cover. Usually they could survive on their own, but the Lord uses the compassion of people to more easily satisfy their needs, especially in very severe weather.

Most of the time the Lord supplies the needs of people not directly, but through the help that others provide. This is true not only for children, the incapacitated elderly, the ill, the poor; it's also true for us. None of us exists completely independently. We need supermarkets for our food, service stations to fuel our vehicles, law enforcement officers, employers – and employees, too – all the various people who in some way provide what we need in life. The Lord helps us through others.

And the Lord uses us to help others. No matter your occupation or role on life's trail, you are His method of reaching others with His help. Not that you can supply everyone's needs fully. But the situation you are in is by His placement and is a vocation, a service to God by how we help.

Which can wear out! He, however, keeps giving us time and ability and sufficient resources so we can give some help to at least some – which we want to do as we remember His great help in our greatest need: forgiveness of sins because of Jesus.

Keep me remembering, Lord, that I am Your tool when I help other people and even the winter-feeding birds. Amen.

Blizzard: The Sound of Death

Don't go in the way of the wicked or walk in the path of evil people. *Proverbs 4:14*

The blizzard had lessened – at least in the city, and he had to get home. But when he saw the wind-driven snow across the countryside, he heard the sound of death – he knew he never would see home, if he tried. And driving the next day, he saw five- and ten-foot drifts, which would have entombed him.

Usually on the path of life "the sound of (spiritual) death" is muted by outward appearances or our inner desires. What can be wrong in going to a party with friends even if there might be alcohol or other drugs involved? It's just harmless flirting with an attractive co-worker, isn't it? True, some friends don't care anything about the Lord, but they are so much fun to be with. Sure, I have to skip worship, but my team depends on me.

Not that any of these activities automatically kill one's faith in Jesus. But alert spiritual ears can hear at least a faint "sound of death", whenever one wants to participate in something which somewhat conflicts with God's way. Have any of us never been guilty of having taken at least a few steps along one or more spiritually dangerous paths?

If Jesus had not heard "the sound of death" in each of the temptations He faced, it would have meant eternal death for us. But He always stayed on His Father's path so that He could forgive our wrong turns and finally bring us home.

Help me be honest with myself, Lord, so I don't close my ears to "the sound of death" in order to do what I want even though it isn't quite right. Amen.

The Fresh Morning After

The Lord is gracious; we're not completely wiped out, because His mercies ... are new every morning – great is Your faithfulness. *Lamentations 3:22-23*

The morning after a blizzard or heavy snowstorm can be spectacular! Crisp clear air! Beautiful white snow hiding ugly trash heaps! Even awesome snowdrifts, at times surrounding individual houses!

Every morning we awaken to a spectacular day of God's love for us! No matter what the previous day of sin has been – no matter how guilty we might still feel over long-past (and forgiven – how foolishly and unnecessarily we so often let guilt still torment us) evils, each day the Lord says to us: Of course I know your record of sin and that you still have your ugly, rebellious sinful nature; but I gave all that to My Son on the cross so those are gone from My sight, and I see only His perfection covering you to make you pure before Me like fresh-fallen snow.

Which does not mean: if past sin and evil are gone – and will be gone each morning, I don't have to be concerned about whether I sin or not. Such attitude is rebellion, not faith.

Instead, God's fresh mercies humble us and increase in us the thankful determination to follow His path even better this brand-new day than yesterday.

Lord, thank You for the peace You give me because of Jesus so that I can leave my sins in the past and concentrate today on thanking You for Your daily faithfulness by how I live. Amen.

The Gift of Life

You created my inner being and wove me together in my mother's womb. I thank You for how marvelously and wonderfully I am made. *Psalm 139:13-14*

What a miracle! How marvelously God made each of us in our mother's womb from two almost microscopically small cells! Truly He has created us! But when did "you" actually become "you"? When did you become a separate person, a living "soul"? Only when you were born? Or only when you began to look like a human?

What about Jesus? When did He become human? Not at His birth, for God's angel told Joseph months in advance: "Her Child *is* from the Holy Spirit" *(Matthew 1:20)*. Jesus, eternal God, received His humanity when He was conceived in Mary's womb by the power of God the Holy Spirit. Which means that also you became "you", when you were conceived.

How many children have been killed through abortion? How many of those abortive mothers now grieve for a child, whom she could have birthed, but chose not to for whatever reason?

Which leads us to pray that more and more individuals will value God's gift of life and preserve it. May we also pray for and comfort those who mourn in guilt over the abortions they have had. The good news is that Jesus died for every sin and evil; no matter how guilty one might feel, He says: You can have peace, because I gave Myself also for every wrong you ever have done and still will do. Which is the only comfort any of us can have.

Thank You, Lord, for the gift of life – and of peace. Amen.

Driving in Near Blizzard

Help me as You promised so that I may live, and don't let me be disappointed in my hope. *Psalm 119:116*

Sometimes you just might have to make a trip even in near blizzard conditions - perhaps to the hospital or your job or for some other emergency. What a stressful drive that is! You glue your eyes to the center stripe – you flinch as the car hits small snowdrifts – you pray other drivers are being as alert as you are. Yes, you pray – as you trust the Lord's protection.

Whether under such weather conditions or facing other extremely stressful situations, prayer and trust help us get through what has to be done: perhaps it is surgery with no assured outcome – perhaps a chemotherapy treatment regime – perhaps a soldier off to war – perhaps a fireman facing an inferno – perhaps trying to resolve a family estrangement – perhaps having to give a presentation in front of a hostile audience. The Lord does not promise such trials will not confront us on our life's trail.

But He has promised His help. And we can count on His help, since He has already helped us so that we have eternal hope by giving us Jesus to take us past our sinfulness into His everlasting presence.

So we pray – and we keep alert to depend on His promises as well as His guiding words because of how stressed we might be.

Whether life is greatly stressed today or not, help me always to depend on Your promises of help and protection and forgiveness. Amen.

Black Ice!

If you think you stand, be careful that you don't fall.
1 Corinthians 10:12

One very dangerous winter condition, whether on highway or sidewalk, is black ice! No matter how alert, you can't always spot it. Often nothing happens; but at times your car suddenly slides out of control with possible disastrous results, or, you find yourself flat on your back with perhaps a broken hip.

Sudden temptation can make you fall, too. Unjust treatment might spark violent anger to lash out with fist or kick or worse. Irritated weariness can express itself in cruel words. Pornography is only a computer click away. Friends can challenge your faithful path of life with a sneer. Credit cards can make it easy to impulsively buy more than you can afford. A stubbed toe might incite curse words. Self-righteous thoughts can flare up when learning of someone's evil doing: "I would never do *that*" – but haven't we done "*the other*" of sin? How quickly we can give in to sudden temptation!

So the Lord warns us not to be over-confident in our faith, not to depend on our own ability, when tempted. Instead, we must always be humbly aware that only His power from His Word, which we try to keep in mind, can keep us in faithfulness. Which we don't do perfectly: we never live even one perfect day without falling somewhat.

That is why we daily need that comforting Word of forgiveness through Jesus to pick us up and encourage us as we continue to walk His way.

Keep me alert today, Lord, to struggle against temptation, no matter how sudden or unexpected. Amen.

I'm Going to Hit Him!

People are appointed to die once and after that the judgment, so Christ also was sacrificed once to take away the sins of many people. *Hebrews 9:27-28*

The last conscious thought he had, as the pickup crossed in front of him, was: "I'm going to hit him!" By God's plan his next conscious thought was: "Can I open the door to get out?" But in-between he had no awareness of the crash, the airbag, the swerving of the vehicles into a light pole.

Some accident victims have only that one last thought: "I'm going to hit him" with no more earthly thoughts at all: sudden death comes with no time for preparation, no time to come to faith in Jesus for entrance to eternal life. The same is true with an immediately fatal heart attack, aneurysm, or stroke.

To have faith, however, does not mean one is consciously thinking of Jesus every moment. If it did, then every time you go to sleep, you would not have faith. Instead, faith is that over-all dependence on Him as the only One Who can take us safely to and past the judgment of God into His promised blessings. The more we keep Him as our Savior on at least the edge of our minds, the better we will follow Him. But He knows our faith even when our minds are engrossed in living.

Some are afraid to fly because of the danger of sudden death. But every time we drive, we are, as someone said, "only an inch away" (turning the wheel an inch too far) from sudden death. So, when traveling by any means, we place ourselves in His hands – for time and for eternity. That is our daily faith.

Lord, thank You for watching over me eternally through Jesus, as well as in whatever happens this day. Amen.

Wood Heats Only Twice?

Come, let us sing joyfully to the Lord; let us shout happily to the Rock Who saves us. *Psalm 95:1*

Most people can't enjoy the comfort of wood heat: not enough burnable trees, air quality problems, no time for the wood gathering, no storage space once you have it. Also, many who could have it, don't want to put up with the inconvenience involved, for traditional wood heat doesn't respond to a thermostat. Many, however, prefer its steady warmth: once warm, a room stays warm without furnace fan fluctuations.

Traditionally people say: "Wood heats you twice: when you get it and when you burn it." Actually, it heats you much more often: not only getting and burning, but also sawing, splitting, stacking, bringing it in, and finally taking the ashes out! Each piece of that "solid sunshine" generates lots of heat!

The warmth of God's love doesn't give a comfort limited to when you first realize you have His forgiveness because of Jesus and then only whenever you really feel guilty. Instead, His forgiveness is continual – which we realize when we daily admit we need it because our sinning is not just minor, but each sin deserves eternal punishment.

In addition, God's love extends beyond forgiveness into every part of our lives: His blessing to give us all we have – His help whenever "rattlesnakes" of temptation or trouble strike – His protection in danger – His healing from sickness or His strength to endure it – His guidance for our path of life. All of which is why we thank Him joyfully with word and song and life no matter how troubled life might actually be.

Thank You, Lord, for the on-going warmth of Your love for me. Amen.

Will It Never End?

In my trouble I call on the Lord and He answers me. O Lord, save me from lips that lie and from tongues that deceive. *Psalm 120:1-2*

As a winter stretches on and on with no let up from freezing temperature, blustery winds, and never-melting snow and ice, one might wonder bitterly: will it never end?   We sometimes ask the same about lengthy illness, financial hardship, family unrest, neighborhood conflict, or other on-going troubles.

We who try to follow God's path for life sometimes also have to bear on-going persecution by those who seem to delight in opposing what we believe and how we live. At times this happens, as some pastors and members experience, within one's own congregation, where all should be united and delighted in working together for the Lord, but where some constantly are finding fault or otherwise showing their dislikes.   Perhaps you have so suffered and asked: will it never end?

Or have you ever been guilty of causing such heartache? Has a pastor, a family member, a neighbor, a co-worker been the object of your nit-picking or gossipy attacks?

If you are one of the sufferers, you can only pray the Lord's help to endure – and to keep you away from retaliation, even if it's only sinful thoughts during nights when you lie awake hurting. If you should be one of the hurters, examine yourself and pray the Lord will change you to act with Christian kindness to everyone. And He Who earned forgiveness for both sufferer and hurter promises to help each, as needed.

Lord, help me endure what I must – and help me never be one of the hurters, no matter how much I am tempted.   Amen.

Cabin Fever

Trust the Lord with all your heart and don't depend on your understanding. *Proverbs 3:5*

An extremely severe and long winter can infect people with "cabin fever". They become irritable, depressed, fidgety, short-tempered, gloomy – the walls of the house seem to be closing in – nothing seems worthwhile. Have you ever experienced this?

Perhaps you have – or will – not because of winter, but because of being shut in for a while by illness or permanently with physical limitations which will never let you get back to normal activity. "What's the point of living? Why? Why me?" you might ask. "Why me?" also can invade our thoughts, when our situation is far less serious than permanent disability, for we all have the tendency to self-pity.

Only rarely can we find an answer to the "Why me?" question, even if our condition resulted from our own carelessness or sinful action (because many others acted exactly the same and are physically unscathed). We need to recognize first, however, that this is not God's punishment; He punished Jesus for all the sins of all of us – the only punishment left is hell for those who refuse to let Him forgive them.

Instead of wanting answers to feed our understanding, we need to deal with our realities through our trust that God allowed and even guided this condition as part of His plan for our individual lives. We know we can trust Him because of Jesus. So, how can we now serve Him in spite of any limitations we have to put up with?

Lord, help me trust Your Son and Your plan for me whatever my limitations. Amen.

January Thaw

He sends His word and melts the ice, makes the wind blow and the waters flow. *Psalm 147:18*

Most winters in most cold areas will have a January thaw. For a day or so daytime temperatures rise above freezing, the sun shines, snow and ice begin to melt, and cold-hardened people even go outside in shirt sleeves! Everyone knows that winter isn't over, but what a "rainbow" to enjoy right now with the assurance that winter will not last forever!

For most of us the trail of life sometimes gets to be more "trial" than "trail". Maybe many "rattlesnakes" of trouble or opposition continually strike at you – maybe life has become a rut of boredom in the monotony of routine. Life feels "blah"!

But every once in a while the Lord will show us at least a little "rainbow", a blessing to enjoy. It might be as ordinary as a child's hug or a friend's smile. It might be a compliment from a spouse, who usually criticizes or says nothing. It might be feeling at least a little better health-wise. It might be completing a long-worked-on project. It might be that "January thaw" or the beauty of softly falling snow. Whatever the "rainbow", how important to remember, to treasure it, since life rarely suddenly or completely changes from "trial" to "trail".

Our greatest treasure, the One we have every day, is Jesus and what He has done to save us. But the Lord also gives us those little extra "treasures" to lift our spirits, as we notice and remember them.

Lord, help me notice at least one "January thaw" blessing You place along my trail today. Amen.

The Beauty of Icicles

So if anyone is in Christ, he is a new creation. The old things have passed away. They have become new.
2 Corinthians 5:17

Winter doesn't even need "January thaw" to produce icicles. A little sunshine with just the right outside temperature can melt snow just enough to send a drip that freezes, then another and another until a glistening icicle hangs down, a crystal clear beauty, sculptured one drop at a time.

The warmth of God's love gradually melts our cold hearts to form us eventually into a new creation of spiritual beauty. First comes His hot love through His Law to melt down our defenses of our sinning, so that His warm message of Jesus as Savior makes us new in His sight: He sees us now, not as the sinners we are, but as beautiful as fresh-fallen snow, for He forgives us.

But neither we nor others see us that way all at once. Much sinful slush mars our "snow-coat" of being forgiven. So the Lord keeps using His warm love through His Word, as we read it and hear it and think daily of His forgiveness, to gradually make us become as beautiful as, not icicles, but as beautiful as the crocus or the snowdrop flower, which stick their little blossoms through a late winter snow to brighten dreary days.

We wish our becoming new would go more quickly, especially when sometimes we seem to "freeze back" into some ugly sin which we despise. But we remember how He sees us and how He is gradually working in us, so we are thankful when even we can see a little new "beauty".

Don't let me make excuses for my sinning, Lord; work in me so that others can see at least some of Your beauty through me. Amen.

The Flight of Snowbirds

In this body we sigh as we long to put on and live in the body we get from heaven. *2 Corinthians 5:2*

Bird migrations take place in spring and fall. "Snowbirds", however, migrate during the winter months. Northerners, wanting to escape at least some of the cold and snow, flock to southern states, especially Arizona and Florida, Texas and New Mexico, for a few weeks or months of warmer temperatures. Of course, some southern winters are not so comfortable; then they get teased about why they had to bring their weather with them!

Which only proves that no place on earth is "paradise". We want peace and comfort and enjoyment. But the harsh realities of life are everywhere, not so much bad weather as health conditions, personal conflicts, and especially sin; sooner or later the "Rattlesnake" ruins every "garden of Eden".

Our continual search for better living conditions is not just a desire to escape trouble; it flows from the longing everyone has for an eternal home of blessing. Some believe that after this life, there will be nothing. But why, then, does every culture have some kind of religion to reach some kind of after life? The challenge is: how to get there!

Every religion except one says: It's up to you to deserve it by the good you do or the punishment you suffer! The one exception is God's good message: You can't – your sinning keeps you out! But I have provided the way in through My Son, Who did enough good and suffered enough punishment to let you enter My eternal paradise. Jesus is our eternal confidence! Because of Him we joyfully follow the path of life He gives us.

Help me make the best of today, Lord, as it brings me one day closer to Your Paradise. Amen.

Into The Desert Of Life*

Then the Spirit led Jesus into the wilderness to be tempted by the devil. *Matthew 4:1*

"I could never live in the desert," he had told himself. But the Lord does not listen to what we think. So he was called to work for Him in the high desert country of New Mexico. There he soon found that it not only was part of God's kingdom, but also a special part of His creation to enjoy. The secret was to see what is instead of to long for what was somewhere else.

Life itself can become a desert. At times it is easy – and smooth as peaches and cream. Usually it's more like roses with some thorns. But sometimes life feels more like falling into cactus prickers! Illness, accident, heartache, or the effects of age can make life seem as desolate as a desert!

Especially do we despair that we've come into the desert of life when we are tempted to sorrow for what was or to lust for what will never be.

Yet, God helps us endure as we use His Word, especially His assurance that through Jesus, Who came into this world of evil to save us, we have forgiveness for all our sins, even for our self- pity. His promises of being with us and controlling all that comes also helps us see the little "rainbows" He gives even when all might seem bleak.

Help me endure, Lord, when You have allowed life to feel like a desert. Amen.

* Edited versions of these February devotions were originally published in **Portals of Prayer**, October 1993.

Truth Or Consequences?

He who believes and is baptized will be saved, but he who doesn't believe will be damned. *Mark 16:16*

Yes, there actually is a town named "Truth or Consequences". Re-named in 1950 for the Ralph Edwards radio program of that time, T or C (as New Mexicans call it) is situated on the Rio Grande river in southwestern New Mexico.

What a sober spiritual reminder that name is! God's Word teaches: either believe My truth about Jesus being the only Savior or you will suffer the consequences of your sinning: eternal damnation.

What a waste that so many people reject this truth, because Jesus has already suffered the consequences for the sins of everybody, but His work does not benefit anyone who refuses to believe it.

Since we trust Him and know that He forgives our sins and will give us eternal life, we have a responsibility to all the others for whom He suffered and died, especially to those whom we already know as friends. God has put them into our lives so that first we can show them by our deeds that we "know the truth". Then they will perhaps be able to hear as we tell them why we live the way we do: because of our Savior.

Help me show my faith, Lord, so those who know me will want to have You, too. Amen.

The Land Of Enchantment

He (the Holy Spirit) will come and convict the world of sin, righteousness, and judgment. *John 16:8*

New Mexico's state motto is: "The Land of Enchantment". The sky, the air, the mountains, the desert, the open spaces, the mixture of cultures all work together to make many people quickly agree: "I can't exactly explain it, but it is enchanting."

Can we explain why we believe God's message that Jesus is our Savior? It has to do with realizing the guilt of our sinning; but many people feel guilty yet do not believe. It surely is not just a decision of human reason; for many hear the very same words yet do not believe. So, why do some believe and not others?

No answer can be given – except that the Holy Spirit causes some to trust in Jesus to forgive them while others absolutely refuse to believe that this can be true for them.

The Holy Spirit does not, however, do this "in a vacuum". He uses the means of His Word: the Law to make us see our need and the Gospel to make us depend on our Savior.

His Word also keeps us in this faith, as long as we keep using it. Which is why God commands us to hear it publicly preached each week.

Lord, bless the preaching of Your Word in all Christian churches; and help me willingly attend each week. Amen.

With A Little Imagination

We didn't follow any clever myths when we told you about the power of our Lord Jesus Christ and His coming. No, with our own eyes we saw His majesty. *2 Peter 1:16*

Just outside of T or C are Turtleback Mountain and Elephant Butte. With a little imagination you can actually see a turtle on the mountain ridge and an elephant in that butte.

Many so-called scholars say that the Christian message is just the product of human imagination, "myth" they term it, not actual history. Isn't it amazing that already the New Testament specifically denies that the apostles spoke any "myths"? To those who refuse to believe, there can be no proof. But we who do depend on Jesus know that God's message deals in facts.

There is the fact of our sinning. Who dares to deny that each of us sins every single day? Our suspicious thoughts, our unkind words, our selfish deeds, our failures to do good when we have the opportunity – these are just samples of the fact of our sinning.

But better is the fact of the peace we know because of this message about Jesus. Somehow we can relax in God's presence, and we can even tell our guilty conscience pangs to be quiet, because God's Word assures us that Jesus has taken care of all our sins there on the cross.

Such are the facts of faith, which then carry over into the facts of Christian living.

Thanks, Lord, for faith based on facts. Amen.

Seeing What You Look For

You meant to do me harm, but God meant to do good.
Genesis 50:20

Some people look at the desert and see only bleakness, desolation, dry dirt. Others see a variety of plants and animals, found nowhere else, with subtle variations to appreciate – and the vastness! and the light! What you see usually depends on what you are looking for.

Some people look at life and see only trouble and evil and ugly. Some days that's also what we see: the negatives, the "rattlesnakes", even though God's blessings and forgiveness are still with us those days. It depends on what we are willing to look for.

One of God's great promises to His children is to work in each day of our lives for good, good for us and for others. But why should we believe that promise, especially when some days don't seem to have any good in them?

We *can* believe Him, because we know the greatest good He has already worked for us: the suffering and death of His Son. How could that be "good"? It gives us eternal life, as we trust that what He did on His cross was for us.

That's why we don't have to see only the "rattlesnakes" in life. Though we can't deny them, we also keep looking to see how He is working for good in what happens, just as He has promised.

Thank You, Lord, for assuring me that You are working; help me see it today, if possible. Amen.

Spectacular Desert Beauty

Who is a God like You? You forgive sin and pass by the wrong of the remnant of Your own people! *Micah 7:18*

How thrilling to be hiking through the desert and suddenly see a prickly pear cactus in bloom with its brilliant fountain-like flower! At other times after a rainy season the desert's beauty can be absolutely spectacular!

Why? Why such glorious blooms and carpets of color out where few will enjoy them? Some say it is just "nature's way" to attract insects for pollination purposes. But some of those cacti reproduce through root suckers, spreading under the ground, so, why such unneeded beauty? Perhaps it is God's way of still saying: "What I made is good!"

He made us "good" also. But that didn't last long, and daily we show it no longer is true of us humans. Plants and animals do not sin, but we sure do!

Which means that the most spectacular aspect of God to us is not the beauty of His creation, but the wonder of His love. On a cross He showed how much He loved all sinners. By pardoning us daily through our faith in Jesus, He tells us individually: "I love *you*!"

So this day we will appreciate the beauty we might see, but we are most thankful for what a forgiving God He is. And we will try to act in "beautiful" ways toward others for His sake.

Thank You, Lord, for loving sinful me. Help me follow Your way better today so that someone might be attracted to the beauty of Your love in Jesus. Amen.

The Beauty Of Dirt?

The Lord God formed man out of the ground and breathed into his nostrils the breath of life, and so man became a living being. *Genesis 2:7*

The beauty of dirt? You might not believe it until you see all the colors of dirt along a certain stretch of interstate highway through the high desert of New Mexico: red and yellow and gray and brown and various other shades! Yet, it is just dirt!

God said that He made us people out of dirt. How sad that so many treat others like dirt! Prejudice against those of a different skin color, a different nation, or a different Christian church is one way. Meanness toward those who can't defend themselves is another. Rudeness to people one doesn't know or like also fits into this type of sinning. Can anyone say: "I never act that way"?

But we do, at least at times if not oftener, even though "they" are people like us: same blood, same feelings, same Creator, same Savior Who died for all.

Perhaps we will begin to change our attitudes if we think more about His suffering for *our* sins as well as theirs. Especially if we know that someone else loves Jesus, even if not from our church, we can act with friendship instead of automatic suspicion.

Lord, help me not treat anyone, especially not fellow Christians, like dirt. Amen.

Beautiful, Beautiful Rocks

Then, as Christ has welcomed you, welcome one another in order to glorify God. *Romans 15:7*

Many who visit T or C enjoy "rock-hounding", hiking in the desert, along the arroyos, or on the mountains in search of pretty rocks: semi-precious ones, such as carnelians, or just some that would look nice in landscaping. The beauty of these rocks, however, depends on what each person sees in them, for what is "very pretty" to one is a "leaverite" (leave it right there) to another.

People seem to come in as many varieties as rocks do. Although all of us are sinners, which can make us seem rather ugly to those who see our sins, still God has made each person with at least some pleasing characteristics and the potential of doing what can be helpful to others. But often someone else has to see those possibilities and give encouragement for that person to become what God wants him or her to be in this life and especially in His Church.

So, God calls us to forgive and accept and encourage each other so that we all will better serve Him as we live this life, for He considers each of us *very* precious in His sight. He gave His own Son to wash away the dirt of our sins by shedding His blood on the cross, didn't He?

Help me to praise You, Lord, by how I accept and encourage my fellow forgiven sinners, whenever I see them. Amen.

Greedy For Rocks

Be sure of this, that no one who is immoral, unclean, or greedy (a greedy person worships an idol) has any share in the kingdom of Christ, Who is God. *Ephesians 5:5*

When out gathering desert rocks for landscaping purposes, one almost can get "greedy", since so many look so interesting. Surely that is not sinful, however (as long as it's not illegal to take them), because they have no real value.

Read greed, wanting more and more of things for self and being tempted to get them by any means, is neither trivial nor uncommon in our culture. God condemns greed as an evil which His people cannot participate in, for to be greedy means a person worships a different god than the true God.

How much we are tempted by modern advertising to become greedy: buy! buy! buy! get more! get more! get more! you must have this and this and this to be happy! The devil doesn't have to attack faith directly to destroy it! If he can just make a person greedy, he has succeeded, usually without that person noticing any spiritual loss.

God warns us against this form of unbelief; but He also holds out His arms of forgiveness to welcome us back, if we may have turned to another god for a time. Jesus suffered for every sin and evil so that through faith in Him we could be returned to the only true God.

Lord, my God, guard me against greed. Amen.

A Recreational Paradise

In others the seed falls among thorns. They hear the Word, but as they go along, worries, riches, and pleasures of life choke them, and they don't produce anything good. *Luke 8:14*

Sierra County, New Mexico, is a "recreational paradise"! It has desert – it has mountains – it has the two largest lakes in the whole state! In summertime its weekday population numbers about 13,000; weekends the count is about 50,000 (and up to 100,000 on holiday weekends), counting all the water enthusiasts who camp along the lakeshores. How sad that very few of those thousands bother to take time for public worship at any of the more than twenty Christian churches in the county.

But isn't this becoming the standard across our entire country? So much interest in life's fun – so little concern for God's message of eternal life through Jesus, Who gave His life for sinful people, even for those who ignore Him.

Will we "follow the crowd" out to the lake or the mountains or wherever they go away from His Word on worship days? Some claim they "worship" in His creation better than in a church. God's Word does not come, however, through the lapping of waves or the rustling of breezes. Instead, He has chosen to use the lips of men, who explain and apply His written Word for the comfort, guidance, and strengthening of His people, who gather together for that Word.

Thanks for the fun of recreation, Lord; but guard me so I never let it become more important to me than Your Word in public worship. Amen.

Turtleback Mountain Climb

I cling to the truths You wrote – O Lord, don't let me come to shame. *Psalm 119:31*

A moderately strenuous trail will take you up Turtleback Mountain, which overlooks T or C. You can do it in half a day – if you find the trailhead down near the river. This interesting hike begins with switchbacks, then straightens out to a narrow trail, literally only one person wide, which follows the very ridge of the mountain to its peak. It's challenging, but not really dangerous – unless you get off that trail which outlines you against the sky. Watch where you are going, stay on the trail, and you will enjoy your day-trip.

Life for a child of God, one who depends on Jesus as Savior, always will have some strenuous and challenging times; the devil and his worldly helpers (sometimes in your own family) make sure of that.

What challenges us, however, is nothing compared to how strenuously Jesus concentrated His efforts to rescue us from Satan's sometimes sly and sometimes brazen attempts to "crowd us off the trail" (of faith) into "unbelief, despair, and other great shame and vice".

As each day we "cling to the truths" about Jesus, which are written in His Word, however, He will keep us safe on that day's trail.

Thanks for saving and protecting me, Lord, so far along the trail of life. Help me today to remember Your love for me, especially if the way gets strenuous. Amen.

Treat At The Top

Instead, they were longing for a better country – I mean heaven. *Hebrews 11:16*

It's quite a view from the top of Turtleback: the Rio Grande stretching like a green-bordered life-line north and south with two reservoir lakes almost at your feet, the 10,000 foot Black Range fifty miles to the west, and to the east a desolate desert. Quite a treat, that view is. Then if you add the enjoyment of a picnic lunch or at least a candy bar, what could be better? Which is the feeling one often gets when you've put out some effort to reach some beauty of God's great creation.

But we look for something much, much better! Eternity with its blessings will far surpass even the most enjoyable experience we ever will have in this life. God promises He has prepared it for us.

Not that we deserve entering it – just the opposite. No matter how strenuously and strictly we try to obey Him in this life, we can never "make it to the top" on our own: daily we "get off the trail" by following our sinful desires.

So Jesus came to *be* the way through His life, suffering, and death. By trusting Him as the *only* way, we can look ahead to what will be "far better" and, until we get there, live thankfully for Him in spite of our failures, for we are forgiven through Him.

Thank You, Lord, for not only giving me so much to enjoy in this life, but especially that for Jesus' sake You will give me the joy of eternal life. Amen.

Not As Easy As Expected

Be faithful until you die, and I will give you the crown of life. *Revelation 2:10*

You would think that coming down a mountain trail would be easier than going up, but usually that's not true. Going up you were fresh and excited – coming down you are tired and probably your feet hurt, too! It's just not as easy as you might expect.

Some days in life are like that – some periods of life are also. You may begin a day and think it will be great, only to find the "rattlesnakes" of temptation or someone's sin attacking you unexpectedly as the day goes on.

As life goes on and comes toward its end in this world, "the golden years" often are also not what was expected: our bodies wear down, our finances dwindle because of inflation or other unexpected difficulties.

When life is not as easy as expected, we then can get that added temptation of: why should I try to be faithful to Him, if He lets this happen to me?

Why be faithful? Because He promised to keep every temptation under His control, never too much that we can't overcome it with His power. Why be faithful? Because He gave Jesus to cover over every time we do sin. Do we need any more reasons?

Keep me faithful also this day, Lord, no matter what "rattlesnake" might try to attack me. Amen.

The Enemy: Bermuda Grass!

God's Word is living and active. It cuts better than any two-edged sword. It pierces until it divides soul and spirit, joints and marrow. And it can judge thoughts and purposes of the heart. *Hebrews 4:12*

Nothing plagues a gardener or a landscaper in the high desert climate worse than that enemy: Bermuda grass! Not content to stay in the lawn, it creeps into the plantings and into the garden to choke out everything else. You can pull it or hoe it or dig it out so you think you've got it all, but next week or next year it sprouts again from just a little left over bit of root. Even weed killers don't eliminate it permanently.

Sounds like self-righteousness, doesn't it? No matter how humbly we trust in Jesus to forgive us, soon the pride of our sinful nature sprouts again to tempt us to compare ourselves with what others do or don't do so that faith, sometimes without our fully realizing it, must face the enemy: self-righteousness!

We can't kill self-righteousness by ourselves – only God's Word of Law can. As we use that Word daily, He keeps cutting off our pride by causing us to admit our continued sinning. Then His Gospel Word does its work of making us trust only in the righteousness of Jesus' perfect life for us, which He gives us in exchange for our sinful lives, which He took to the cross.

Keep me aware of my sinfulness, Lord, so I neither pride myself over others nor trust in what I do, but depend only on what You have done for me. Amen.

Enjoyment Or Work?

By dying in His human body He has made you friends in order to have you stand before Him without sin or fault or blame if, of course, you continue in your faith to stand firm on the foundation and are not moved from the hope of the good news you heard. *Colossians 1:22-23*

Given extreme temperatures, little moisture, and Bermuda grass to struggle with, if you want even a xeric landscape at your home in the desert, you have to put in a lot of effort. Anticipating the final results will determine, however, whether that effort will be enjoyment or work for you.

Entering eternal life requires much effort. The real effort was done by Him Who gave His human body through death to make us be friends with God instead of enemies. Also, having faith and continuing in faith – so we finally reach eternal life – come by the effort of the Holy Spirit, as He works through God's Word, the Bible.

Yet in a human way we feel that our effort is also required. If we don't use His Word, the Holy Spirit can't work. If we don't struggle against the temptations and pressures attacking our faith, but instead just give in, all will also be lost. Christian faith and Christian living can seem like work!

But since we know where our trail of life is taking us because of Jesus, we consider it enjoyment to use the power the Holy Spirit gives us in this struggle to "continue in faith".

Holy Spirit, keep working in me today, as I think of Your Word about Jesus, so I willingly keep on struggling to live the faith in Him that You have worked in me. Amen.

So Little Water!

The wages paid by sin is death, but the gift given freely by God in Christ Jesus is everlasting life. *Romans 6:23*

Beyond Turtleback Mountain east of T or C is an area named: *La Jornada del Muerto* (The Journey of the Dead Man). This 90-mile stretch of desert had no dependable source of water, but was used by the Spanish to avoid the rough country and Indian attacks along the Rio Grande. Death by thirst was a real possibility.

We all travel a journey at the end of which is not just the possibility, but the certainty of death. Unless the Lord returns first, each one of us will die.

After dying, we each should then receive what we have earned by how we lived this life: hell, eternal death! God says that is the pay for sin, and sin has been not merely an occasional, but a constant companion as we live the days of life.

Yet, we look not for what we have earned, but for what God will give us: eternal life. For He did not make life a water-less desert, but sent the "water of eternal life" through His Son, Jesus Christ, our Lord. Pouring out His life-blood on the cross, He paid for the gift we will receive.

So, refreshed daily by His forgiveness, we have strength and desire to travel His way on the trail of life, even when we cannot avoid the rough country and the attacks the devil puts in our way.

Thanks for the "water of life", Lord, which keeps me in faith so that I will at last receive Your gift of eternal life. Amen.

So Much Water!

How can a young man keep his life pure? By living as You tell him to. *Psalm 119:9*

Elephant Butte Lake, northeast of T or C, has more water than all the rest of the lakes in New Mexico combined. Stored behind a dam built in 1916, water from this reservoir is used to irrigate farms along the Rio Grande, generate electricity, and provide water recreation for people as well as sanctuary for birds.

God's Word, which calls us to public worship each week, is like a reservoir for us who are His people. In the Bible He has stored up for us the guidance, the power, and the comfort we need to live in this life, which can be so beautiful at times, but which also has its difficult, desert-like times. Most of all, however, from His Word comes the message of His love in Jesus, Who came and obeyed and paid with His life for us and all sinners.

All these blessings are in the Bible, but do not benefit anyone unless it is opened by the proclamation of preaching and the study of personal reading. Even then, those heard and sighted words must be accepted and applied by us to help us on the trail of life.

So, as we worship publicly and privately, we do so with the prayer:

Use Your Word, Lord, to keep me in faith so that You can guide me in life. Amen.

So Quickly Dehydrated

**So let us come boldly to God's throne of grace to receive
mercy   and   find grace   to help us   when we need it.**
Hebrews 4:16

The dry heat of the high desert can easily deceive you.
Working out in the sun or in the shade or even inside a building,
especially if you are doing something enjoyable, doesn't seem
so draining. Pretty soon, however, your mouth feels like cotton,
because you've forgotten to drink water regularly and you've
started to become dehydrated.

When we leave our use of God's Word in public worship, we
are refreshed and energized to meet the responsibilities and
opportunities that the week will bring.   Through our daily
devotions we also receive guidance and help from His Word.

But the stresses and temptations of life, the "rattlesnakes", are
such that we dare not rely only on our specific worship times to
keep us strong and faithful. As each day wears on, we need to
return in our minds to what God has told us, for example: what
was the worship service about last Sunday? what did God's
Word tell me through the devotion today?   Also we need to
frequently pray:

*Be with me, Lord in this day, in each situation to help,
guide, and protect me. Especially keep me thankful that You
love and forgive me because of Jesus, my only Savior. Amen.*

Thunderstorms And Flash Floods

When distress comes, or a flood of raging waters, it will not reach them. You are my Hiding Place; You protect me against trouble. *Psalm 32:6-7*

Desert thunderstorms can be magnificent with sheets of rain pouring down, lightning flashing all around, and thunder echoing off the mountains and down the canyons. These storms also are exceptionally dangerous: lightning kills more people in New Mexico than anywhere else in our country, and flash floods down the arroyos easily can sweep vehicles away to send passengers to a watery death.

Our lives can have storms and floods totally unrelated to weather conditions. Major health problems, crime attacks, explosive emotional outbursts, accidents at home or at work or on the highway are just some of them. Although God does promise to protect us, He doesn't say we won't ever experience such painful events or be unaffected when natural disasters occur. So what good is His promise? What does He mean?

God's protection keeps us safe in faith by assuring us that He sets limits on what He will allow to happen to us so that we can endure what happens without being overwhelmed into despair. We might cry, but we will remain confident of His love and guidance, because He kept His promise of a Savior, didn't He?

No matter what happens today, Lord, I trust Your promise to help me endure any trouble that comes. Amen.

Irrigating A River?

"This is My body, which is for you... This cup is the new testament in My blood..." Every time you eat this bread and drink the cup, you are telling how the Lord died until He comes. *1 Corinthians 11:24-26*

"The Rio Grande is the only river that has to be irrigated to keep it from drying up!" joked a park ranger at Bosque del Apache National Wildlife Refuge north of T or C. She meant that a "low-flow channel" had to be built next to the river, where it is very wide and shallow, so it wouldn't dry up in the heat of summer; the river needs that special help.

God also provides special help for us through the channel of His grace which we call Holy Communion. His proclaimed Word gives us comfort, guidance, power, and peace. But He knows we sinful humans need even more, extra help with a personal touch. So He touches us with the very Body and Blood that Jesus gave and shed on the cross, when He suffered and died for our sins. Here He personally assures us: although it was for everyone who has ever sinned, I also was thinking specifically of you when I was on that cross.

Ordinarily we receive Holy Communion with fellow believers in public worship. But your pastor can also give you this unique assurance and strength, when you have special need, if you go to him privately for this great "rainbow" of God's love.

Holy Communion also is our confession of faith in Jesus as Savior; for by it we are publicly saying: I am a daily sinner who always needs forgiveness and help, and I trust that Jesus is the only One Who can give me this forgiveness and help

Lord, thank You for Holy Communion. Amen.

The Peaceable (?) Kingdom?

I urge Euodia and Syntyche to agree in the Lord. And I beg you, my true fellow worker, help them. They fought side by side with me in telling the good news. *Philippians 4:2-3*

Especially from late fall to early spring Bosque del Apache Wildlife Refuge attracts birdwatchers from around the nation. Ducks, geese, sandhill cranes, and other water-loving birds flock there by the thousands, protected from their enemies and provided with food through the cold months. All these different species get along quite well, but what a racket they make, especially the geese! It does not sound very peaceable, even though they have nothing to fight about.

God gathers us into local congregations where we find forgiveness through Jesus, spiritual food to empower us for faithful walking on the trail of life, and fellowship with brothers and sisters in faith. Surely in this place of refuge and spiritual strengthening we should also find peace and harmony!

All too often, however, attitudes in congregations don't seem to differ much from out in the unbelieving world.

Do we forget where we are? Do we forget Whom we serve? Do we forget to follow Him when we are close enough to each other to see our shared sinfulness? Do we forget forgiving?

Lord, forgive me for my sin in any lack of peace in my congregation; and somehow help me be a peace-maker, whenever needed. Amen.

Let Someone Know!

My fellow Christians, if you find anyone doing wrong, you who are spiritual should set him right. But be gentle and keep an eye on yourself; you may be tempted, too. Help one another carry these burdens. *Galatians 6:1-2*

When hiking or driving out on the desert or into the mountains of New Mexico, you really should let someone know where you are going and when you plan to return. If you should get lost or stranded, so few people in so much area means no one might come your way for days. But communities are organized to search for those who do not return when expected, if they are notified.

This concern for those who get lost in the wilderness areas of New Mexico is to be mirrored in the Christian congregation. One reason for our being drawn together by God is to reach out for any member who wanders from the faith or even gets lost. Not only the pastor but also each of us as members of our congregation has the responsibility to pray for and encourage our fellow members so they don't turn away from Jesus as the only Savior by outright evil living or by just not showing faith in living.

Of course, if you realize that you are slipping away from that faith – if He Who gave His life for you doesn't seem too important to you at times, it is essential that you let someone in the congregation know, so they can try to help you overcome that "rattlesnake" of unbelief.

Thank You, Lord, for people who do care for me spiritually. Help me be alert to help anyone who seems to be slipping away from faith in You. Amen.

The Trash Of Sin

So you, too, because you are in Christ Jesus, think of yourselves as dead to sin and living for God. *Romans 6:11*

Even in New Mexico with so few people out in so much space almost anywhere you hike you will find some trash to mar the beauty of God's creation. Littering seems to be second nature for most people.

Sounds like sinning! Only sinning is not "second nature for most people" – it is inescapable for *all* people. Every day in every way we are guilty of sin – even "all our righteousnesses are like filthy rags" in God's sight (*Isaiah 64:6*).

This is why Jesus had to come into this sinning world; if He had not come to endure God's punishment upon all sins, no one could ever be saved. Also, it is because we recognize and admit our own sinning that we trust in Him for our forgiveness (the Holy Spirit causing this faith, of course).

Although we never will do a single perfect deed in this life, God calls us from sinning to godly living. No matter how well we live, we do not earn eternal life. But with faith God gives us a "second nature", the new nature of being one of His children, a new nature which wants to thank God for His undeserved love by living as He commands, as much as possible.

Help me fight against my wanting to sin, Lord, in order to better live Your way in what I do today. Amen.

How Green Grows The Desert

The wilderness and the parched ground will be glad, and the desert will be happy and blossom. *Isaiah 35:1*

Without rain the desert truly is barren. But when the "monsoon" season comes in New Mexico, especially if it brings more rain than normal, the desert can become a carpet of brilliant colors. Some years even Turtleback Mountain has a sheen of green covering its normal barrenness. Such is the power and the glory of water.

Such is also the power and glory of the "water of life" which God gives in His Word, which we are called to each week. In the desert of this unbelieving world life would be hopeless and barren with no peace and nothing to cover over the ugliness of sin. But God works to change people from enemies into His friends, people who are beautiful in His sight because of the beautiful Savior He sent for us.

As we keep receiving His "water of life" when we worship, He gives us guidance and power to do beautiful deeds of kindness and helpfulness to others, as we walk the daily trail of life. We do need to apply that guidance and that power to the situations of our lives, however, or else we will be just as "ugly" in our deeds as all the unbelievers around us. This we will do, because His "water of life" does shower upon us as we worship publicly and privately.

Help me this day, Lord, in what I do so that no one will think my deeds are unbelieving "ugly", but will know that Your life is working in me. Amen.

A Melting Pot Of Cultures

In the same way, many as we are, we are one body in Christ and individually parts of one another. *Romans 12:5*

One fascinating aspect of New Mexican life is how much it truly is a melting pot of cultures: Native American, Hispanic, and Anglo contribute the most, yet Asian and African add some spice to the mixture. There isn't perfect harmony; but since each has had to live with the others for so long, each has influenced the others in order to give the 47th state a fairly harmonious blend.

In our individual congregations we may or may not see many colors or cultures present. Because we each have different abilities and personalities, however, God intends each congregation to be a "melting pot", which combines each one's uniqueness into a living tool for the One Who combined His divinity and humanity into a living Person, Who could and did obey and die to save us all.

Our congregational "pot" is not by accident of geography, however, but by the guidance of God, Who has worked faith in us and specifically brought us to the particular congregation we are members of. His purpose? That we might help each other be more faithful to Him as individuals and as a congregation which serves Him in the part of His creation and His kingdom where we are. That united faithfulness can then result in more deeds of helping people and in more bringing of people to His message about Jesus than each of us could do individually.

Help me, Lord, to appreciate the role You have given me and each one in my congregation. Help us to overcome our human differences so that we can do more to reach other people with deeds of kindness and words of witness about Jesus. Amen.

A Land Of Heroes

But you stay with what you've learned and found to be true. You know from whom you learned it. *2 Timothy 3:14*

Southwestern New Mexico could be called a land of heroes except most of the remembered historical figures of the area were notorious rather than notable: Billy the Kid, the Apache Kid, Geronimo. The real heroes of New Mexico, however, were the ordinary people: the tribal people and the Hispanic and Anglo settlers – their everyday efforts went largely unreported, but produced the culture and character of this state.

Sadly, so many "heroes" of our day produce the culture and destroy the character of our country, as their violence, immorality, and extremism are imitated by so many of all ages.

God calls us to be His heroes, people who live their faith in Jesus, so that others see what it means to be His in life as well as in name. Knowing and imitating others who are faithful can encourage us, but faithfulness only results through the Holy Spirit working in us with the inspired Word of God and causing us to trust in Jesus for daily forgiveness.

That's why we made the time for daily devotions: to read them, to think about them, to try to put them into practice all day long.

Lord, help me live for You so others can be encouraged by my example of faithfulness each day. Amen.

The Gila Cliff Dwellers

But according to His promise we expect new heavens and a new earth where righteousness lives. *2 Peter 3:13*

The Gila Cliff Dwellers National Monument is about 150 highway miles west of T or C, a pleasant day's trip. The people who lived there long ago had a seeming paradise: safety and relative comfort in their sun-lighted cave homes, a year-round creek, game to eat, and a spectacular view! Yet, that ancient tribe abandoned that site after about 75 years. Paradise lost!

Which only goes to show that paradise never can exist on this earth. No matter how satisfying life might seem for a while, the fact of sin eventually will ruin it – and if not sin to ruin it, in death we lose it.

So God has promised to remake this earth, destroying it on Judgment Day and re-creating it for eternity with sin never to enter it. Then life will be what He originally intended: peace and joy and satisfying obedience forever.

But not one of us can even hope for that life in paradise on our own. Instead, our hope is built on the righteousness of Jesus. Because He gave Himself for us, we have not just "hope" but *confidence* that He will give us that paradise – that future joy helps us live for Him now.

No matter how much I might enjoy today, Lord, help me keep in mind that You have much better planned for me and all Your people of faith so that I will joyfully live this day Your way, no matter if the day is not "paradise". Amen.

Like Heaven Coming Down!

This is a statement that can be trusted and deserves complete acceptance: Christ Jesus came into the world to save sinners. I am the worst of them. *1 Timothy 1:15*

One late afternoon they saw an especially brilliant sun amid some still strong storm clouds; it reminded them of God's eternal glory. She even said: "It's just like heaven coming down!"

Of course, heaven's glory will never be on this earth, for God in His glory will destroy everything at Judgment Day before re-creating it all.

Still, in a sense God did send heaven's glory to earth, for His glory is not so much shining magnificence as it is His gracious love. When Jesus came from what we call heaven's "glory", He brought God's *real* glory with Him so that by His life and death here, we might through faith in Him enter the heavenly glory there.

How we each need the trip of Jesus into time to be the Savior! Paul wrote that as far as he knew, he was the worst of sinners. Yet, doesn't each of us have to admit that? We see a few of the sins of others; but we know our own sinning in explicit detail, for we have done each one. So, along with Paul we are humbly thankful that He came down for us. This is why we praise Him each week in public worship and each day by our living.

Thank You for Your glorious love, Lord, for a sinner like me. Amen.

An Extra Blessing: Beautiful Sunsets!

I think what we suffer now isn't important when I compare it with the glory to be revealed to us. *Romans 8:18*

Every so often, New Mexico sunsets can only be described as: unbelievable!   You almost have to see them to believe it possible! Glistening silver! Fiery red! Glowing gold! True, most sunsets are rather ordinary, but sometimes: Wow!

The sunset of life tends not to be spectacular. Some are blessed with health and energy even in well-advanced years. Most notice bodies that slow down and wear out with frustrating speed. Others, of course, never make it to "sunset" years.

However, we do not face the end of life with fear, but with joy, no matter when the Lord says it is time. Not that we want to die, but we are willing, for we know where we are going even though we don't know when or what will happen until "when" comes.

We know, not because we can look back with satisfaction at how we lived, but because Jesus made satisfaction for us, when He lived here. We know, because God's Word tells us that we are safe into eternity by His grace alone (His work in Jesus) through faith alone (we only receive what He gives, we cannot earn it) according to the Scriptures alone.

"Rattlesnakes" do trouble us all along the trail of life. But the eternal "rainbow" is waiting. So we are content and try to be as faithful as we can until then.

Thank You, Lord, for being with me in all of life: joy, desert, sunset, always. Amen.

First Signs Of Spring

We are saved, hoping for this. But if we hope for something we see, we really don't hope.... But if we hope for what we can't see, we wait for it patiently. *Romans 8:24-25*

In southwest New Mexico the first real sign of spring is the delicate greening of globe willow trees. Each part of the country has its special signs which assure us that the harshness of winter won't last forever, and the glory of spring is surely coming! Of course, we don't actually need a psychological encouragement, because we've experienced the change of seasons each year. Still, the first sign of spring does lift one's spirits.

We know our trail of earthly life with its "rattlesnakes" of trouble and temptation will not last forever; but the coming glory of eternal life is not so sure for us, since neither we nor anyone we personally know has experienced it. We have words of promise: because of Jesus, Whose cross is the entry, we can be sure God will accept us in spite of our unworthiness. Yet, because these are only unverifiable words, Scripture calls this our "hope" – if it were absolutely proven, it would no longer be "hope".

Which is why the Lord keeps giving us "signs of (eternal) spring": His words of promise which we keep hearing – His Body and Blood in Holy Communion, which say by word and sight: "given and shed for you" – His having us baptized to be His adopted children. Also are those special times when His promise of forgiveness because of Jesus is really meaningful to us so that joy and relief replace feelings of guilt and despair. Eternal life still is not proven – it remains our "hope" – but we are encouraged in knowing that it is our destination.

Thank You, Lord, for Your "signs of (eternal) spring" to help me endure the sometimes "winter" of this life. Amen.

Drifts Of Daffodils

By your loving one another everyone will know you're My disciples. *John 13:35*

Even a single daffodil has a striking beauty. But especially when they multiply naturally to form drifts of daffodils, a landscape can become almost breath-taking!

Christian love is not a feeling, but the action of helping someone. The little deeds of a smile, a hug, a compliment, are Christian love just as much as listening patiently, helping to get a job done, paying for someone's needed supplies, giving for God's work. Whether these or similar deeds take place in one's family or toward others, they are Christian love when we do them because of our thankfulness for Jesus having done for us the greatest of all deeds of love: sacrificed Himself for our sins. Each act of Christian love reflects His love for us to others and is beautiful.

But especially can others come to know the beauty of Jesus' love for sinners when they see deeds of Christian love mutually practiced and unitedly carried out by His followers as they are gathered together in a congregation.

The message of Jesus as Savior is our motive and power – our deeds of Christian love are our initial witness to others about that message.

Help me act with Christian love as best I can today, Lord; and especially help me be kind and helpful and friendly to those You have placed with me in my congregation. Guide us to work together in Christian love projects in our community so more people will come to know that Your love is also for them. Amen.

Here Come The Swallows!

Then he came to his senses and said: "... I'll start out and go to my father and tell him, 'Father, I've sinned against heaven and against you. I don't deserve to be called your son any more. Make me one of your hired men.'"
Luke 15:17-19

Not only at Capistrano but throughout the country swallows regularly return to the nesting area where they were born – many other birds do also, but swallows get the most publicity about their habit.

Which teaches us something about children and family values. Because no family life is perfect but is marred by sin, some children are attracted by various temptation "rattlesnakes" and so choose to leave a family emotionally and spiritually as well as physically. But if a family has been sincerely teaching about following Jesus and also has really tried to walk His way, especially with deeds of forgiving Christian love, even though that child may leave for a "distant (spiritual) country", there always is the possibility that the family commitment to Jesus might bring him or her "home", back onto His trail of faith for forgiveness and of living according to His commands.

What an opportunity parents – and grandparents – have! Sinning in family relationships cannot be completely avoided. But forgiving and loving and explaining one's own reasons (as well as admitting one's doubts and struggles) for following Jesus are the ways God uses in a family to help all the family be in His family.

Lord, not only forgive me for my failings in family relationships, but help me neutralize those by how I show Your love for sinners through my kind, loving and forgiving attitudes and actions in daily family living. Amen.

Martin Houses For Rent

From morning until evening he explained the matter to them, earnestly telling them the truth about God's kingdom and trying to convince them about Jesus from the Law of Moses and the prophets. *Acts 28:23*

Just because you might put up martin houses doesn't mean martins will nest in them. They might, because martin "colonies" can get so crowded that some have to find new nest houses. But martins are quite choosy – for reasons we humans don't really understand. However, would-be martin "landlords" keep patiently trying – and usually are eventually rewarded with chattering "tenants".

Jesus has opened up God's house for all sinners – He didn't just suffer and die for some, but for all. Obviously, however, all don't immediately flock into faith, even though it's what they need most of all. So, how to help others enjoy the faith that we have?

Much patience! Much explaining of why we trust in Jesus instead of believing in something else, much faithfulness in how we ourselves follow Jesus, and especially much kindness (Christian love) in our relationship with the person who is wandering through life without Him.

Some never will come to Jesus – their pride keeps them going "my way" instead. But some might join us in faith and enjoy the peace and help which we already experience.

Lord, help me be patient and loving with _____, a person whom You know I care about, but who does not care about You. Use my words and deeds so this person will, if possible, come into Your family of faith. Amen.

The Chatter Of Martins

Don't say anything harmful but only what is good, so that you help where there's a need and benefit those who hear it.
Ephesians 4:29

One especially enjoyable aspect of landlording a colony of martins is how they chatter with one another. We don't know if they are sharing useful information or gossiping or just making sounds, but it seems more like conversation than how most other birds twitter.

What about our conversations? Conversations are mostly gossip – we can't help but talk about people and what they do. However, there is "good gossip" as well as "gossip". Good gossip speaks approvingly of the good others do – good gossip tries to explain the actions of others in the best possible way – good gossip reflects on the events of life and tries to see God's guiding hand – good gossip shares helpful information – good gossip will also include the good news about Jesus in a very matter-of-fact, life-related way.

Sadly, we too easily follow the "rattlesnake" of sinful gossip: reveling in the sins of others, putting the worst interpretation possible on what someone else has said or done, trying to make others look bad in the mistaken idea that then we will look better. None of us is totally isolated from such gossip. Which means we daily need to speak to Jesus in repentance for so many of our words as well as for our sinful deeds. He then again assures us: I've already silenced those spoken sins before our Father, and I'll help you try to speak in ways that will help and benefit, not hurt others.

Keep me alert today, Lord, so I avoid "rattlesnake" gossip and instead speak in "rainbow" ways with and about others. Amen.

Beautiful Bird Music

Sing to the Lord, you people that He loves, and praise Him as you remember how holy He is. *Psalm 30:4*

How beautifully birds sing! People used to think their music was praise to God; instead, it has more to do with attracting a mate and defending claimed territory. Even so, how interesting that God gave them the gift of music for such vital life chores instead of growls and hisses, which so many animals use.

Music, both for hearing it and in making it (playing an instrument, singing, humming, whistling) truly is a "rainbow" gift from our Creator. Music can soothe and refresh us (by taking our minds off our troubles) – it can excite and inspire us.

Music, however, has been given to us not merely to absorb into ourselves or to give to others, but especially to give back to God. We call this praise. But praise is not merely melodies. Praise puts words to music, because praise always has a message. Praise recounts what God has done and is doing for us, His people who belong to Him because Jesus bought us by His life, suffering, and death.

Not that God needs our praise – He needs nothing from us sinners. But we, both individually and with each other, need to hear the praises given to honor and thank Him, so He can use those words to teach and comfort, to guide and strengthen us. Merely seeing a rainbow or hearing a melody is open to any interpretation the human mind desires. But combining words with the music put His message more deeply into our minds and hearts. So we sing our praises as we worship, and in doing so, we remind and teach each other how great and loving He is.

How good You are, Lord, to have given Your people music to enjoy and to use in praising You. Amen.

Bluebirds? Here?

Jesus heard them and said: "Those who are healthy don't need a doctor, but those who are sick. Go and learn what this means: 'I want mercy and not mere sacrifice.' I didn't come to call righteous people but sinners." *Matthew 9:12-13*

Bluebirds? *Eastern* bluebirds? Here in southwest New Mexico? Yet there they were in late winter, a small flock, feeding and flitting about so far from their normal territory.

Ever had unkind thoughts about certain visitors to your congregation's worship services? Some can seem so different because of color, clothing, or cleanliness that a very human reaction can be: What are they doing here? Or, what if a person with a bad reputation (or proven crime) or one who has deeply hurt you by some sin comes? Is your reaction: "How *dare* that person come?" Which questions about others ignore this similar question: "How dare *you* come to worship?" Yes, why do you attend? Because you are such a good person, and this is your duty along with your social club friends? If so, you've missed the whole message about Jesus!

We attend not because we are good, but because we aren't good enough no matter how hard we try – and we don't try very hard at times! We all are sinners who need the comfort of being assured that God doesn't turn His back on us because of our continued sinning, but instead keeps welcoming us, because Jesus came "not for righteous people but for sinners" – *us*!

Which is why we will struggle against the "rattlesnake" of self-righteousness to welcome whoever comes; for they are just like us: sinners – and we all need the same medicine: Jesus!

Lord, I'm ashamed how sometimes I look down on others; help me be friendly with all who come to Jesus. Amen.

Will They Stay?

Then you are no longer foreigners or strangers but fellow citizens with the holy people and members of His household. *Ephesians 2:19*

They didn't! In spite of nest boxes quickly put up those bluebirds left. Nor did they stay the next year when they flew in briefly.

People visit a worship service, some formally join the congregation; but a realistic question, which also applies to long-term members, is: Will they stay? For the devil does all he can to disrupt even the best congregation in order, if possible, to scatter members and turn away visitors. His methods? Primarily his attack is to get people to think of each other and to react to each other just in human nature ways as though the congregation is supposed to be a social gathering of likable people. When this becomes the attitude, then people will eventually get on each other's nerves, cliques will form, just "my way" will be emphasized, and conflict will erupt.

To prevent this we need to keep remembering that we gather together as part of the Lord's "household", His family – we are fellow "citizens" in His kingdom. Doesn't matter what we were or even still are as sinners; now we are "holy people", because Jesus made us "holy" in God's sight by taking away our sins. Of course, we try to *be* holy, that is, we try to live up to whom God has made us. But since we don't always, because we can't, we have to keep being reminded by the preaching about who we actually are and why: forgiven sinners who forgive and who try to serve our Forgiver individually and together. When that is the congregational attitude, people will stay.

Bless my congregation, Lord, so we clearly keep in mind that we are Yours and want always to follow You. Amen.

Birds In Their Habitat

All were one at heart as they went to the temple regularly every day. They had their meals in their homes and ate their food with glad and simple hearts, praising God and having the good will of all the people. *Acts 2:46-47*

The bluebirds didn't stay, because that area was not their normal habitat. Most birds are quite site-specific: the habitat needs to be just right. Some can live almost anywhere, but some live only near the desert, others only high in mountains, still others only along the ocean.

We followers of Jesus are like birds who need a specific habitat – in two ways. First, our faith in Him cannot exist very long if we separate ourselves from each other and try to "go it alone, just me and Jesus". God's people are His *people*, His *family* or *household*, not His "persons". Of course, sometimes, but rarely, He guides a person into life circumstances where no other people of God live close enough for coming together. But then that isolated person (or family) will make efforts to gather with other of His people, whenever possible, in spite of long distances, for the Lord directs us to hear His message of Jesus as Savior together and to help one another. Our natural habitat is to be with fellow people of faith in Jesus: a congregation.

However, we also need to be rather "site-specific" about "habitat", that is, we need to be united with those people of faith who believe very much the same as we do. That "habitat" is called a Christian denomination. If there isn't unity in the teachings believed, there won't really be much unity at all.

Help me, Lord, to participate faithfully in my congregation, both in worship and in work. Amen.

Unused Bird Houses

I'm saying this to help you, not to hold you by a rope but to show you how to live nobly for the Lord without being troubled about other things. *1 Corinthians 7:35*

Those bluebird houses were never used, not even by wasps! Sometimes would-be martin "landlords" never get any tenants – wrens may never nest in boxes hung out for them. Disappointing!

Some individuals find that the Lord leads in life so that, although he or she has love to give and much desire to give it, no marriage partner appears or no child is conceived. Not just disappointing, but unfulfilling! Lord! Why? Same thing can be felt about abilities a person might have but without opportunity to use them. Lord! Why?

Yet, the Lord is guiding whatever our trail might be. And even if it is not close to what we inwardly desire, He wants us to open our hearts to those around us who need the Christian love we can give: people who are lonely, disabled, or ill; children who need help learning or need an adult role model because of an unkind family environment; others in need. The Lord wants us not to merely look at what we want, but to look for the "mission" He wants for us. Same is true also if our inner desires are quite fulfilled; still He has a "mission" for us – still He wants to use us by being helpful to others.

That's why He broke us out of the prison of selfish sinfulness by the work of Jesus: not so we live for ourselves, but to live "nobly for the Lord" no matter how "other things" might not be as we might like.

Lord, use me also today in some way to do what You say about helping others. Amen.

Fruit Tree Pruning

I am the true vine, and My Father takes care of the vineyard. He cuts away any branch of Mine that bears no fruit, and He trims any branch that bears fruit to make it bear more fruit. *John 15:1-2*

A late winter, early spring orchard chore is pruning fruit trees: broken, rubbing, out of place, too long, and too dense branches have to be cut off so the tree does not waste its energy on unproductive leaves, but bears more of the desired fruit. If trees could talk, they might complain at the hurt – but later be pleased at being able to do more of what their nature is: to bear as much good fruit as possible.

It hurts when God "prunes" us! Perhaps He does it through disappointment, illness or accident, economic hardship, even someone sinning against us so that we feel not only hurt, but deserted; sometimes His "pruning" is to let us experience the consequences of our sinning. Why does He allow such things?

Because when our trail of life goes too easily, we gradually begin to rely more on our abilities and thinking than on His guidance – it's just human nature. That's when and why He "prunes" us: so we will look at ourselves to see where we may have wandered from His path, even if it was only in not taking time to ask His guidance in whatever activity we were pursuing.

His purpose never is punishment, for Jesus was punished in our place; instead, He aims to draw us closer to Himself so our faith in Jesus is renewed and our desire to live His way is strengthened. And when we think, as we can at times, "that's enough pruning, Lord", then we listen as He responds: I know what I'm doing – just wait, and you will see.

"Prune" me, Lord, however I need it. Amen.

Tree Planting Time

The people scattered by the persecution that broke out over Stephen went as far as Phoenicia, Cyprus, and Antioch, and they spoke the Word only to the Jews. But among them were some men from Cyprus and Cyrene who came to Antioch and started talking to the non-Jews, telling them the good news of the Lord Jesus. *Acts 11:19-20*

Late winter, early spring also is the time to plant trees. True, the landowner could plant seeds or cuttings, but it's safer and quicker to purchase and plant seedlings or potted older trees, since trees take so long to grow anyway.

How does one "plant" a congregation? A pastor can just canvass an area, make calls, put out publicity, and begin holding services; many congregations have so begun. More often, however, a number of believers in an area will work together with a pastor so a faster-growing congregation is born. Either way those who already have faith need to share that faith with neighbors and other friends for a new congregation to grow.

The growth power is, of course, not in the ability of the already-Christian people – it's in "the good news of the Lord Jesus" which they tell. Words about our being sinners and Jesus giving Himself for our sins have to be spoken by people – that's God's planned way.

Which is true also for older congregations. Those with faith in Jesus need to tell others what they believe and why, if any congregation is to grow, not just survive.

Lord, please give special blessing to those in new congregations as they tell the good news of Jesus. And help me to do so also. Amen.

Never Should Have Lived

**All who heard him were amazed. "Isn't this the man,"
they asked, "who in Jerusalem destroyed those who call on
this name?"** *Acts 9:21*

Sometimes a tree isn't in the right landscape place so the
landowner transplants it to a more desirable location, the best
time being when it's still dormant. But once half a dozen semi-
dwarf apple trees were transplanted after they had already
leafed out and were blossoming. They never should have lived!
Yet all but one did! Which might prove the old saying: "Where
there's life, there's hope!"

Applying this to the trail of life we might say: "Where there's
physical life, there's spiritual hope" regarding a person you
know who apparently has absolutely no interest in Jesus. That
person may be trapped in an addiction, physical or moral, which
seems unbreakable. Just as likely, however, the trap might be
that life is going along so well that no need for religion of any
kind is felt. No point in trying to "tell the good news", right?

But the miraculous can happen! Some who seemed beyond
hope have come to faith! In fact, what about us? Perhaps we
never were addicted or never were so caught up in just enjoying
life that we had no religious interest. Still, God's message had
to overcome our pride so we would admit we were helpless
under the power of sin; then His Word about Jesus made sense:
He had to do everything to set us free from the punishment our
sinning deserved. If the Lord has worked that faith in us, He
can work it in anyone. So, we won't give up praying for even
the person who seems unreachable and trying to share our faith,
when a reasonable opportunity arises.

*If possible, Lord, use me to help _____ come to faith
in Jesus for eternal life. Amen.*

Why Did It Die?

Everyone's own desire tempts him, draws him away, and tries to trap him. When desire conceives, it gives birth to sin, and when sin grows up, it gives birth to death. *James 1:14-15*

A very productive French plum tree that year blossomed out as beautifully as in other years. Yet about a month later it just died! Why? Not a late freeze, no apparent insect or weed spray damage, not drought – no reason was ever figured out – it just died.

Why does faith die in some people, as in Judas, who betrayed Jesus, and in Hymenaeus and Alexander (*1 Timothy 1: 19-20)*? Why do some individuals we know no longer have any faith in Jesus?

The reason is one's own sinful desire which is not confronted with the power of God's Word but is allowed to grow: perhaps greed for riches or just for things – perhaps sexual lust for a person – perhaps desire to escape one's struggles into the high of alcohol or harder drugs – perhaps the anger of revenge which becomes hate.

No one is immune to sinful nature desires. That's why we need God's Word, not just to tell us "No!", but especially to assure us that, because even sinful thoughts and desires have been punished on Jesus' cross, we don't have to give in to them, but can live God's way, which is much better.

But we have to be alert and on guard and remember His Word, because desires can be such attractive "rattlesnakes".

Turn me away from my sinful desires, Lord, so I do not turn away from You. Amen.

Apple Blossom Time

Give me again the joy of Your salvation and a willing spirit to strengthen me. *Psalm 51:12*

One of the satisfying joys in having an apple orchard is apple blossom time. First of all, it's the beauty of those trees covered with white blossoms. Added joy comes from the fragrance of those blossoms. And then there is the expectation of bushels of apples in a few months.

Joy – underlying, sustaining joy – is one of the "rainbows" the Lord gives us, His people. Just think! We have no right at all to look forward to eternal blessings! God should throw us out of His holy presence forever into punishment forever because of our sinning. But He hasn't – and He won't! For He piled all our sins upon Jesus on the cross and then threw all His anger at our sins on Jesus. So has He saved us! What a relief! That's why we trust in Jesus as our Savior!

And so, what joy we have! Joy at being forgiven! Joy that God is with us! Joy that He will always help us! Joy, that underlying peace we have in spite of our daily sinning.

Our joy may not always be visible in smiles, because life isn't always easy. But joy in our salvation gives us confidence and strength as we walk with Him along the trail of life no matter what may come.

Thank You, Lord, for assuring me that I will have Your eternal blessings because of Jesus. Help me remember this today, especially if I have to face some circumstances that are not humanly joyful. Amen.

A Late Killer Frost

That is why we are not discouraged. No, even if we outwardly perish, inwardly we're renewed from day to day. The light trouble of this moment is preparing us for an everlasting weight of glory, greater than anything we can imagine. *2 Corinthians 4:16-17*

One of the fearful realities in having an apple orchard is a late killer frost. Although a degree or two below freezing might not hurt too much, into the 20s will surely turn those beautiful blossoms at least slightly brown so fruit will not set. Overnight the joy of apple blossom time can turn into the frustration of probable fruitlessness. Of course, an underlying comfort is: next year might be an even better crop after resting this year!

We have the joy of being saved through Jesus. Sometimes, however, the immediate pileup of troubles and temptations seems larger than any joy we might have. Life can get too painful to do anything except cry!

Still, underneath our long, worried faces is our comfort: This, too will pass! I don't have to despair, for He is in control – and He won't let it get to be too much. After all, since He rescued me from all my sins, He won't forget about me now, but will help me endure.

But sometimes the pile weighing on us will never get any lighter and may finally kill us. That's when our comfort is: He will help me bear this all the way to the end of life, and then He will give me the joy of eternal life! I know He will! Jesus is my proof! And so we *can* endure.

Keep me confident of Your care, Lord, no matter what You allow to oppress me, since I know You will finally take me to Yourself for eternal joy. Amen.

Why Did Those Survive?

He comforts us in all our suffering to make us able to comfort others in all their suffering with the same comfort with which God comforts us. *2 Corinthians 1:4*

Amazingly, even after the severest late frost a few apple blossoms will survive and set fruit. Apparently they had just enough protection deep in the tree leaves that the freeze didn't destroy them.

Some individuals experience so many burdens and yet remain positive, even cheerful. Perhaps he is a quadriplegic who lives independently, displays no self-pity, and almost always sees the bright side of life. Perhaps she has one illness after another or numerous family heartaches, yet keeps her confident faith in the Lord. Why? Why does the Lord allow so much to burden them, and why are they able to withstand what we fear would crush us?

They are able, partly because they realize that despair or self-pity would only worsen, not improve their situation; but mostly because they are comforted in knowing that Jesus suffered much more than any sinner could suffer so that we sinners would not have to suffer forever. Being so comforted, they are then used by the Lord to comfort and encourage and even at times inspire others by their example along with their words about faith in Jesus and how it comforts them.

Lord, continue to strengthen those I know who have so many burdens on their trail of life. When sufferings come to me, help me to endure them patiently because I know Your love in Jesus, and perhaps even use me to comfort others who face similar troubles. Amen.

Water Rights

Share what you have with the holy people who need it.
Romans 12:13

New Mexico has hundreds of *acequia* (ah-SAKE-ya) associations, formed to divert ground or river water into ditches, mostly hand-dug generations ago, for irrigation purposes. "Water rights", originally assigned by how much land a family owned and how much labor it provided in digging the ditch, determine how much water may be used according to the *acequia* schedule. Since arid New Mexico rarely has too much water (except in flash floods which damage rather than help the land), water rights are jealously guarded to make sure no one gets more than his legal share.

Our sinful nature says: "Mine! Just for me!" But God says: "Share!" Not indiscriminately, however! God clearly says, "with (those) who need it", but not with those who are just lazy (*1 Thessalonians 3:10*). He blesses us with enough so we can share with others and still have enough for our own needs.

Our reason for sharing is only partly because He commands this. Mostly we share, because He has shared with us, not just the physical blessings we have, but especially His Son, Who shared our human life so He would not "share" the punishment of our sins (as though: He did His share, now we do ours), but took it completely so we could share in His eternal blessings.

Keep me from selfishness, Lord, so that I will be able and willing to share the blessings You have given me (time as well as things) if You bring someone who does need help onto my path of life today. Amen.

Ditch Preparation

Examine yourselves to see if you really believe. Test yourselves. *2 Corinthians 13:5*

Before the new irrigation season begins, the "mayor domo" (ditch boss, manager) will inspect the ditch and, if needed, organize the owners to take out fallen branches, widen sides that have been narrowed by weeds, block up gopher holes, and dig out bottoms where silt has collected. With proper ditch preparation little precious water will be wasted.

Along the trail of life we need to inspect ourselves to see the sinning we've not only done, but have become accustomed to. Each day we should look at our lives to admit specific sins and ask God's forgiveness. Which does not mean we aren't forgiven unless we ask, because that would make forgiveness at least somewhat dependent on something we did. Instead, Jesus did everything on the cross to forgive all our sins. But we examine and ask in order to more clearly realize how much we are forgiven, so we will be continually thankful. Probably this self-examination is best done at the end of each day's trail trip.

In addition, we need to examine our beliefs in a specific way from time to time. Am I believing the teachings His Word proclaims? Especially am I trusting only in Jesus, or have I been drifting back into self-righteousness, whether by pride in my "goodness" or by comparison with someone else's sinning? This belief self-examination is best done each week at public worship. God does not command us to attend public worship just to go, but so we might remain in clear faith and grow.

Help me to be honest with myself, Lord, about my sinning and my believing so I will better appreciate Your forgiveness and will believe only what Your Word teaches. Amen.

Deep Irrigation Also Preparation

Two or three should speak God's Word, and the others should decide whether what is being said is right or wrong... You can all speak God's Word one after another so that everyone learns something and is encouraged.
1 Corinthians 14:29,31

Some New Mexico *acequias* allot double water time for each owner at the beginning of the irrigation season. This allows a deeper soaking of the fields so what is planted will have subsoil moisture to draw on as it grows.

When we use God's Word, whether reading it personally or hearing it preached or studying it with others, we may not see an immediate connection with our life that particular day. But we are receiving God's guidance and power in preparation for facing the various "rattlesnakes", which inevitably will attack us. This holds true also regarding the doctrinal teachings we learn; they draw us closer to Him so that we want to live faithfully for Him. Every time we use His Word, however, we need to remember His most important message: He gave His Son to make us sinners His.

Such using of His Word is how He puts His commands and doctrines and good news message deeply into our minds and hearts so that we are prepared to use and follow what He teaches us, whenever the "rattlesnakes" of temptation or trouble strike at us.

Help me, Lord, so that, when "rattlesnakes" do attack, I will use the guidance and power You have been giving me, whenever I've used Your Word. Amen.

Irrigation Borders

His disciples saw Jesus do many other miracles that are not written in this book. But these things are written so that you believe Jesus is the Christ, God's Son, and by believing have life in His name. *John 20:30-31*

Since one's share of irrigation water is limited, a pasture is divided by low berms, called "borders", to keep the water from spreading so thinly that is does no real good. First one section is well-watered, then the next, and so on, although perhaps the furthest section might have to wait until the next irrigation cycle. In this way, borders are used for the most efficient use of the available water.

The truth about God, Who He is and all He has done, is limitless – which means it's more than we limited human beings can grasp. So God has revealed to us only what we actually need to know about Himself. The "borders" God has set are the written Scriptures of the Old and New Testaments. We can wonder much about why God created the world even though He knew sin would corrupt it or what He did before creation; we might like to know more about the life of Jesus, His childhood and youth. But we don't need such information in order to come to faith in Jesus for life with God so He didn't include that in the Bible.

By our reasoning we might also speculate about things of God and think: It must be this way (as many have done, giving rise to a great variety of non-Christian religions). But He commands us to stay within the "borders" of the Bible so our beliefs will be what He says, not what we imagine.

Thank You for bringing me to faith, Lord; protect me so I never fall away by believing teachings which contradict what You have revealed in the Bible. Amen.

The Profuse Beauty Of Wildflowers

As you know God and our Lord Jesus, may you enjoy more and more of His grace and peace. *2 Peter 1:2*

Wildflowers can grow just about anywhere: out in desert heat, from a crack in a mountain cliff, backyard or garden (but called "weeds" there); with some water and adequate soil conditions they will sprout and grow into spots of color. But with enough water wildflowers can blossom so profusely that an otherwise barren field can become a carpet of color.

The "water of life", the message of God's love for us through Jesus, causes faith to sprout in us to give us peace through forgiveness and beautiful "flowers" of loving deeds. The more we receive of that "water" of His Word, the more we will enjoy being His and living His way.

Unless we only "soak up" His Word into our minds, but don't try to apply it to our emotions and our actions! A person could memorize many Bible verses and be able to tell the details of Jesus' life and death, but have no peace or power, if this is only knowing the words without trusting the Speaker.

As we use God's Word, we need to apply it to ourselves. Does God forgive sins because of Jesus? Then let go of guilt! Does God promise to care for His people? Then turn away from worry! Does God give strength and guidance for living? Then give up all excuses and follow Him!

This is how we more and more become truly beautiful to Him and also "enjoy more and more of His grace and peace."

Help me more fully trust Your Word, Lord, so my living becomes more helpful to others, satisfying to me, and pleasing to You. Amen.

The Dark Side Of Ice Plant

But people who want to get rich fall into temptation and a snare and many foolish and harmful desires that drown them in destruction and ruin. *1 Timothy 6:9*

Ice plant seems to be the perfect high desert ground cover. It survives summer heat, doesn't need much water, rather quickly fills an area, and has an interesting flower display. In addition, juice from its tender stalks sooths burns and other skin irritations almost as well as aloe vera does. Yet ice plant has its "dark side". It can literally choke out other plants in its area, and then for no obvious reason sections of it might die, while all of it might be killed by a really hard freeze.

Most people think that having more money would make life's trail much smoother: the area called "bills" could be quickly covered, more luxuries could be enjoyed, and paying for health care would be less stressful. Why else are lotteries so popular (especially when the jackpot gets into the upper millions)?

But having more money has its "dark side". So often the more you have, the more you "need", because money just buys things, which never fully satisfy our inner restlessness. Money also almost has an inherent magnetism, which draws one's attention away from dependence on God's care and guidance, because "I've got the money to do what I want."

If the Lord grants us more money, even riches, we can receive it as a "rainbow" and not let it become a "rattlesnake", if we keep remembering how He gives us what no amount of money can buy: eternal life at the cost of His Son's life and death.

Help me wisely use the money You've put under my control, and help me trust You, Lord, when there doesn't seem to be enough. Amen.

Tender House Plants

So I try to please everyone in every way and don't look for my advantage but for that of many people so that they may be saved. *1 Corinthians 10:33*

Most houseplants require special care: the right amount of light, humidity, and temperature as well as protection against insects and diseases. If you want healthy, beautiful plants inside your home, you willingly make that extra effort.

Some of God's people are like tender houseplants. They so often seem to stumble in trying to follow His trail – they might be fearful to attempt any new way of serving Him – they may easily become offended by what others do or say, while at the same time being offensive themselves. Although they probably don't realize it, they need extra patience and gentleness from their fellow trail companions, if they are to survive spiritually, because they focus too much on what they do and want instead of concentrating on what God's will for life actually is. They can be very irritating to live with!

But aren't we also in our own way? Our desires often cloud our understanding of what God wants His people to do, either in our individual lives or together as a congregation. Without realizing it, we, too, offend others. As we rely on Jesus for forgiveness of sins, we usually think at most about sins we are aware of; humbly we need to admit to that sinning against others, which we don't even realize.

Which is why, since not only the Lord but also others forgive us, we try to be patient and gentle and forgiving with others. We want them to remain in His family along with us.

Guard me, Lord, so I don't get so irritated with others, but give them extra Christian love instead. Amen.

Then There Are Dandelions!

I said to myself "I'll try pleasure and enjoy myself." But that also was pointless. I said about laughter, "it doesn't make any sense", and about pleasure, "what does it accomplish?" *Ecclesiastes 2:1-2*

One must admit that dandelions have pretty yellow flowers – and blowing the ball of seeds can be amusing. But so quickly it can ruin the looks of a lawn! Its initial beauty and even its sometime uses for salads or wine making, just aren't worth it! What a nuisance *weed*!

Isn't mere human pleasure like that? And laughter? Our culture teaches that we should have fun, be happy. But one cannot live on smiles or jokes, which actually give us only "fun". What we really want, our actual inner need is, lasting satisfaction, based on accomplishments. Yet even what we accomplish does not satisfy, since it is only temporary, soon forgotten by others and quickly becoming rather "hollow" to us. Why? It's the temporary nature of our lives – and the sinning in our living. These inescapable facts make us feel guilty and uncertain so that underneath our outward appearance is the haunting question: what will finally become of me?

Which question is unanswerable – unless we trust the good news God's Word gives us, the promise that we have an eternal future, because Jesus accomplished what was humanly impossible: He made satisfaction for our sinning. When we believe this assurance that we are safe eternally through Jesus, then, although guilt sometimes still gives us that unsettled feeling, we can relax and also enjoy "the lighter sides" of life.

Thank You, Jesus, for giving me the lasting satisfaction of knowing I have eternal life through You so that I can smile and laugh and even have fun in this life. Amen.

Roads To Nowhere

There is one God, and One Who brings God and men together, the Man Christ Jesus, Who gave Himself as a ransom to free all people. *1 Timothy 2:5-6*

Along an interstate in southwestern New Mexico hill after hill has roads to nowhere. Nothing of interest, no mining site, no impressive view at the top, just jeep tracks apparently made by people out "having fun". The damage to the fragile high desert environment, however, may never be healed, especially since others will also probably investigate: where does this one go?

Many people claim: There's only one god, and many roads lead to Him (or "Her" according to some). But the Bible says: Yes, there is only one God. However, there is also only one "road" to Him – and that "road" is Jesus. All other religions are "roads to nowhere" with eternally damaged results.

Non-Christian religions all believe that humans have to make their own way to "god": be good enough, do enough good, suffer enough – then "god" will ignore your sins and accept you into eternal blessings (although some "religions" don't believe in afterlife at all, instead: just be good and do good so you'll be happier now).

But the truth is what God says in His Word: sin puts an uncrossable distance between Me and sinners. But My Son, Who became also human, laid down the bridge of His cross and paid the "toll" by His suffering and death so that the way to Me is now free!

Use me today, if possible, Lord, to help someone at least begin to see that You are the only way and Your way is completely free. Amen.

Got Enough Gas?

Give the Lord the glory due His name. Bring an offering and come to His courts; worship the Lord in holy garments. *Psalm 96:8-9*

All rural people, but especially those living far from town, keep an eye on the gas gauge. "Got enough gas to get to town?" is a continual concern. Some install a second gas tank on a pickup or have a five gallon can filled and available to be safe. Sure isn't fun to run out of gas along a country road.

Along the trail of life we sometimes hear a "rattlesnake" which sounds pleasantly soothing instead of dangerous. It's that one which says: You don't need to go to church this week – after all, you don't get to go hunting/fishing/to a special sports event/on a family outing every week – anyway, you'll just hear the same old thing from the preacher, and you know it already, right, so??? And our sinful human nature is all too willing to agree: Yes, I've got enough spiritual gas – this once won't hurt.

But who knows better: us sinful humans or God? He commands public worship each week, not because He needs our presence, but because, whether we realize it or not, every week we need the message His Word proclaims that Jesus "dresses" us in the "holy garments" of forgiveness which He washed clean by His blood. This is the "fuel" that will keep us on the daily path of faith until we finally "get to (His eternal) town".

Since I know I always need Your power for the path of life, Lord, help me so I never choose to skip public worship. Help me also to pay attention at worship in order to hear Your guidance and to appreciate Your assurance that through Jesus I have Your forgiveness every day. Amen.

Following In The Darkness

You will guide me with Your advice and finally take me to glory. *Psalm 73:24*

Have you ever, while driving on a little-traveled highway through an isolated area where you had never been before, felt uneasy about whether you were on the right road? But a friend had given you a map with directions, so you just had to trust that your friend knew the way. Even in a familiar area one might begin to feel uneasy if the night is dark enough (or stormy enough) so all landmarks are blotted out.

Today's trail of life is unknown territory – we've never come this far before. Even if our physical situation hasn't changed (same home, same neighbors, same fellow workers), we really can't see what waits for us around the next hour's bend: could be "rainbow", but could be "rattlesnake" (especially if there's a stress element involved, such as: "what will the doctor say?").

But we have our Friend's guiding map, the Bible, which tells us to keep looking to the landmark of His cross so we can keep going toward His glory with Christian love to others, trust in His plan for us, and faith that He truly is our eternal Friend, Who will never mislead us, as we follow Him.

Thank You, Lord, for assuring me that You will guide and help me whatever might come on my trail of life today. Help me use and follow the map You've given me, Your inspired Word, the Bible, not only as I'm doing now, but all day long. Amen.

In Danger All The Way

It is given to you to be for Christ, not only to believe in Him but also to suffer for Him as you have the same struggle you once saw me have and now hear that I have.
Philippians 1:29-30

Every hiking trail, every traveled highway, every step of life has danger. A slip at a cliff, a real rattlesnake, a drunk or inattentive driver, a criminal's assault, a former friend's hatred, a fall at home, these and more can cause us real pain and suffering. On the trail of life we truly are in danger all the way.

What's more, we who follow the trail of life His way are in even more danger. Those who reject Him will in various ways show their opposition to Him by attacking us. Sometimes it's minor: a snub, a jeering insult. But sometime they truly cause suffering: destroying one's reputation or job, inflicting harm – even a martyr's death, initiating costly lawsuits. Such things have happened to followers on His path, going all the way back, not only to the early Christians, but even to the whipping room and the crucifixion hill where Jesus suffered and died. We are not to be surprised if some day we also have to suffer for Him.

Jesus was in danger throughout His life. Yet He was protected until that time when God fulfilled His eternal plan to deliver us sinners from eternal suffering. So we can be sure also that if we do have to suffer for Him, God will bring us through it according to His plan. Which is why we don't have to live in fear, but can bravely endure even the painful attacks of those "rattlesnakes" who hate Him. We won't enjoy it – we won't refuse to bear it either.

Give me courage to remain faithful to You, Lord, whenever someone opposes You and takes it out on me. Amen.

Spring Winds Keep Blowing

So, whether you eat or drink or do anything else, do everything to glorify God. *1 Corinthians 10:31*

In New Mexico the spring winds, often kicking up dust clouds, blow from March sometimes into May. In North Dakota the wind blows nearly all year round and strong enough so that 10mph could almost be called a "calm" day. Fierce Santa Ana winds also regularly rattle California areas. When the winds are blowing, one just has to accept their irritating monotony.

Many necessary things in daily living can get irritating in their monotony: house work, laundry, lawn mowing, taking out the garbage, putting up with another person's ingrained habits, the humdrum of most jobs – almost anything can become a deadening "same old same old".

But the Lord says that even these ordinary, monotonous routines of life are pleasing to Him – if we consciously do them as thankful service to Him. For Jesus also was carrying out God's plan, when He did the ordinary things of life during His 30 or so years on earth – He wasn't always doing miracles or suffering for our sins. Every deed of His life, the repetitious routine things included, was needed to earn our forgiveness.

So, everything we do in life, even boring things, will honor and please Him, when we do each one the best we can.

I have to admit that I don't always have a good attitude, Lord, when I do what I continually have to do. Thank You for having paid also to forgive that sinning. Please make me more willing and cheerful today so that what I do, whether routine or special, will honor You. Amen.

Finally! Hummingbirds!

I long to see you, to share a spiritual gift with you to strengthen you.   I mean when I'm with you I'll be encouraged by your faith and you by mine. *Romans 1:11-12*

The arrival of hummingbirds is a much anticipated spring event for many people. Hardly bigger than some insects, their antics are amazing as they hover at feeders and flowers, dart and swoop at amazing speed, and challenge one another at food sources. Quite a "rainbow" entertainment show they put on just by being themselves.

We eagerly look forward to special guests who are coming: family (grandchildren especially), enjoyable relatives and friends, especially if we haven't seen them for a long time (although we may also enjoy slipping comfortably back into our usual routine, once they have gone).

We naturally think that any such visit was all our mutual deciding: we invited – they worked out the travel arrangements. But the Lord was actually guiding – He allowed it for His purposes, which are partly just the relaxation and fun we have, but also for us to influence and encourage each other. Good visits include time for good talking – not only about past activities and about plans and dreams we hope will come, but also about how the Lord is leading us on the trail of life. Since He is most important for our lives, can we leave Him out of our visiting? What we say of Him and His love for us sinners just might be the special encouragement we and our guests need, when we are no longer together.

How I want to see loved ones, Lord, family and friends whom I've not seen for a long time. Grant that they might be able to come and visit so we can enjoy and encourage each other, especially in our faith in You. Amen.

The Palms Of Our Praise

The large crowd that had come to the festival and heard, "Jesus is coming to Jerusalem," took branches from the palm trees and went out to meet Him. *John 12:12-13*

We call today "Palm Sunday", because it was on this day (one week before Easter) that Jesus entered Jerusalem on a donkey, while people sang praises to God as they laid palm branches on the road before Him. Now for centuries Christian churches have used palms to mark this Sunday.

Some wonder how the crowd on Palm Sunday could sing praises, then five days later shout: "Crucify Him!" The fact is: it wasn't the same group. Scripture clearly says that the Palm Sunday people of praise were those who had come for the Passover festival. The mob members, thirsting for crucifixion blood, were cronies of Barabbas as well as others who had been enlisted by the chief priests against Jesus.

The contrast, however, should caution us about our possible fickleness. When life is going well or excitement fills us in a stirring church service, we can easily sing our palms of praise to Jesus. But when we are away from His presence or are challenged by the opposition of unbelievers, how easily our praises become silence or even are changed into joining those who reject Him. With shame we must admit that some days we are guilty of this contradiction.

Yet, we give our palms of praise to Him this day, because we know that on that first Palm Sunday He was coming to His cross for sinners, including us. And in our praise we also pray:

Lord, help me give You the praise of my lips and of my living every day no matter who might oppose me. Amen.

Monday of Holy Week   Read: Matthew 26:47-56

The Rope Of Our Unwillingness

So the troop of soldiers ... arrested Jesus, bound Him, and took Him first to Annas. *John 18:12-13*

We assume the soldiers bound Jesus with a rope to lead Him off to those who would condemn Him. But no rope was needed! Jesus could have escaped when they had all fallen to the ground at the sound of His voice. He could have urged His disciples to fight so He could escape in the confusion. But He did neither. Willingly He went with them, bound not by the strength of a rope, but by the power of God's plan to provide escape for us from the consequences of our sinning. The soldiers didn't know this, of course, so they used a rope.

At times in daily life don't we use a mental "rope", not to tie up Jesus, but ourselves? This "rope" limits us in our living for Jesus. It is the "rope" of "I can't"! Most days what God calls us to do is not difficult, the ordinary deeds of kindness, honesty, helping. But some days include real challenges: to forgive immediately the one who has hurt us, to speak calmly when anger boils in us, to do what God says is right even though we could get away with what is wrong, to obey Him when those around us want to disobey! "I can't" is often our inner cry in those times, and that "rope" limits our faithfulness.

But is it "I can't" or "I don't want to"? We know the answer. We also know the escape Jesus gives us when the "rope of unwillingness" winds itself around us. He is our escape! As we think of not just His willingness, but that He did suffer and die for us, the Holy Spirit works in us to give us power to be faithful daily.

Lord, make me willing to obey You and then help me do it. Amen.

The Rooster Of Our Pride

And Peter remembered Jesus saying, "Before the rooster crows, you will deny Me three times." *Matthew 26:75*

No, Lord! Peter had proudly boasted! I will die for You instead of deny You! How loudly the rooster of Peter's pride was crowing! Until the morning rooster crowed and Jesus looked at him from across the courtyard! Then Peter remembered – and wept in bitter shame.

How quickly the rooster of our pride can also crow! As we hear of how someone has sinned, our rooster might crow: Well, I would never do that! As we look at some special way we have served the Lord, our rooster might crow: Yes, look at what I have done! As we think about our living and compare it to others, our rooster might crow like that Pharisee did: Thank You, God, that I'm not like those sinners (*Luke 18:11*)!

How blessed we are, if, when our rooster crows, we catch sight of Jesus looking at us with the mirror of His Law, which says: "Cursed is everyone who doesn't follow and do *everything* written in the book of the Law" (*Galatians 3:10*).

That look of God's Law leads us to blessing. Only when the rooster of our pride dies, can we then see Jesus' look of loving forgiveness, His look from the cross where He erased even our rooster of pride.

In His forgiving look we realize the peace He gives us. No pride in us then, only humble thanks for His acceptance in spite of how often our rooster tries to crow.

Lord, keep me humbly thankful for Your forgiveness. Amen.

The Moneybag Of Our Greed

Then (Judas) threw the money into the temple and left. He went away and hanged himself. *Matthew 27:5*

Judas, how could you? Betray your friend and teacher for money? Judas, how could you? Kill yourself in despair? But that's what greed will do to a person! Whether greed for money or greed for things or greed for excitement or greed for anything! Greed never is satisfied: the more it gets, the more it wants. Greed finally destroys and kills!

Obviously, in life we need a certain amount of money and things and change from daily routine. Our sinful human nature, however, tempts us toward more than just some or enough: Wouldn't that be nice to have? *and* that? *and* that? So, more money is needed – and if $1,000 would help, why not $10,000? More, more, more!

The only way to empty the moneybag of greed is to see Jesus as He really is: the One Who has promised and proven He will care for us into all eternity. More importantly, by His suffering and death for our sins He has acted to take care of us forever. Since He did that at such great cost to Himself, will He not care for us as we live?

The fact is that He cares and provides for our needs – and even much more. At times we may just barely get by – perhaps you've even suffered bankruptcy – still, we have enough to live. We can pray for what we would like; but we can enjoy and be content with what we have, as we wait to see how He will provide as life goes on.

Lord, thanks for all You do and will provide, especially the blessing of eternal life. Amen.

The Crown And Whip Of Our Cruelty

Then Pilate took Jesus and had Him whipped. The soldiers twisted some thorns into a crown and placed it on His head. *John 19:1-2*

Scourging, beaten 39 times with a whip, was a cruel enough punishment. To that the soldiers added a crown of thorns, mockery, slaps, and spit. How could they be so cruel?

They? Is not cruelty part of our human nature? We are most likely not physically cruel, but words can prick like thorns and even looks can cut deeply into another person's feelings. Who of us has not also at times, usually in anger, done some little thing which we knew would hurt another person? We didn't have to, probably felt guilty afterward, but cruelty can easily show its mean face in our deeds or words.

Jesus came into our world with full knowledge of the cruelty He would experience. He also knew our cruel deeds, as well as the cruelty of everyone else who has ever lived, for which He would have to suffer. He did not flinch from this pain, for there was no other way to spare us from suffering far worse than human cruelty: the eternal punishment of hell.

As we thank Him for enduring all this for us, we also ask Him to work in us so that the Holy Spirit might keep us from any kind of cruelty, no matter how angry we become.

Lord, I need Your help to lessen and even eliminate the cruel words and deeds that I so easily inflict on others. Amen.

The Nails Of Our Daily Sinning

When they came to the place called Skull, they crucified Him there with the criminals, one at His right and the other at His left. *Luke 23:33*

The mallet blows echoed across that barren skull-shaped slope. Excruciating pain quivered throughout His body as the nails dug deeper through His hands and feet into the wood of the cross. Yet these pains were only the beginning. Still to come: the sharp jar of the cross jammed into place, the weight of His body tearing at those nails, the aching of muscles, the gasping for breath, the thirst, the sun's rays burning in the morning, the lonely darkness for three afternoon hours.

But even that physical pain was not the worst. Spiritually He suffered beyond human imagination. The very agony of hell, not just as one person might suffer, but for the sins of all people – punishment compressed from all the Old Testament peoples and from all our New Testament billions, compressed by God into one punishment on that one day! No wonder He cried out in near despair: "My God, My God, why did You forsake Me?" (*Matthew 27:46*)

There Jesus hung, so did He suffer. We don't want to admit that what we do wrong could cause Him such agony. Yet He was on that cross primarily because of the nails of our daily sinning. Yes, even the "little" sins we quickly forget put Him and kept Him on His cross. He was there because of us. In His love He endured what we deserve so we might receive forgiveness, peace, power for godly living, eternal life.

Lord, thank You for suffering in my place; help me struggle against even the "little" sins I so often am guilty of. Amen.

Can There Be Any Hope?

Pilate was surprised He was already dead. .... When the captain told him, Pilate let Joseph (*of Arimathea*) have the body. *Mark 15:44-45*

When standing beside a grave of a dear one, we can feel devastated. Life seems meaningless and hopeless. That's how Jesus' followers felt after seeing Him buried. He had so many ideas, He had such great powers, He promised so much! "We were hoping He would be the One to free Israel," said some (*Luke 24:21*). Death, our last and greatest enemy! Can there be any hope, when even Jesus ended up dead?

Of course, we know there is hope, even confidence. We know that Jesus' death was only a planned pause in His battle plan to give us life without end. He had to die as well as suffer because of our death-causing sinning. When He died, however, He was not in that tomb – only His body was – He was in His Father's hands, in His presence, in Paradise. Yet in the shock and sorrow over His death the disciples didn't remember that. How could they? They had never actually understood that.

We, however, should remember, for we know the meaning and purpose of Jesus' death, and we know He didn't stay dead. Still, our feelings can cloud our remembering. Yet only for a while! God has given us tear ducts for more than just to moisten our eyes. Tears release the pressure of our emotions so we can hear again the promises of Jesus. Then we are comforted, no matter how hopeless a grave seems. Those who have died, trusting in Jesus as Savior, are not in any grave, but are with Him in eternity. And so we are comforted.

Lord, comfort me when sorrow at the death of one I care about tries to overwhelm me. Amen.

When God Said: Yes!

"Don't be afraid," the angel said to the women. "I know you're looking for Jesus, Who was crucified. He is not here. He has risen as He said." *Matthew 28:5-6*

They couldn't believe their eyes! The tomb was open and empty! They could hardly believe their ears! An angel said He was alive! Filled with a mixture of fear and joy those first Easter women ran off – without saying a word to anyone – until Jesus met them on the way. Then they went and told the disciples: He is risen!

Actually, Jesus did not have to rise from the dead to earn our salvation. He had accomplished that completely by His suffering and death on the cross. There He had proclaimed: It is finished! Completed! Nothing left to be done – salvation has been won!

But how could we know that, if He had stayed dead and buried like any other human being? How could we know that God had accepted His sacrifice as payment for the sins of all of history? If He had not risen, no one could know whether He was Who He had said He was, the Promised one of God, the Savior, or just another slick-talking pretender with grandiose ideas about himself.

But He did not stay dead! On that Easter morning God said: *Yes! He did enough! Yes! He absorbed all My punishment for sin! Yes! He is the Savior, the only Savior! Yes, people! Trust in Him as your way into My peace as you live and finally into My presence eternally!* Truly, when Jesus rose from the dead is when God said: Yes!

Lord, I give You thanks and praise and glory – for Jesus, my risen and living Savior. Amen.

Fools For Christ

I think God has made us apostles come last in the procession like men condemned to die... We are fools for Christ's sake. *1 Corinthians 4:9-10*

No one likes to be made a fool. Even on April Fool's Day we may smile, but we don't like being tricked into looking foolish.

Sometimes we hesitate to follow Jesus' way on the trail of life, because we are afraid others might ridicule us as being fools. At times it isn't even others, but our own selfishness which argues that we are being foolish. How?

To give generously for God's work, when we could spend that money on our own enjoyment – to disrupt our own plans to help a complete stranger – to patiently listen to a troubled neighbor, who says the same thing over and over – to risk your life when someone is in danger – to work for less pay with a company after being offered more elsewhere – to "turn the other cheek" when being insulted – to keep helping someone who never even says thanks – to volunteer an extended commitment for a mission or service project – to attend public worship instead of going to a championship sports event – to insist on sexual purity at the cost of popularity: according to human standards these are foolishness.

So why willingly do any of these or similar things? If an action truly helps someone or is being faithful to our Lord, then even if others judge us as "fools", we cheerfully will be such "fools for Christ", because according to human thinking He sure was a "fool" to suffer and die on the cross even though He had the power to escape it. But He did it for our eternal good.

Help me, Lord, not to fear to do what is good today no matter if others do ridicule me for it. Amen.

Just By Chance?

And the Lord will guide you continually and satisfy you even in times of drought. *Isaiah 58:11*

Just by chance they saw the ad for 9+ acres along a New Mexico arroyo. Just by chance they had enough money meant for retirement housing to buy RnR ("Rattlesnakes and Rainbows") without debt. "Just by chance"?

So often things happen in life, which we might think are "just by chance"; we had not expected them – whether negative (car accident, illness) or positive (making a new friend, finding something long looked for), but they happened.

Except that nothing for a child of God happens "just by chance"! The Lord guides everything that happens, even the troubling things, for He keeps them within His planned limits so He can work through them for our good. As we are thrilled by the unexpected "rainbows" He guides to us, so we can willingly accept the "rattlesnakes" He allows, for nothing happens "just by chance".

Proof of this is Jesus in His life and death for us sinners. He wasn't born to Mary "just by chance" – it was God's foretold plan. He didn't suffer and die on the cross "just by chance" – it was God's eternal plan to save us sinners.

True, He lets us sin – and He lets those who reject His love go their eternal way. But for us who trust in Jesus, He guides so that nothing *ever* happens "just by chance" but for a good purpose according to His plan.

Thank You, Lord, for teaching me that I can be sure that You are in control and guiding in whatever happens today or any day. Amen.

Three Times A Crossing

No one can say, "Jesus is Lord", except by the Holy Spirit.
1 Corinthians 12:3

Their place, RnR, isn't the easiest to find even with directions: "Just before the road crosses the arroyo the third time, turn across it into our lane." But some, perhaps looking at the scenery, don't follow the directions and drive right on by.

The Bible gives the directions for how to receive forgiveness of sins and eternal life. But it also has so much history, so many laws, such a variety of prophecies as well as hard to pronounce words and some difficult to understand doctrines that people get distracted and do not find the message that Jesus is the way. Primarily, however, because of self-pride or an over-whelming sense of guilt or both no one by nature wants to depend on Jesus' suffering and death to be accepted by God. The Holy Spirit has to convince a person.

Yet He does not act like thunder out of a bare sky; He has bound Himself to using the quiet Bible words as we share them with friends, who not only hear our words of faith, but especially see the effects of faith on the trail of our life. Which means that we need to figure out ways to both share and show our faith with friends who don't depend on Jesus. We don't know if or when the Holy Spirit will finally convince that person, but we keep trying – and praying – for that friend.

And think what special joy we will have if in eternal life one or more will tell us: And I'm here, because the Holy Spirit used you to help me find Jesus.

Guide and use me, Holy Spirit, to somehow be Your tool to reach _____, my friend, who does not yet trust in Jesus as Savior. Amen.

Taking Care Of God's Creation

The Lord God took the man and put him in the garden of Eden to work it and take care of it. *Genesis 2:15*

When you own property, what do you do with it? Some don't seem to care and their land becomes an unsightly jungle or an ugly junk heap. But most want to beautify their property with landscaping and plantings, with gardening or even an orchard. This almost innate desire actually goes back to God's command to Adam in the first paradise: he wasn't to just sit around loafing, enjoying the view; he had work to do in God's perfect creation. What that work was, we don't know, for there weren't any weeds yet – those came after the fall into sin (see *Genesis 3:17-19*); but he worked to "take care of it".

No question about the work we have in taking care of any land we have: planting and weeding, watering and harvesting, pruning branches and fighting insects.

Also, our taking care of God's creation extends beyond our immediate property; we are responsible to Him for the whole earth. Not that we will go to the irrational extremes of those who seem to think that individual plants and animals are more important than people. But we need to live as wisely as we can in order to help preserve this present creation, until we enter His promised new creation of everlasting life.

How we live here on earth does not earn us entry into that glory. Jesus has earned it completely so He can give us free admission. But how we live now shows how thankful we are that we will live with Him there.

Although I am so insignificant, Lord, guide me to see ways how I can better help to take care of Your creation. Amen.

Projects Without End

It is God Who works in you, both to desire as well as to do what is pleasing to Him. *Philippians 2:13*

Ahh, what plans they had! Landscaping here, plantings there, gardens, more fruit trees, the house site, a mountain-like trail up the ridge, even a bird sanctuary habitat – so many projects! "And what will we do when the projects are done?" he asked; to which she replied: "We'll never get done with projects!"

And we are God's "project", as long as we live on earth. Who we are now is not what we were nor what we will be! Once we did not know Him – now through faith in Jesus we are His! And see the changes He has worked in us compared to some time ago! How He has worked! But how much He still has to do to make us be what He wants, for we still have ways that bring shame to His name and guilt to our consciences – which shows we are His not-yet-done "project"; in fact, we will never be totally "done" until we are finally in His eternal glory.

He does not, however, just snap His fingers to end our tendency to anger, our occasional curse word, our desire to "get even", our sometimes loveless words or selfish deeds. These require our attention and effort.

Still, any "project progress" will not come by our power or will. We are *His* project so our desire and effort and changing come from Him. Yet these happen only as we think of what He wants in our living and especially what He has done for us sinners. In Jesus we are already accepted – He sees us as already "complete" since He forgives us. That fact is what gives us the desire and the power to please Him more day by day.

Help me, Lord, to please You more today than yesterday, especially in this area of my life: _____. Amen.

Irrigated Blessings

Their life will be like a well-watered garden, and no longer will they have to starve. *Jeremiah 31:12*

The high desert country of New Mexico is truly desert, not sand like the Sahara, but with such sparse rainfall that little of food value can grow to enable people or most animals to survive. RnR, however, has the rights to 45 minutes of irrigation water, channeled spring water, about every 19 days. With that water how the desert does produce: pasture, fruit trees, garden! Not enough land to provide everything a family might need to survive on, but it shows how water produces and sustains life.

So also the spiritual "water of life"! Left to ourselves trail life is only desert: bleak plodding along, temporary pleasures to shift attention away from on-going troubles, sin, and guilt (with attempts to escape through drugs, sex, excitement – but without lasting success), and finally death! Into this hopelessness, however, came the "water of life"! God channeled His limitless love into the Person of Jesus, God come to earth. His love is not feeling, but action, the action of obedience and of sacrifice, done in His life and by His death on the cross because of our sins. Now the message of that love becomes the spiritual "water of life" for sinners. As we "drink" it by trusting in Jesus, we do not starve eternally, but receive life with God now and forever.

But this "water of life" does not merely *give* life; it also produces blessing in us who are spiritually alive and through us to benefit others. This is why we "drink" daily by using His Word to keep aware of His love for us in Jesus: so we might be better blessings, "brighter rainbows", to others.

Use me, Lord, to be a blessing to someone today. Amen.

Free Water?

Oh, come to the water, all who are thirsty! You who have no money, come, buy and eat. Come and buy grain without money, and wine and milk that costs nothing. *Isaiah 55:1*

That irrigated water just keeps coming! From a spring some dozen miles up the canyon! And it's free! Except for a minimal cost each year to pay the ditch boss and keep the ditch in repair – so, it isn't really "free". Nor is well water free: well has to be drilled and maintained, etc. And, city water? It's surely not "free"! In fact, is anything in life absolutely "free"?

Well, air is free – and sunshine – and rain – these are free, creation gifts from God. And how about "people things": the love of a spouse, the smile of a neighbor, the kindness of a friend, the hug of a child – aren't these "free"? Not really! For each depends to a certain extent on how we act toward those individuals. Even a grandchild would eventually turn away in fear if grandpa was continually mean – and how long will a marriage last, neighbors smile, or friends be kind, if we act only selfishly? No, "people things" are not actually "free" either.

Yet God gives for free the best blessing of all: His forgiving love in Jesus. Without any payment on our part, in fact, in spite of our opposition to Him, He gave Himself for us. Jesus entered our world of sin, endured the attacks of sin, took sin upon Himself, suffered the consequences of all the sins of all time. All this He did without any deserving or payment on our part – since we can't. True, we now thank Him and try to live for Him; but this is response, not payment. And all He did was done even for those who never let themselves be rescued. He did it all for free!

Thank You, Lord, rescuing me for free. Help me show my thanks better in my living this day. Amen.

Art's Work

A man and his friends can destroy one another, but there is a friend who sticks closer than a brother. *Proverbs 18:24*

When it's their turn to irrigate, the water has to be diverted from the irrigation ditch into their side ditch. At first they had a cumbersome "gate" of 8' long planks, which had to be manhandled into place at the cost of loss of water and an aching back. "Don't think I can do this when I get to be 80," he said. So friend Art devised a simple lever gate, which changed a ten minute grudge into a ten second smile. A friend: one who willingly helps if able to, not as a "got to", but as a "want to".

Help from a friend can take many forms: encouraging smiles, listening ears, guiding words, sympathetic tears, as well as physical effort. Help from a friend also requires response – thanks, kindness, caring, helping – or friendship will disintegrate into feelings of being taken advantage of. Friendship also requires forgiving, because no two people ever can get along without ever offending each other.

One "friend", however, will never desert us in spite of how we have and do and will offend Him, our Friend Jesus. He didn't think "got to", when His coming was planned, even though if He didn't help, there would be no hope for any sinner. He came completely on a "want to" basis – in His pity for us helpless sinners. And no matter how we fail to thank Him, refuse to follow Him, and perhaps even have walked away from Him to go our own way alone again, He never gives up wanting to help, trying to help, and actually helping us with His forgiveness and blessing as we turn to Him again day by day. Truly, He is the friend who is better than a brother – but He also is our Brother.

What a friend You are, Lord! Help me willingly to help my friends and also others whom I see today to be in need. Amen.

Not Always What Seems To Be

He lies in his hiding place like a lion in his den, waits there to catch the helpless, and takes the poor away. *Psalm 10:9*

As they sat under an old apricot tree next to the irrigation ditch, it looked like a large rock in the water was rocking back and forth. But it was only the shadow of the leaves making an optical illusion. Things are not always what they seem to be.

Especially so with many unbelieving people! Some pretend friendship, all the while having plans to take advantage of the person, usually financially. Some groups also seem innocent on the surface, but are being used by organizers for their hidden purposes and so mislead well-meaning people. Some charities claim to aid needy causes, but use most of the contributions for "administrative expenses". Cults and false prophets use selective Bible verses to snare unsuspecting individuals. And, of course, temptation to sin often conceals itself under an attractive appearance of reasonableness.

On the other hand, a person who might at first seem unfriendly or dull might just be shy, and some situations which seem forbidding might be very fulfilling, because your help was much needed.

Which means that we dare not automatically judge anyone or anything on the basis of first impressions. We need to look more carefully and use God's Word to help us determine whether what is being offered is an opportunity for good or a trap of sin. The primary purpose of God's Word is to assure us of forgiveness of sins because of Jesus. But God also gives us guidance through His Word to help us avoid evil and do good.

Keep me alert, Lord, so I am not misled today by the outward appearances of people or situations. Amen.

Mighty Cottonwoods In Decline

You made my days a few inches, and my whole life is nothing to You. *Psalm 39:5*

Their irrigation water originally formed Rio Alamosa, "River of Cottonwoods", so named because of the many ancient cottonwoods up and down the valley. For hundreds of years those mighty trees have survived and grown because of that water – some are 50' or more tall with trunks 6' thick. But they are declining: great branches break off when heavy with occasional wet snow or shaken by strong winds – every few years one just dies. And, due to changed conditions, including how these giants suck up the available water and give so much shade, no young cottonwoods seem able to grow as replacements. How long before they are just gone? Nothing lasts forever!

Except for us! As years pile up with increasing speed, we realize we will not "last forever" in our earthly bodies. Inwardly we may feel hardly older than ten years ago, but physically we just can't do everything as well or as quickly as then. So soon we will be gone, no longer residents of this earth. Except! We will *not* be "gone"! Once alive, we live forever! No one escapes death or "forever"! The question really is: will we only exist, separated from God in hell, or will we live in His presence with more blessing than we can now even imagine?

The answer is determined by our relationship to Jesus: do we trust in Him or do we ignore Him? By the Holy Spirit's power, which we receive as we remember the good news of Jesus daily, we will remain on the path of faith past death to be with Him in person.

Keep me in faith, Lord, serving You day by day until finally I see You in person forever. Amen.

Fences Make Good Neighbors

"Please let's have no quarrel," Abram told Lot ... "Doesn't the whole land lie before you? Please move away from me. If you go left, I'll go right, and if you go right, I'll go left." *Genesis 13:8-9*

When the world was all open range, fences were not needed – space alone could separate neighbors sufficiently. But now even in the large open areas of New Mexico and other western states residents know: "Fences make good neighbors"; fences keep in my activities and keep out yours so we aren't as likely to quarrel. Disagreements and conflicts still do erupt, since our selfish sinfulness never fully respects any fence; but where people are so crowded together that no fences can be built to define personal space, no wonder so much tension, fighting, and violence result. Unselfish friendship would eliminate the need for fences; but since that isn't practiced fully by anyone, fences and double-locked doors and security systems are required.

Still we are called to be helpers to others, especially those who are close to us, such as neighbors. It's not "just by chance" that we live exactly where we live. The Lord has specifically placed us next to those who live next door, in the next apartment, on the next ranch. Some may not want to be bothered by us; but yet we need to be alert to their times of need so that we can help them, if possible. Only God knows how He might be able to bless them through us. Our physical helping might even open them to the spiritual help we can give them by eventually sharing how Jesus came to release all of us sinners from the eternal consequences of our sinning.

Lord, help me see how I can help my neighbor today, since I know You do want to bless them through what I do. Amen.

They'll Find The Low Spot!

Then one of the twelve, called Judas Iscariot, went to the ruling priests. "What will you give me?" he asked. "I will betray Him to you." *Matthew 26:14-15*

"Fences make good neighbors" – but animals, as well as people, believe that "the grass is always greener on the other side of the fence", so if there's a low enough spot in the fence or a break or a hole big enough, soon the neighbor's cattle (out in the country) or the neighbor's dog (in town) will be on your property or in your garden with unavoidable damage as a result.

The devil always keeps probing to find the "low spot" in our spiritual defense. With Judas it was greed (*Matthew 26-27*) – with King David it was lust (*1 Samuel 11*) – with Peter it was fear (*Mark 14*) – with Moses it was anger (*Exodus 2*). What is your "low spot"? For we all have such areas of life, where we easily give in to temptation – perhaps it's pride or fear or anger or lust or lack of trust or pessimism or self-righteousness or self-pity or interest in gossip or selfishness. Which of these or other areas must you admit to as being a big problem because of small defense?

What can we do about our weaknesses? Realize most of all that Jesus forgives us every time we fail Him, even bringing us back to Himself if we fall away, if we let Him (as He did with David, Peter, and Moses – and He would have received Judas back also except he despaired in his guilt). That forgiveness gives us both peace about our past and power for our future, as we ask Him to help us be especially on guard against those so tempting temptations.

Raise my defenses, Lord, against those temptations I so easily give in to so that today You keep me from them. Amen.

A Fence With No Purpose

Then some Pharisees and Bible scholars came to Him from Jerusalem. "Why do Your disciples sin against the rules handed down by our fathers?" they asked. "They don't wash their hands when they eat." *Matthew 15:1-2*

Across parts of RnR are old fences. Originally each enclosed an area where cattle would graze until the grass was low; then they would be moved to the next area. Without cattle, however, those fences no longer have any purpose – except as nostalgic reminders of what once had been.

Traditions can become such "fences with no purpose". If no longer understood, they don't remind anyone of the past except for the statement: "We've always done it this way". Traditions serve a good purpose, if they are understood: they can teach us how others lived and believed and, therefore, how we still need to live and believe. Some traditions need to be maintained or even restored, because they still can have value in our lives. But sometimes traditions lose all meaning. Life has so changed that what happened or was done in the past, important as it was then, has no relation to us today. Then it's time for mere tradition to be changed so that new and meaningful patterns can be established and practiced.

Some of the past, specifically the teachings of God's Word about the way of eternal life and His commands for God-pleasing living, dare never be changed. Those who reject Jesus as Savior want to discard all traditional teachings about Him and to eliminate all the commands of God. But sin has not changed, so the way to forgiveness does not change.

Help me adapt to how life has changed, Lord, so I can give up any traditions which are now meaningless; but guard me so I never give up Jesus. Amen.

Making Good Use Of It

It is good for a man to be generous and ready to lend and fair in doing his business. *Psalm 112:5*

They had nearly an acre of RnR in pastureland, but no animals to graze it. They had dreams of turning it into a bird sanctuary habitat, but that was years off. So they let the neighbor use it free for emergency grazing until then. After all, why not make some good use of that part of their property?

We all have so much stuff, some of which just sits there, rarely or ever getting used. We had a reason for getting each thing at the time, but what good are such little used items now? Could perhaps they be put to some good use by someone else?

Some possibilities: the willingness to lend and the generosity to give. Perhaps a neighbor or friend could use something we have. Maybe we have reason not to give it away yet, but we surely can lend it willingly. And just maybe we should give it outright to someone who will use it. Or, if you have enough to dispose of, how about a yard sale? That can be a valid choice, since "one person's junk is another person's treasure". Or perhaps a charity thrift store could offer your things at minimal prices to needy people who will better value something they pay even a little for, since they don't want to accept "charity"!

When it comes to our eternity, however, we can't pay even a little bit – we have to accept the "charity" of Jesus, Who paid completely for our home in eternal life by His cross sacrifice. But part of our thanks for His so giving Himself for us is to make good use of what we have, also by giving to others.

What should I give away of my things, Lord, so good use will be made of them? Help me see and then give, because You gave Yourself for me. Amen.

The Tax Man Cometh!

That is why you also pay taxes. Men in government serve God and are busy doing their work. Pay to all whatever you owe them. *Romans 13:6-7*

April 15th! A day of dread for perhaps most Americans! Even if a refund is due, it's an anxiety-producing chore to get that income tax return sent in. Which is partly why so many pay others to fill out the forms – another reason being, of course, the instructions can be so complicated that the average person can't easily understand them and might fail to pay in enough or might miss possible deductions.

Does anyone like paying taxes? Yet we enjoy the services which taxes provide. Our dislike, however, stems from: having to subsidize some benefits we are not eligible for, thinking that rich people can find more tax breaks than we can, and government waste. Still, it is our Christian duty – so God has commanded, because government in spite of its shortcomings is how He carries out His plans in the world!

Think how He used government to fulfill His plan to give us eternal life! Hate-filled leaders manipulated Jewish religious government and cowardly Pilate used the authority of Roman government to get Jesus crucified! But God was working to carry out His justice of punishing all sinning so He could set sinners free forever as they trust in what He did through Jesus.

Now freed, we thank Him by our living, which includes our paying to support His work being done by His people and also through the government.

Help me, Lord, to pay my due taxes willingly, even cheerfully, and especially to give generously for Your work of freeing those who are still trapped in their sins. Amen.

Sunset Ridge

Who knows what is good for a man in his life, in the few pointless days of his living? He spends them like a shadow.
Ecclesiastes 6:12

The first few years they would eat an evening picnic on Sunset Ridge, while watching the fleeting sunset (mostly blocked by other valley ridges) and talking over plans for the next day. After the house was built, however, they hardly ever climbed that ridge to eat a meal – the courtyard table was more convenient.

Many of life's trail habits change, as time goes by. We might occasionally look back and think: "It was enjoyable when we used to …..", but changed circumstances keep us from renewing those patterns. The fact is, we never know whether what we find good to do now will seem as good in the future. No point, therefore, in fixing our hopes too much on present patterns, since like fleeting sunsets nothing permanently lasts in life.

Except for the good which comes through Jesus! Good radiated from Him as He lived on earth. But at His "Son-set" (His death on the cross) that good seemed as temporary as an evening sun's last rays. And if He had stayed dead, our lives would be absolutely pointless, merely brief shadows, lost in the darkness of nothingness.

His "Son-rise", however, has eternally changed our existence: we walk a trail which actually goes somewhere with Someone. It twists and turns with many changes; but this "Son", in Whom we trust, is always with us – and we will finally be with Him always.

Keep me confident of Your Presence, Lord, no matter the changes I have to make, as life goes on. Amen.

Cross Crest

The Lord looks at the world from heaven to see if there is anyone wise, who comes to God for help. They have all turned away altogether and become corrupt. Not one does right, not a single one. *Psalm 14:2-3*

Their first summer at RnR they made a 4' cross from bare cottonwood limbs and erected it on the brow of a ridge, which they named "Cross Crest". That cross can be seen from the entire property and continually reminds them to keep our beautiful Savior in mind always on the trail of life.

The overall view from Cross Crest is quite beautiful. In season you can see the blooming orchard, flowering plants and shrubs, the wildflowers and cacti, the landscaping and gardens, the trails, the house site – "beautiful" because you're too high up to see the weeds! And weeds there are aplenty, because God's creation has been corrupted by sin (*"The ground will grow thorns and thistles for you"*, He told Adam after he first sinned. *Genesis 3:18*).

From eternity He, however, was not "too high up" to see the "weeds" of sin! So Jesus' cross became necessary. And from it He saw every sin everyone ever did; He saw them – and suffered for them under God's absolute justice. Now with our sins hidden in the shadow of His cross, He sees us as beautiful people, as long as we depend on Him alone to forgive us.

Which is why we try to live beautifully with people we live and work with day by day.

Lord, help me to live this day so that others will see the beauty of Your working in me. Amen.

High Point

May I never boast of anything but the cross of our Lord Jesus Christ, by Whom the world is crucified to me and I to the world. *Galatians 6:14*

Usually twice a week their morning hike takes them up the mountain trail to "High Point", tallest elevation on RnR at 5545', where the view of the surrounding valley and the San Mateo Mountains to the north is rather impressive. They do it for the exercise, however, with the view an enjoyable bonus.

On the trail of life we make great effort to be the best we can be. Sometimes the Lord then blesses so we achieve a real high point – perhaps a championship, perhaps public recognition, perhaps even celebrity. Then can come a "rattlesnake", the temptation to think too much of ourselves, as though we had accomplished this just by ourselves and not by His blessing.

Some then also are tempted to boast about past championships or public recognition or celebrity to keep up their pride no matter how little they now achieve.

Yet one "high point" of life does give us lasting worth. It is that rather low hill outside Jerusalem where on a cross, raised toward heaven, the God-man Jesus achieved the impossible for us! He became God's method to punish our sins while forgiving us sinners!

We are thankful for and enjoy various high points on the trail of life. But we find our peace in life and our strength to achieve good as we live in the "high point" of His cross.

Help me do the best I can today and every day, Lord, because of what You did for me on Your cross. Amen.

The Last Stop

"Your brother will rise again," Jesus told her. "I know he'll rise again in the resurrection on the last day," Martha answered Him. *John 11:23-24*

Remnants of a horse-drawn wagon were found under some brush, hauled down to the entry lane, and whimsically named, "The Last Stop": it could go no further. A few years later an arroyo flood covered it with gravel so now it is only a disappearing memory.

According to human logic we might think the same about our bodies: we age – we die – and the "remnants" are cremated or buried – and eventually will be completely forgotten. Our bodies are strictly temporary residences, right?

But we confess in the Christian creeds: "I believe in ... the resurrection of the body" – don't we mean it? Well, doesn't that merely refer to a glorious *spiritual* body? However, did Jesus rise with a "spiritual" or a physically *touchable* body? "A ghost doesn't have flesh and bones as you see I have," He told the disciples (*Luke 24:39*). As He arose physically, so shall we! The cemetery is not "the last stop" for our bodies!

When we die, we are separated from our bodies to live in God's presence as non-physical persons. But on Judgment Day we shall get our bodies back – recreated, sinless, glorious – so we can live physically forever in the new creation. This is our Christian "hope", made sure for us by Jesus' death and *resurrection*!

Lord, help me care for my body with healthy habits of eating, sleeping, and exercise so I have more energy in serving You now, as I look forward to living with You in my recreated body forever. Amen.

Just A Little Adjustment

Don't neglect to welcome guests. This is how some without knowing it had angels as their guests. *Hebrews 13:2*

An old log-hauling long-bed trailer had been left at RnR, almost obstructing the driveway. Too big and broken-down to roll away, it was an eyesore problem. Then one day they shoved one end only about a foot into a position parallel to the drive – that small change in perspective gave it a "just right" character.

Inviting guests to visit is one thing. But when you have other planned activities, a friend who stops by or especially a stranger at the door can feel like quite an imposition. Self-pity over "how am I going to do what I had planned" can even make one only barely hospitable. That's when a change in our perspective will be helpful.

Typically we look at situations from our point of view: what I need/plan/want. But what might we see, if we ask ourselves: what does God want at this time? True, sometimes we must say: I don't have the time – I can't help right now. But if we trust Him to help us eventually work out what we had originally planned, instead of a "rattlesnake" problem we just might find an opportunity which becomes a "rainbow" joy, when we see how we did provide the help He intended.

In all of history only one plan never was delayed or changed: His plan of saving us through Jesus.

Keep me calm and kind, Lord, if my plans have to be changed by the need of someone whom You bring into my schedule today. Amen.

April 21

Read: 1 Corinthians 5

Waiting For Moonrise

But we were hoping He would be the One to free Israel.
Luke 24:21

Moonrise the previous night had been so spectacular that they climbed Sunset Ridge anticipating an even greater show when full moon came up. But for some reason it wasn't nearly as good as expected.

The trail of life so often seems that way: well-laid plans just don't work out – long-expected experiences are less than thrilling – perhaps a business fails, a friendship evaporates, illness ruins retirement, or marriage is disappointing. Also at times our trust in public figures is crushed by their incompetence or unethical behavior. How depressing! And there's little, if anything, we can do about it!

Except trust! That God is in control no matter what has happened! As He was, when Jesus was crucified! Evil people and the devil thought they had won, for Jesus was dead! They didn't realize that "the Christ had to suffer this and so go to His glory" (*Luke 24:26*). God used that seeming tragic end to give eternal glory to those who trust in Jesus, not as political figure, but as eternal Savior. Although we are disappointed when He vetoes one opportunity, we can have confidence that He will open up another for us.

And even if life truly does seem just to be getting worse and worse, as it does for some individuals (perhaps you or someone you know), when we trust in Jesus, at least each day is "one day closer to glory".

Please help me patiently bear any disappointment that might come today, Lord, with trust You are controlling all things in the way You know will be best for me, even if not easy. Amen.

Stars So Bright

When I look at Your heavens that Your fingers made, the moon and the stars that You set up, what is man that You should think of him or the son of man that You should come and visit him. *Psalm 8:3-4*

New Mexicans claim that you've never seen stars until you see them on a moonless night from the open desert! Even with unaided eye you can see more than you can count! And then looking at the Milky Way with just binoculars, you literally see millions more! Of course, other open areas, whether desert or mountainous, make the same claim; but in New Mexico one can actually walk paths at night, if they are wide enough, just by starlight!

So many stars – such vast distances! Who are we that the Creator of them all should, humanly speaking, be interested in searching for our planet, such a very small speck of dust in the whole universe? And why would He want to, since, having found us, He also would find our rebellion against Him! Surely He has better things to do, human reason would conclude, such as taking care of all those stars, than caring about us!

Yet, having created also us, He did not have to search for us. He cares about us so much that He not only came to "visit" us – He came in the Person of His Son to live among us and then die so we could leave our rebellion to be at peace with Him.

Unbelievable! But this is the Gospel truth which we now trust for eternal blessedness!

Thank You, O God over all, for caring about us sinful humans and about me personally, sinner though I am. Help me live my life today in a way which shows my thanks to You. Amen.

Stars All Night Long

He decides how many stars there should be and gives all of them names. Our Lord is great and very strong, and there's no limit to what He knows. *Psalm 147:4-5*

At first when overnighting at RnR, they slept in a tent with a mesh roof so they could see the stars any time they woke up at night – unless they had put on the rainfly to keep dry!

How awe-inspiring – to see all those stars, yet God is greater than them all.

How interesting – to learn to identify the planets, some of the constellations, and even certain individual stars as well as to know where they will appear during any night as our planet moves in constant rotation on its annual circuit around our medium-sized star.

And how comforting – to be assured that He Who made them all and named them all and "sustains (them) by His mighty Word" (*Hebrews 1:3*) also made us and knows us by name through our Baptism and watches over us individually. Darkness does not hide us from His knowing eye. Also, He sees our needs even more than our sins, for He has hidden our sins from Himself by covering them with Jesus' pure life and suffering death. Which is why even more constant than the stars is His caring love to help us.

Whenever I look at the stars, Lord, remind me that You always see me to forgive all my sinning because of Jesus and to give me help in all my needs. Amen.

Satellites Zipping Across The Sky

Since by God's wisdom the world by its wisdom didn't get to know God, God decided to use the foolishness of our preaching to save those who believe. *1 Corinthians 1:21*

Not too long after twilight at RnR occasionally a speck of light can be seen zipping south to north across the star-filled sky. What a testimony to human intelligence and ingenuity earth satellites are! Even more impressive are the feats of placing human feet on the moon and robotic machine feet on Mars as well as other space exploits. Then, too, are the many advances made in medicine, communications, transportation, and daily civilized comfort to improve life here on earth.

But all such human "wisdom" cannot find the answer to life's biggest challenge: what to do about sin? In fact, by "majoring" in the relatively "minor" things of life, people feed their pride and so lead themselves away from the only solution for sin by claiming either "forget it, because there is no god" or "if you live good enough, you'll be o.k. – if there is any life after death."

So God had to reveal the one-and-only way to escape sin and its punishment, the way of Jesus, God come to earth: I'll punish Him for all sin and forgive them!

Sounds too simple to proud, "wise" humans! But there is no other way, says God.

Keep me humbly thankful, Lord, for rescuing me from my sinning no matter that others at times might ridicule my faith in Jesus as the only Savior for me or for anyone. And make me brave to speak lovingly of Him to others, when You give me that opportunity. Amen.

Who's Out There?

When the disciples saw Him walking on the lake, they were terrified. "It's a ghost," they said, and they cried out in terror. Immediately He talked to them. "Have courage," He said. "It is I. Don't be afraid." *Matthew 14:26-27*

Some nights when they slept in the mesh-tent, a gusty wind would flap the ground cover to sound like perhaps a person or an animal was prowling around just outside the tent. Never happened, but darkness has a way of igniting unwarranted fears.

Fear easily attacks when we face a future made dark by uncomfortable possibilities of health, economics, conflicts, or uncooperative individuals. What will happen? How will it turn out? What will I do?

Fear has value: it can warn us to be more careful in what we want to do, to plan better what we might say. But fear also can be paralyzing to prevent us from doing the best we can; it also can be sleep-depriving and health-destroying.

In our weakness we can't completely avoid fear; yet we can be encouraged when we keep reminding ourselves that we will not face this fear-arousing thing alone. Perhaps no human friend can possibly understand what we fear. But Jesus stands with us to help us endure even if what we fear actually happens. He not only cared about us on His cross for our eternal life; He also cares about what happens as we live daily life.

Help me keep Your presence in mind, Lord, whenever I fear, so that I know You will help me get through whatever actually comes. Amen.

Hours Of Dawn And Twilight

The path of the righteous is like the morning light that gets brighter until it has reached the brightest of the day. The way of the wicked is completely dark, so they don't know what they stumble over. *Proverbs 4:18-19*

If you wake up at dawn, at first there isn't enough light to read by; gradually, however, the sun's light strengthens to enable you to see what you need to do. At the other end of the day the reverse happens: increasing twilight darkness dims your vision so it's easy to stumble.

Just as dawn and twilight do not stand still but continually increase, so spiritual light and spiritual darkness are not static: one always tries to overcome the other. And all life long we experience that struggle.

If we do nothing, if we neglect the source of light, the Bible, by staying away from public worship and by being too busy to have daily Bible reading, darkness will overcome us and life will become one stumbling disaster after another until eternal darkness envelopes us.

So we need to use His Word regularly – hearing it every week in public worship and reading it every day in personal devotions. Still, the prince of darkness, the devil, will try to blind us into missteps in hopes of making us fall. But as we look to His light, always seeing how Jesus conquered our darkness by the victory of His cross, the Holy Spirit will keep us in faith and on the path that leads to eternal light.

Help me turn away from any excuses, Lord, which would keep me from hearing Your Word with others each week and from using Your Word each day. Amen.

Darkness Flees The Light

Once you were darkness, but now you are light in the Lord. Live as children of light, since light produces everything good and righteous and true. *Ephesians 5:8-9*

It goes without saying that light and darkness cannot co-exist: as the sun rises, darkness flees. True, clouds can dim it's light, but rarely can they produce total darkness.

By human nature we were in spiritual darkness. But the Son, by entering time, brought eternal light into this sin-darkened world. Then He left us with the on-going source of that light: the inspired Word of God, the Bible, through which He has now made us "children of light" by bringing us to faith in Him as our Savior. With His light shining on our way, we can now walk the trail of life, doing what is "good and righteous and true".

Sadly, so easily, because we still have that dark (sinful) human nature, we let clouds of darkness dim His light so that we wander off instead of fully walking on His path. Actually, this happens to a certain extent every single day: we sin.

So His light reminds us: live according to Whose you really are; keep turning to My Word of light and let it shine on you with its forgiveness and on the path ahead of you with its guidance. One way of doing this is to ask ourselves in every situation: Is this good to do? Is it righteous according to His Word? Is it being true to Him Whom I follow?

Lord Jesus, thank You for wiping out the darkness of my sins on Your cross; help me in my life this day to better follow the light of Your guidance because I am comforted always by the light of Your forgiveness. Amen.

So Cute, So Deadly!

No one can tame the tongue – a restless evil, full of deadly poison. *James 3:8*

Some think mice are cute – she would rather face a rattlesnake than a mouse – with good reason! Not only because their droppings contaminate food and eating utensils, but also because at least in New Mexico they sometimes carry the deadly Hanta virus, which can kill a person in just a few days unless promptly given drastic medical treatment.

The tongue of a baby sure is cute. But as it grows with the child and into maturity, that tongue quickly becomes an uncontrollable deadly weapon! It learns to lie and gossip and curse and hurt with harsh words. Which we know from personal experience on both the receiving and the giving ends!

Of course, that piece of flesh in the mouth isn't really at fault – it only does what the person wants: "What a person says with his mouth flows from his heart" (*Luke 6:45*). So we can't control our words just by deciding to control our words. Instead, we need to ask the Lord's help to fill our hearts with His good so we will speak what is good.

Still, as with all other areas of godly living this doesn't happen automatically – at least at first. We do have to ask for specific help – we do have to determine to think of the good He has revealed – we especially need to concentrate on His forgiveness for our verbal sinning. In this way He gradually can transform our tongues from being such "rattlesnakes" into being "rainbows" of truth and kindness – at least most of the time.

I'm ashamed, Lord, at how I sometimes speak! Thanks for having suffered to silence the punishment my words deserve! Help me, because I sure need it! Amen.

Into The Mud Hut

This is why you should take God's whole armor; then you can resist when things are at their worst and having done everything, you can hold your ground. *Ephesians 6:13*

Only one room remained from an adobe home built in 1916; they called it the "Mud Hut". But the wind could whistle through spaces between the adobe bricks, gophers sometimes dug up through the dirt floor, and those mice kept coming through various holes. They wanted to use it, since wrestling the tent bedding was a chore, so they defended it as best they could by stuccoing the walls, pouring a concrete floor, patching holes, and setting traps for those mice. And after once spotting a prowling bear, they never slept out in the tent again!

The Lord provides us with spiritual defenses against the invaders of: our own sinful nature – unbelieving people around us – and the devil masterminding all the attacks. His "armor" is: the truth of His Word, the message of forgiveness and eternal life through Jesus as revealed in that Word, the words about Jesus which we speak to others (which we also listen to and are strengthened by), the fact of our faith which makes us remember we are His children and can live as His children, and very specific Bible passages which help us not only recognize invading attacks but also apply God's strength to resist them (*Ephesians 6:14-17*).

They couldn't keep all the mice out – nor can we completely avoid sinning. But being forgiven daily, we not only fight to defend against the temptation "rattlesnakes" – we also make "rainbow" advances in doing good to others as He desires.

I need Your help also today, Lord, to be defended against the attacks which come and to be guided toward good when these opportunities appear. Amen.

Let The Rest Of The World Go By?

Tell them to do good, to be rich in good works, to be glad to give and share. *1 Timothy 6:18*

Only about 20 people live in the valley up from Monticello – which makes for mostly peace and quiet with only minimal neighborly contact, unless one desires it. Most people seem to like at least some periods of solitude, but so much "quiet" (except for daytime bird sounds with sometimes coyote yapping and owls calling at night)? Still, nearly everyone tries to make their own little "nest" to which they can escape and not be bothered by the rest of the world.

Which cannot completely be, of course, both because no one is totally self-sufficient – we need things and services from others, and because God has placed us on a trail of life which always leads us to people who need us. Exactly how and how much we can help others varies for each of us according to the situation we have been guided into (even if this was our personal choice). But always God is directing us "to do good, to be rich in good works, to be glad to give and share".

For so has He acted toward us! His rich goodness we can see in His creation around us, in people who care about us, and in how He provides for us (even if we don't have abundance, we still have so much – you are not starving right now, unless you have chosen unwisely). Most of all He has shared His eternal love with us by giving Jesus so we, who cannot deserve it on our own even one bit, can have an eternal home

Lord, keep me from being only self-centered; open my eyes to see, my heart to care, and my hands to share, as You have so directed. Amen.

Until He Returns

"Men of Galilee," they asked, "why are you standing here looking up to heaven. This Jesus, Who was taken away from you to heaven, will come back the same way you saw Him go to heaven." *Acts 1:11*

The disciples stood there stunned! They had seen Him suddenly appear and disappear a number of times in those forty days after His resurrection, but this! All of a sudden He just began to float up and up until He disappeared into a cloud. So they just stood, staring! Until two angels said: Why are you standing around? Get to the work He has given you! He'll come back some day – until then carry out His orders. Which for them right then were: wait in Jerusalem, praying – which included trying to understand what all this meant that they had heard and seen of Jesus and had read of God's promised One.

Throughout the nearly two thousand years since then His followers have continually needed to be reminded to work for Him until He returns. We who trust in Him know that nothing we do can add anything to the work He completed so we can one day join Him in heaven. As a result, we are tempted to conclude: we don't have to do anything – just go our own way. Our thankful faith does urge us to serve Him, but our sinful nature wants to do for self instead of for Him.

Which is why the New Testament books include so many verses of instructions and explanations why we are to obey Him (examples: *Romans 6, Galatians 5, 1 Peter 4*). Because Jesus did all His work for us, we now have work to do for Him. He has saved us so that we can serve Him. By our serving we earn nothing – with our serving, however, we thank Him.

Help me thankfully serve You today, Lord. Amen.

The Birthday Of The Church

When they came together, they asked Him, "Lord, are You now going to reestablish the kingdom of Israel?" ... "When the Holy Spirit comes on you, you will receive power and will testify of Me in Jerusalem, in all Judea and Samaria, and to the farthest parts of the world." *Acts 1:6,8*

Even on Ascension Day the disciples were all mixed up about why Jesus had come. They still thought "the kingdom" He had preached was earthly power. They heard the word "kingdom", but human ambition closed their ears to the words "of heaven" (*Matthew 2:39*). In reality, they were not yet "Christians" by New Testament definition! Until Pentecost, the special coming of the Holy Spirit on the 50th day after Jesus' resurrection!

The real blessing of that day was not their miraculously speaking languages they did not know (*Acts 2:6*); instead, it was their finally understanding what Jesus had actually done. Pentecost can be called "the birthday of the Church", because on that day the disciples began to believe and to testify that Jesus was the One Who made sinners acceptable to God by the sacrifice of Himself on the cross. This faith is what makes the Church *be* God's Church, and to testify with this message has been the primary work of the Church ever since. Personal daily obedience and loving help to others in need also are our work; but to "testify" to Jesus is essential. For what eternal good does it do anyone to see an example and to be helped physically if the message of Jesus for eternal life is never heard? Our task as Church, however, is not an either/or choice, but a both/and attitude: speak the good news that Jesus is the Savior and show by faithful, helpful living that we do believe in Him .

Lord, help me and my fellow followers of Jesus to share and show our faith daily on the trail of life. Amen.

April Showers...

The land you're crossing into to take over is a land of hills and valleys, watered as the rain falls from the sky, a land the Lord your God is looking after and His eyes are always watching. *Deuteronomy 11:11-12*

"April showers bring May flowers." But often those showers don't come in New Mexico until May – and sometimes not even then, if desert drought is severe. Still, after the moisture, whether gentle rain or downpour storm, the beauty comes.

Along the trail of life come sometimes showers, sometimes storms. The "showers", the ordinary stresses of daily living, we don't mind too much, because we also have times of relaxation as well as expressions of love and friendship to enjoy; then we easily can say: "God is good to me."

But when "storms" drench us, those hurtful "rattlesnakes" of emotional conflict with others (which we sometimes also cause) or serious health problems or economic hardship, then another "rattlesnake" easily slithers into our outlook: "Does God really care about you, to send this to you?" In the middle of a "storm" we can seriously doubt that any "rainbow" will come out of it.

Yet that is God's promise! His "eyes are always watching" us, not to see our sins, because He knew them all before we were born – that's why Jesus died for all people including us; He knew then the wrongs we would do now, so He paid for them in advance. Now God's watching "eyes" are looking out for us in our troubles so that He can finally work out a "rainbow" of good after the "storm" passes.

Whenever a real "storm" comes, Lord, help me trust You to bring me through it to enjoy however bright a "rainbow" You then give me. Amen.

The Joy Of Gardening

"What is God's kingdom like," He asked, "and what will I compare it with? It's like a mustard seed a man took and planted in his garden. It grew to be a tree, and the birds in the air nested in its branches." *Luke 13:18-19*

Gardening is the world's oldest occupation, for Adam's job was to take care of the Garden of Eden (*Genesis 2:15*). Is that why gardening feels so natural for so many people? More likely the joy of gardening comes from seeing plants quietly grow – and the gardener helped in the process! Of course, the gardener only plants and waters; God actually grows the plant.

A similar joy results when we see God's kingdom, His rule, grow in ourselves: when a troubling "rattlesnake" ceases its bite (perhaps our quick flashes of anger lessen), when we are able to make more "rainbows" for others because our willingness to help increases. And we helped in the process – or did we?

God Himself actually works any good change in us through the power of His Word. Yet, just as a garden seed left in a seed packet cannot grow, so also the "seed" of God's Word accomplishes nothing in us if it just stays inside a dust-covered Bible. We have to in a sense "plant" it in our minds and think about it and try to follow it – but that's all we do. The Holy Spirit then gradually works the change in us.

So we don't get proud when we notice any improvement; we only give thanks that God both forgives sinners like us (because of the work Jesus did to make us spiritually alive) and keeps working to make our words and deeds more pleasing to Him.

Lord, thank You for having made some progress in me. Work in me also today, because You and I both know how much more I still need to grow. Amen.

For Food And Beauty

As the ground produces its sprouts and a garden makes the seed sown in it come up, so the Lord God will make righteousness and praise spring up in the sight of all the nations. *Isaiah 61:11*

A person gardens not only for the joy one feels, but especially for the food and beauty produced. God created plants not for their own sake, but to bless us: vegetables to feed our bodies, flowers to uplift our spirits. Which would have been enough for life forever according to His original creation plan.

But not any more, not since a certain "rattlesnake bite" infected us all with sin unto death (*Genesis 3*). Now we need righteousness, perfection, if we are to be healed spiritually and live eternally.

However, we can't find such righteousness from anything of this world or by our efforts. Even if we could accomplish the impossible and do everything absolutely right from this moment on, there would still be all our past wrongs showing our death sickness.

So God had to create righteousness for us by "planting" His Son on earth to do every right deed as well as make up for all our wrong deeds.

By faith in Him we "eat" this "fruit of righteousness" and are healed of our sin sickness so we can live: for Him while on earth, with Him in eternity.

Thank You for making me righteous in Your sight, Lord; help me today to do right and keep from wrong. Amen.

Water, Fertilizer, And Mulch Needed

"Master," he answered him, "let it stand one more year, and I'll dig around it and fertilize it; it may have figs next year. If not, cut it down." *Luke 13:8-9*

As plants grow, they use up the nutrients and moisture in the soil so fertilizer and water must be added to keep them producing food and beauty. Composted animal manure is best, but man-made fertilizers are more convenient for most gardeners (as well as farmers) and do the job adequately, if they have the proper ratio of three essential elements: nitrogen, phosphate, and potash. Depending on soil conditions, too much of one or not enough of another will harm rather than help particular plants. Sufficient and consistent watering (with mulch to conserve that water and protect the plants) also is needed for a good harvest.

For us to produce the fruit of godly living, we need the "water and food" of God's Word. How often? He says every week in public worship for a major application as well as daily "mulching" through personal Bible reading.

We need His Word in the proper "ratio", however, which is: His Law to make us keep admitting our need for forgiveness because of sin, His good news about what Jesus has done to cover up our sins, and His Law again to guide us in daily living. Without regularly receiving these three spiritual "nutrients", we cannot produce the good works which please Him.

Thank You for the "mulch" of Your Word in this devotion, Lord; help me today to do what pleases You. Amen.

So Much Better Taste

How blessed is the man who fears the Lord, who takes great delight in His commandments. *Psalm 112:1*

The reason garden vegetables taste so good in contrast to most store-bought produce is the difference between harvesting a fully ripe tomato and one which had to be picked half-green for shipping purposes. Supermarkets may be more convenient and less expensive, but gardens (and farmers markets) give you fresher produce with so much better taste.

Following the desires of our sinful nature often seems easier and more appealing than obeying God's commands. "Just do it," whispers the "rattlesnake", especially if it seems that no one you care about will ever find out what you did. But afterwards comes the nagging guilt feelings, which tell us that God knows – and so often that cared about one eventually finds out which makes us feel worse.

Far more satisfying is to turn from the enticing path of sin to follow the narrow trail of obedience to Him Who has blessed us with the food we need, those who care about us, and, best of all, His loving forgiveness for us in Jesus. When we do what He says, not only do we escape the trouble that sin always produces, but we also feel good for doing what is right and we get along better with other people. True, unbelievers might ridicule us, when we don't join in with their evil deeds; but that's a small price to pay for pleasing Him instead of them. Yet we can be faithful only as we keep receiving and thinking about the message of Jesus' obedience in our place all the way to His cross.

Especially when sin seems so appealing, Lord, keep me remembering Your sacrifice for me so that I follow Your way and realize each time that Your way is truly better. Amen.

The Aroma Of Garlic

Yes, we are the aroma of Christ to God among those who are saved and among those who perish – to some an aroma of death that kills, to others an aroma of life that gives life.
2 Corinthians 2:15-16

Garlic: a very healthful vegetable – and it tastes so good, say garlic lovers. Yet a polite garlic eater might tell a friend: "You may not want to get too close to me today," since many people are offended by garlic's lingering "aroma". Why should the same thing be so pleasing to some and so distasteful to others? Just personal preference decides regarding garlic as well as so many other things of this life.

Is the contradictory reaction to the Gospel, the message about Jesus as Savior of sinners, also just personal preference? Do we trust in Him because He pleases us? Do others reject Him because He doesn't?

Not really, for initially even we did not like what we heard of Him – and sometimes we still don't! For if He is "Savior of sinners", then we have to admit that our sinning makes us need saving, and our pride doesn't like that! I'm not *that* bad, we protest – until we are honest with ourselves: yes, I am "that bad", so I need Him! Those who reject Him never come to that admission or else believe they are *too* bad for even Him to save.

But what worked to destroy our pride objections (without making us despair) while not convincing others? To that question there is no Scriptural answer. There is only the need for us to be thankful that somehow the pleasing "aroma of Jesus" has worked to bring us to faith in Him for eternal life.

Help me, Lord, so my actions today are like a pleasing aroma to those with whom I live and work. Amen.

The Beauty Of Cut Flowers

No one has a greater love than he who gives his life for his friends. *John 15:13*

Blossoming flowers truly are beautiful in their growing location. But to enjoy their beauty inside our homes and for special occasions, they have to be cut, in effect, killed. Flowers, of course, have no consciousness of such self-sacrifice in giving us joy.

How we help others along the trail of life is like being a beautiful flower to those being helped and also in God's sight, for helping always involves some sacrifice of time, effort, and sometimes cash. But how much are we willing to sacrifice to help someone else? Would you sacrifice your life? Sometimes people do – for someone they love. But how about for an enemy? Would you give up your life for someone who despises you? That's asking too much of anyone!

Yet that's exactly what Someone did, that Someone being Jesus! According to our sinful nature we were rebellious enemies against Him – and still show this hostility by our continued sinning. Yet He sacrificed Himself in order to make us His friends, even better, members of His family.

His self-sacrifice is now what gives us ability and willingness to make the sacrifices necessary to be beautiful helpers to others, even to those who do not like us. And if the situation ever calls for it, maybe we might risk and even sacrifice life itself, if needed.

Guide me, Lord, so today I will be helpful to others no matter what I might have to sacrifice. Amen.

Weeds! Always Weeds!

The kingdom of heaven is like a man who sowed good seed in his field. But ... his enemy came and sowed weeds among the wheat... When the wheat came up..., then the weeds showed up too. *Matthew 13:24-26*

Weeds! No matter how diligent the gardener, there almost always seem to be weeds to fight! Yet, as has been said, in spite of their coarseness weeds actually are just misplaced flowers, some even have food or medicinal value. Which would be acceptable in a proper location, but: Not in my *garden*!

Some people in our congregation – because of their unthinking sinning or maybe their personality quirks – can seem like unwelcome "weeds" to us, to be avoided or just endured. Of course, we conveniently forget that because of our sinning and personalities, we probably seem like "weeds" to others, too. So, what to do? Join a different congregation? But we'll find – and be part of – the same "weed problem" there. No part of God's "garden" (the church) is free of "weeds" – the enemy (that first "rattlesnake") makes sure of that!

Before God each of us sinners truly should appear to be an obnoxious "weed". But He sees us as "flowers", worth the price of His Son's life and death. So He keeps working, not to get rid of us, but to re-grow us, still with weedy/sinful aspects, but in process of becoming His "flowers". Which is why we, keeping our own not-yet-"flower" condition in mind and that we are accepted through His forgiving us, can be accepting of our fellow "weeds" and be thankful together that He isn't done working in any of us yet.

Keep me humble, Lord, when I get irritated with others, since I have to admit I'm just as "weedy" in my own ways as they are – but You forgive us all for Jesus' sake. Amen.

Allergy Season I

**My son, don't forget what I teach you, and keep my
instructions in mind, because they will give you a long, good
life and you will be happy.** *Proverbs 3:1-2*

Allergies! As plants produce pollen many gardeners (as well
as others) battle their allergies. Some have such a problem that
they move to a different climate, only to find that after some
years of exposure to new pollens they develop new allergies.
Other allergies to food, dust, molds, and more also plague
many. No one knows exactly why some develop immunity,
while others don't, nor how to definitely cure allergic reactions;
but it helps to avoid exposure as much as possible.

Constantly allowing oneself to be exposed to particular
temptations can break down one's spiritual immunity so that
instead of recoiling from it, one becomes addicted to that
particular sin, whether explosive anger, lying, suspicion, fault-
finding, immoral thinking – what sin allergies might you have?

Although we know we can never be completely cured until we
reach eternal life, as those following Jesus on the trail of life,
we have taken the "medicine" of His forgiveness so they don't
kill us eternally; still such sin allergies make us miserable and
we want relief from them. His prescription is: keep His loving
sacrifice for us and also His instructions to us in mind – these
will help us avoid situations where we know we'll be exposed
to those particular temptations and even give us some
"immunity" when temptations do come. The peace of being
forgiven is always our comfort; but we are relieved when
through the help of His Word we don't give in again when we
are tempted.

*Help me today, Lord, to avoid this particular sin, which I so
often give in to: _____. Amen.*

Allergy Season II

The Lord gives me light and saves me – of whom should I be afraid? The Lord is a fortress where my life is safe – whom should I fear? *Psalm 27:1*

Their friend moved to New Mexico to escape allergies that were literally killing her. After much improvement she went back to Minnesota for a visit – her allergies quickly flared up again. Such can be one's physical sensitivity to certain conditions.

We can have a similar emotional sensitivity, which can affect our spiritual well-being. Deeply hurt by someone's past sinning against us can make us "allergic" to even a slightly offensive word or unkind glance from that person so that old hurts and old fears flood us all over again. Similarly, sometimes between husband and wife just the tone of a comment can cause hurt feelings. Why?

It's that "rattlesnake" again, trying to destroy our peace, trying also to bring back resentments to fuel a desire for revenge, which would take us down its path instead of His trail. There truly is spiritual danger in such emotional sensitivity.

What can be done to overcome such "allergies"? Remember: because God forgives me for Jesus' sake, I truly have forgiven this person for Jesus' sake. Consider: perhaps I am still overly sensitive toward this person because of my human weakness. Remind yourself: I don't have to fear, because the Lord will protect me. Because of our sinfulness we won't automatically dismiss our fearful resentments, but He will help us do so, just as He will keep forgiving us for them.

Help me keep the past in the past, Lord, so I deal only with what really is now in my relationships with others. Amen.

Hiking Before It's Too Hot

My son, pay attention to my wisdom; listen to the understanding I give you, that you may conduct yourself wisely and talk intelligently. *Proverbs 5:1-2*

It's just common sense in southern New Mexico to plan desert or exposed mountain hikes before summer comes when it gets too hot. It's common sense also to take along plenty of water and sunscreen any time you hike, because it will get hot in the searing sun.

Common sense usually is a reliable guide, yet not always, especially not in spiritual matters. Common sense says: if a statement isn't completely logical or scientifically provable, don't believe it – but that rules out most teachings from Scripture, especially the teaching that Jesus was truly God and truly human in One Person as well as the teaching that He as One Person did suffer the complete punishment for all the sinning of all the billions of people who have ever lived. Common sense says: follow the crowd so you don't get hurt or look foolish – but the sinful crowd follows its own desires, not God's way. Common sense says: take care of yourself first – but Jesus says: I'll take care of you, so even sacrifice of yourself to help others.

For most decisions along the trail of daily life then we should use common sense. When a choice must be made, however, we will follow Scripture no matter what our sinful nature feels or what others might say or do, for Scripture is God's sure wisdom and guidance.

Help me live wisely, not foolishly, in any way today, Lord, according to Your wisdom. Amen.

Mud Mountain Hike

Because of the toil of His soul, He will see the light and be satisfied. By His experience My righteous Servant justifies many by taking on Himself the heavy load of their guilt. *Isaiah 53:11*

They didn't expect much from a hike up Mud Mountain just west of Truth or Consequences – from below it looked pretty barren. So why do it? Because it had a trail and might have a nice view from the top. And that trail turned out to be very interesting with a variety of cacti and wildflowers, petrified mud, and "candy rock". Quite an enjoyable hike after all!

Sometimes we reluctantly face experiences that are just routine, distasteful or painful, things that can't be avoided but have to be done: washing windows, cleaning the bathroom, confronting a quarrelsome neighbor, undergoing surgery. One Thursday night Jesus faced His most distasteful and painful task: to carry the heavy load of our guilt into the pain required to "justify" us sinners, to get us declared innocent by the Father because He completed His task. His prayer that night showed His human reluctance: "If it is possible, let this cup pass away from Me" (*Matthew 26:39*). Then, strengthened by His Father and looking ahead to the glorious result – eternal life for sinners, He willingly did what He had to do.

Nothing we confront can ever come close to what He did. But if we pray for willingness, think about the outcome, and keep our eyes open to what we might find or whom we might help along the way, we might just be surprised at how satisfying, if not enjoyable, it was to get it over with. And if it really was as boring or painful as we expected, at least we know it was part of God's plan for us and He helped us endure it.

Lord, make me willing to do what just must be done. Amen.

"Dead Stick Forest"

The Lord laid His hand on me and by His Spirit took me out and put me down in the middle of a valley that was full of bones. "Son of man," He asked me, "can these bones become alive?" "Lord God," I answered, "You know." "Prophesy about these bones," He told me, "and say to them: 'Dry bones, listen to what the Lord says.'" *Ezekiel 37:1,3-4*

On Mud Mountain the trail goes through a "dead stick forest", a stand of ocotillo. Most of the year this desert plant looks like a dead stick with thorns. But given even a little moisture, it blossoms with scarlet flowers at the tips followed by small greenish leaves covering the entire stem of each "stick". Then as the desert dries, it retreats into apparent death again.

God says we were "dead in (our) trespasses and sins" (*Ephesians 2:1*), not just *apparently* "dead" like the ocotillo, which has life hibernating in it, but truly spiritually *dead* – absolutely no ability on our own to come to life before God.

Until the Word of God came to us! Not just any Bible verse but those which made us admit our deadness, our inability to do anything to deserve God's blessings, and then those which tell us that God gives us life through the death of His Son on the cross. Through such words the Holy Spirit creates faith in us to make us "dead bones" live!

Now, just as the ocotillo shows its life by flower and leaf, our having spiritual life from God shows in our looking and being different in daily living from those who are still "dead" in unbelief.

Thank You, Lord, for making me spiritually alive; help me show this today by living Your way in all I do and say. Amen.

Trying To Climb Rathdrum Mountain

No one else can save us, because in all the world there is only one name given us by which we must be saved.
Acts 4:12

When they lived in northern Idaho, three or four times they tried to climb to the top of Rathdrum Mountain. Others told them there was a way; but no matter which logging road they tried, though they found elderberry bushes and once someone's lost revolver, they always came to dead ends – they never quite found the way to make it to the top.

We may not know how to reach every earthly mountaintop. But we do know and believe the one way to reach our goal of eternal life; as Peter confessed, so do we: "There is only one name given us by which we must be saved" – and that name is "Jesus", not as a word spoken like a memorized magician's incantation, but as the expression of our dependence only on His sacrifice for our sins. "Jesus" is the "password" which opens heaven's "door".

Until we are safely inside, however, we must guard against substituting a different name, our own! That's what the "rattlesnake" of self-righteousness wants us to do: think of *our* "sacrifices" instead of only His.

That's why every day we need to pray a repentant prayer of faith, which might be something like this:

Lord, be merciful to me, a sinner – I know You are, but only because of Jesus. Help me live for You today; but no matter how well I do, guard me so I depend only on Him and never on anything by me. Amen.

Unless You Scale The Mountain

Then they went back to Lystra, Iconium, and Antioch, strengthening the disciples and encouraging them to be loyal to the faith, saying, "We must suffer much to enter into God's kingdom." *Acts 14:21-22*

"Unless you scale the mountain, you cannot enjoy the view." What a thrill to stand on a mountaintop and see ranges off in all directions with a river down below winding through a green valley. But you have to climb that mountain to get that view – unless you get there via the shortcut of cable car or helicopter – not the same satisfaction, however.

No "shortcuts" exist on the trail of life to the "mountaintop" of eternal life – there weren't for Him Who made the trail, there aren't for us who follow Him.

The "rattlesnake" tried to mislead Jesus onto a "shortcut" (just "bow down and worship me" and You'll escape all that You're heading for, *Matthew 4:9*). But Jesus could not, for that sin would have destroyed the trail. He had to live without sin every day to take all the world's sin away. No "shortcuts" for our Savior.

Nor dare we try any which attempt to escape obedience or opposition. To follow Him, "to be loyal to the faith", means that for His sake we will have to suffer, inwardly as our sinful desires protest our denying them, outwardly as others oppose our faithfulness. Such suffering does not make us worthy before God – only Jesus' cross does that; but it reminds us of His suffering so we are willing to accept whatever "cross" He lays on us.

You know I don't like to suffer, Lord; so help me not to try to avoid it by being unfaithful to You in any way. Amen.

A Pebble In Your Shoe?

It isn't good for you to feel proud. Don't you know a little yeast ferments the whole dough? Get rid of the old yeast in order to be a new dough, as you are really free from the old yeast, because our Passover Lamb was sacrificed; it is Christ. *1 Corinthians 5:6-7*

Have you ever on a hike had some small pebble in your shoe, but for some reason, whether the hike was almost over or "it isn't that bad", you didn't want to take the time to stop and shake it out? Kind of foolish to put up with an on-going irritation, but sometimes we do.

More serious is when we "put up with" our seemingly "minor" (as we judge them) sins. But these, if left un-fought, can develop into more destructive sinning: coveting (wanting more and more things) can escalate into greed – angry outbursts can lead to violence – occasionally skipping public worship can become indifference to God's Word – bragging about what we do can produce self-righteousness.

Jesus was sacrificed for all our sins, also for what we consider "little" as well as for any other. So if He had to suffer also because of these "small" sins, does that mean we should continue in them or repent of them, that is, turn from them as the sins they are to the way He wants us to totally be?

We'll never become perfect in this life. But that's no excuse for not using the power of His forgiveness to more faithfully follow the guidance of His commands in *every* deed of living.

I am ashamed, Lord, that I'm not always strict with myself in obeying You; help me quit making excuses for sinning, as I often do. Amen.

The Sky's So Blue!

Don't let these things get out of your sight, but keep them in the center of your heart. *Proverbs 4:21*

While hiking down a narrow, high-cliffed arroyo, she exclaimed: "Look how blue the sky is!" New Mexico's sky is almost always spectacular blue, but why was it more so that day at that place? Because their attention was focused up! Out in the open, looking horizontally, one's eyes automatically see a dusty desert haze or even creeping smog from larger cities. But when your vision is narrowed so you just see cloudless sky, BLUE!

The trail of life can get rather depressing when we only look around us "horizontally." So much evil in the world, people we live with being so sinful (including that one who stares back at us from the mirror!), tragedies and catastrophes continually – or perhaps what we see is hospital room equipment next to us or medicine bottles in front of us. So our spirits droop!

That's especially when we need to refocus our attention – in our mind's eye looking up to Jesus, risen and alive, having conquered sin and death so they have no claim on us – in our mind's ear hearing His promises to protect and help us until we see Him in person.

What we need is spiritual "split vision": one eye fixed on Him and His care for us so that the other eye doesn't get blinded by some of the realities of life around us; then we'll have courage and be thrilled by the "rainbows" He also keeps giving us.

No matter what I have to go through, Lord, help me so my attitude never loses its focus on Your forgiving and blessing care for me. Amen.

Eggs On Legs

Aren't two sparrows sold for a cent? And not one of them will fall to the ground without your Father's permission. As for you, even the hairs on your head are all counted. So don't be afraid. You're worth more than many sparrows. *Matthew 10:29-31*

One of the cutest baby birds God has created has to be the baby Gambel's quail. "Eggs on legs" perfectly describes that small egg-shaped body of feathers, perched on a pair of short bare legs. It's almost comical to see a covey of about a dozen scurry quickly one after another with their parents. Soon they lose that baby shape. How many survive to maturity depends on habitat conditions and predator presence, but also on our heavenly Father's permission. He gives them – and all things – life, and He decides how long life will be. His "eye is (not only) on the sparrow", but on each of His creatures.

But especially on us! So specifically does He see us that He knows how many hairs each of us has on our heads! Impossible for Him to know all that, all those hairs? But He is God, Who knows everything!

More important, He knows our need so He will not let sin and the devil destroy us! We are worth too much for Him to allow that! We are worth His Son's life to give us eternal life.

What a comfort! No matter what may come to us today or any day, we don't have to be afraid because of His watching care (which also forgives us when fear does shake us).

Give me more trust in You, Lord, because so often I do let things make me afraid. Amen.

Papa Quail And His Family

And you fathers, don't make your children angry, but raise them in the training and instruction of the Lord.
Ephesians 6:4

Almost as interesting as those "eggs on legs" is the role of "Papa Quail" as a faithful guide and protector for his brood. When they must cross from one bit of shrubby cover to another, he tentatively advances first to check out possible dangers, hurries across the exposed area, and then waits while the little ones quickly scoot over to safety. When in a feeding area, he stands guard, alert for danger, while the chicks are pecking at the weed seeds or grain. Even after they mature, he stays on the job as leader of the covey until the next breeding season. Usually among animals the mother has the primary task in raising the young; but with quail "Papa" apparently is in charge.

Which is God's plan for human families. Mothers have an inescapable nurturing role; but God wants fathers to be vitally involved as the primary provider, protector, and guide. He is not to be dictator with spouse and children treated as slaves. Instead, father and mother have cooperative responsibilities in raising their offspring with father taking the lead. Tragically, this God-intended arrangement is nowadays so often disrupted, making the whole family and especially the children suffer.

Our heavenly Father offers forgiveness and recovery for every failing father and mother, for every damaged child; Jesus suffered and died for every family sin, too, since no parent and no child is totally innocent. Comforted by His forgiveness, we can work together to improve our family relationships, even if we are no longer home with our family.

Lord, have mercy on families, especially fathers, in this world which so strains family relationships. Amen.

Broken Wing Of The Killdeer

I am the Good Shepherd. The Good Shepherd gives His life for the sheep. *John 11:11*

Some other birds and animals may use other tactics, but the killdeer will feign a broken wing and screech noisy calls to distract any apparent threat, skulking animal or hulking human, away from its nest. This act (which probably fools animals, but actually tips off us humans that a nest is nearby so we will be careful not to harm it) is all pretend, of course, since the killdeer quickly flies away once its helpless eggs or nestlings are out of danger. But it shows a willingness to sacrifice its life for its offspring.

It was no pretend act of willingness when Jesus came into the world to give His life for us helpless sinners. Although He was tempted to escape, He would not even when He could (*John 18:1-6*). If He had deserted His mission, not the "danger", but the reality of our eternal death would have been unavoidable, for without Him we cannot defend ourselves against the devil's temptations nor against God's righteous judgment upon sin.

So Jesus gave Himself for us; He did not merely "distract" God's punishment for sin, but took it completely upon Himself so we could be safe – and able to follow Him as our Good Shepherd until we are *forever* "safe".

How I thank You, Lord, that You died for me; help me to live for You faithfully today. Amen.

Lazy And Demanding

And while we were with you, we gave you this order, "If anyone doesn't want to work, he shouldn't eat." *2 Thessalonians 3:10*

One common characteristic of all baby birds is demanding to be fed. Even when already as big as their parents, many still will not work for the food they need. Instead their open beaks and whining cries say: "Feed me! Feed me! Gimme! Gimme!"

So often don't we approach our heavenly Father the same way? How often aren't our prayers merely "gimme" demands? Then we sit back and think, "It's all up to God – I can't do anything about the situation." But if we don't get what we want, we complain that He didn't answer.

One thing we cannot work for: eternal life. Jesus did all the work in our place. He earned forgiveness for all our sins. We only receive it by the open heart of faith, which depends on Him as Savior.

Nor can we earn any other blessing. Each is a gift.

Yet the Lord expects us to use our abilities and time and energy as wisely as possible so that He might provide what we need and even more to enjoy.

The old saying, "Pray as though everything depended on God and work as though everything depended on you", gives us good guidance.

Lord, help me use the time and energy You give me today in the wisest and most productive way possible. Amen.

Foul Weather Friends

Israel went back lusting after the Baals... The Israelites didn't remember the Lord their God, who rescued them from all the enemies around them. *Judges 8:33-34*

Actually, birds like probably every creature are basically lazy. They try to get their food as easily as they can. So they come to feeders, even though these may not provide the best diet for them, as long as the food is offered and the weather doesn't hinder them from finding their more preferred, natural food sources. In good weather bird feeders aren't visited as much. So, in a sense most birds are "foul weather friends".

As are many church members! When trouble enters their lives or when natural catastrophe strikes, then they come for God's help. But let life return to normal, let the stresses pass, and soon no church pew holds their bodies – while it is truly a question whether their bodies ever held any actual dependence on God, instead, just a desire for an easy satisfying of their wants.

On the other hand, everyone who trusts in Jesus as Savior is a "foul weather friend" of His. The only reason we come to Him, humanly speaking, is because we recognize that we need Him: we need Him to take away our sins, we need Him to replace our guilt with peace, we need Him for guidance and strength to get through the challenges of this life, we need Him as the only way to get to eternal life.

But actual faith exists when we recognize our need is continual, not just sporadically wanting Him for other things.

Lord Jesus, keep me always aware and admitting to myself that I always need all that You have to give me. Amen.

Bullies At The Feeder

I wrote something to the church, but Diotrephes, who likes to be their leader, won't listen to us. So, if I come, I'll bring up what he's doing when he talks such wicked nonsense about us. Not satisfied with that, he also will not welcome the fellow Christians as guests and stops those who want to welcome them and tries to put them out of the church. *3 John 9-10*

At most bird feeders especially the smaller birds seem to get along cooperatively with only some fluttering to challenge any who feed too long at a time. But sometimes larger birds will move in and chase all the others off; blue jays especially are such bullies. The other birds don't starve – they manage to get some of the feed, but the "bullies" make life rather miserable for them.

There are bullies in all walks of life. The worst kind are, however, those in congregations who insist on "running the church"; these may be clergy, they may be lay people, they may be those united around the motto: "we've never done it that way before". Such "power" corrupts in a congregation as in any human organization.

God's plan intends local congregations to involve all the members with all their abilities working cooperatively, joined together by clear faith in Jesus, their only Savior, and united under His Word so *His* work, not human desire, will be done as effectively as possible. No room for "bullies" of any kind in any Christian congregation or Christian denomination.

Lord, help me and all the members of our congregation to be workers together in what Your Word guides us to do. Amen.

Feeding Them By Hand

One and the same Spirit works all these things and gives as He wishes to each in his own way. *1 Corinthians 12:11*

Some people can get some birds to eat right out of their hands; most of us have neither patience nor time to achieve this feat.

Which goes to show how each of us has different abilities and opportunities on the trail of life. Some accomplish greatly admired deeds – most of us will never be known much beyond our circle of friends and acquaintances. Some are musicians and some "can't carry a tune". Some are writers and some sell their books. Some lead and some comfort. Some speak several languages, while some have smiles which brighten the attitudes of others. The point being: God has given each of us a unique combination of abilities and opportunities.

We may not always know we have these, until we try them out. Sometimes we might fail and so decide "that's not me". Still there's no value in wanting to be someone else. Instead, since God has made us who we individually are, we are to accept ourselves and do what we can do, both as well as we can and as part of our serving Him. For when we use the abilities He gives us – as cook, truck driver, church usher, or whatever we can do – we are thanking Him for making us the special persons we are. And we are special in God's sight. Though we all to a certain extent waste our abilities and pass by our opportunities ("sins of omission") and then rebelliously disobey Him ("sins of commission"), we are so special that He used His almighty power and everlasting love to make up for all our failures, when Jesus lived our human life and suffered death on the cross.

Help me, Lord, to accept who I am, Your forgiven child, and to use the abilities You've given me as thanks to You. Amen.

Sudden Strike Of The Shrike!

When people say, "All's well and safe!" then destruction will come on them suddenly.... and they will not escape.
1 Thessalonians 5:3

Most birds, especially while feeding, are very wary, because any moment a hawk or a shrike could suddenly swoop down to snatch any careless one for its next meal.

Most tragedies on the trail of life strike suddenly with little warning: one moment a pleasant highway drive, the next a pile of blood-splattered smashed metal – the explosion of a gas pipeline near sleeping campers – earthquake devastation – a slip off a cliff. Suddenly! One's world completely changes or ends!

Suddenly will also come the end of this whole world! Since this world has been corrupted by sinning, God plans to destroy it on Judgment Day before making His new creation where sin will never gain even a "snake's hiss" (*2 Peter3:3-13*). Not even we who trust in Jesus can know exactly when He will do this, so we dare not "take a vacation" from faithfulness for even one day – even toying with such a thought shows the danger of another sudden strike: the "rattlesnake" who always tries to slither its way into our hearts in order to push faith out.

So we must remain "wary", spiritually alert and awake in faith, daily remembering that Jesus is the only One Who can take us through death, whenever and however that might come, to defend us before God's judgment with the evidence of His cross. We do not have to fear any sudden future, when we have Jesus with us daily.

Be in my thoughts throughout this day, Lord, so that I will not fear no matter what may come. Amen.

Peace In His Hands

Into Your hands I entrust my spirit – You have redeemed me, O Lord, my faithful God. *Psalm 31:5*

Hummingbirds are amazing in their maneuverability and their memory (a hummer which survives its long migration flight can return to the exact place where a feeder hung the previous year); but when they panic, they lose all sense. In a carport one might keep flying at a window, though the way out would be only a few inches away. Yet it could die there, trying to get through the glass. And if you come to help it, it will flutter up and down on the pane, trying to evade your hands. Yet, once you close your hands over it, it completely quiets down. Perhaps its heart is racing, but its wings are still and it seems to be at peace – until you open your hands outside the building and it immediately zips away like a rocket!

How often don't we get into a panic when we try to go our own way without asking His guidance or relying on His promises to work life out for good. True, we must plan for and try to work through the problems before us. *But*, "what peace we often forfeit", because we don't rely on Him most of all.

And we can rely on Him, no matter how threatening our situation! He has given us the peace of knowing that He doesn't hold our sins against us, but poured them onto His Son to blot them out of His sight by what Jesus did for us. Since we have peace regarding our most serious problem, we also can have peace about every other "rattlesnake" that attacks us if we only remind ourselves: Ahh, but I am in His hands – and so He will protect me and help me find the best way through this.

Help me remember, Lord, that I am always in Your hands so that because of peace from You I'll be able to think clearly and act wisely in whatever faces me. Amen.

Mr. Mocky

Yes, by His grace you are saved through faith. It is not your own doing; it is God's gift. It is not the result of anything you have done; and so no one may boast.
Ephesians 2:8-9

What a showoff the male mockingbird seems to be! Able to mimic the songs of other birds and even mechanical sounds, he will often perch on a tall pole and go through those "musical pieces" one after the other and every once in a while flutter up a few feet as though in emphasis! Really he is only declaring his chosen territory and trying to attract a mate; but he sure seems to be a boasting showboat!

Occasionally Scripture says that we may "boast"; yet never about our own accomplishments, but only to "boast in the Lord" (*2 Corinthians 10:17-18*). After all, if we have achieved anything, it's only because He gave us ability, opportunity, and blessing. So, instead of "boasting", we are to be thankful.

Especially regarding our being saved, we dare not utter even a twitter about any good we think we have done. Regarding our salvation before God even our "righteous deeds" are no better than filthy rags (*Isaiah 64:6*), because we never can do even one perfect deed in our whole life. Jesus had to do absolutely everything needed for us to escape what we have done, sin, so salvation is all His doing, not at all ours.

Instead of boasting about anything, we can only give thanks with our words and by our deeds.

Thank You, Lord, for doing what I could not do, rescuing me from what I've done. Thank You also for helping me say and do that which does please You. Amen.

Noisy Neighborhood

Don't pay back evil for evil. Be concerned with things that everyone considers noble. As much as you can, live in peace with everyone... Don't let evil conquer you, but conquer evil with good. *Romans 12:17-18,21*

What with the mockingbird's "play list", the chatter of a chat, the unmusical monotone of the cactus wren, and the loud singing of the curved-bill thrasher along with other bird songs and distant cattle sounds, "life on the New Mexico frontier" has a "noisy neighborhood", not a quiet one.

At least it's "natural", however, not like in town with so many barking dogs, screaming sirens, rumbling trucks, and amplified sound systems! Some of that sound is unavoidable – no one would want to silence ambulances or fire trucks. But some of the "noise" is very irritating, especially those continually barking dogs or music that can be heard from a block away! What does one do about unthinking, inconsiderate neighbors?

The "rattlesnake" says: pay them back – call the police – turn up your stereo so they see what it's like! And sometimes we do – which usually only escalates the problem.

The Lord says: be a "rainbow" of good to those offenders in order to develop a friendly relationship so the problem can be discussed calmly. But our anger would rather get revenge!

Until we think again: all the evil we do against God – yet He gives us the good of His forgiveness because of Jesus and even more blessings. So we can at least try to do good, even to inconsiderate neighbors.

Lord, help me do what is good for all my neighbors. Amen.

A Quiet Night

A heart that has left the Lord may be satisfied without His ways, but only with Him does anyone find what is good.
Proverbs 14:14

Some city folks who come out to isolated rural areas cannot stand the silence, especially at night! The occasional hoot of an owl, the once in a while yipping of coyotes, the croaking of frogs, the rasping sound of cicada locusts – not quiet at all for them! On the other hand rural folks on a visit in town wonder how anyone can ever sleep with "all that (highway and neighborhood) racket" going on! But God has created our brains so that most of us self-defensively learn to filter out continued sounds which don't really affect us so we actually hear only what we want to hear. Of course, some can't "get used to" some sounds and need earplugs or soothing background music to camouflage the noise.

Sin might be described as "noise" to God's hearing. His way produces peace and the pleasant sounds of people working together – sin causes conflict with shouts of accusation and anger. Most people are satisfied with such "life as it is". And we also tend to "get used to" sin, not the sinning of others, but our own; for we easily "repent" of our sins – say we are sorry for the "wrong", but don't always try very hard to "do the right", which is the other part of repentance.

God, however, never could "get used to" our sinning. That's why He had to "camouflage" it, cover it up, conceal it under the red blood of His Son so He could look at us without punishing us. Now because we are so "camouflaged" through faith in Jesus, we want to "find what is good" and do that instead of the sins we've grown so accustomed to.

Lord, help me do what is right and good today. Amen.

Remembering Their Example

I recall how sincere your faith was; just as it lived in your grandmother Lois and your mother Eunice before you, so I am convinced it is in you too. *2 Timothy 1:5*

Memorial Day in the United States was first established to honor soldiers killed in the Civil War – later it was expanded officially to honor all military and veteran deaths; informally it has become a day when families honor the memory of all their loved ones who have died. The manner of their dying does not concern us – the example of their life is what we remember and give God thanks for.

One death, of course, we remember each day – both in its detail and for its meaning: the death of Jesus. Actually, that He died an agonizing death on a cross would have little value to us in itself – two others that same day died in much the same way. But it is why He so died that we think of His death: by His dying He "finished" (*John 19:30*), completed, the purpose of His life on earth. He came to die so that we, who by our sinning deserve death forever, can live for eternity.

Yet even how He died and why still would have no value at all for us, if He had stayed dead, for then He would just have been another false hope-giver braggart. But by rising bodily to life again, as He promised and as no one else has ever done, He proves that He is exactly Who He claims to be: the one and only Savior for sinners. Because He died and rose again, we don't have to fear death, but look forward to life forever with Him – and with loved ones who have died in faith.

Thank You, Lord, for Your life and death for me. Thank You also for the example of faith that so many of my loved ones showed me during their lives. Amen.

Time To Mow Again?

Now, who is the faithful and sensible slave whom the master has put in charge of his servants to give them their food at the right time? Blessed is that slave whom his master finds doing this when he comes. *Matthew 24:45-46*

Before he retired, he liked to mow the lawn – because then he could see immediate results, while spiritual results in people (including himself) and progress in congregational planning could be frustratingly slow. Some pastors, in fact, think they never see specific results of their efforts, although years later someone might tell them: what you taught me really did help in my life! Of course, lawn mowing never gets completely done; depending on the season, the grass variety, and the weather, you may need to mow again in less than a week – one just has to keep at it. Still, there is at least temporary satisfaction in seeing that neatly trimmed yard.

Although we humans like to see progress, God does not demand results from us in serving Him. Instead, He requires faithfulness: obeying Him, rather: *trying* to obey His commands (since none of us can obey with never a missed "blade of grass") even when our efforts seem to lead us into more "rattlesnakes" of trouble than "rainbows" of joy, as we live.

Can it be true that He doesn't "demand results"? If He did, then we would have to meet at least a minimum requirement to be accepted by Him. But He accepts us because Jesus produced all the results required to make up for even our imperfect faithfulness efforts. So we have peace in knowing we are totally forgiven, and we have the desire to keep on trying to be faithful to Him wherever He guides us on our trail of life.

Thank You, Lord, that You accept me because of what Jesus has done; help me be faithful to You today. Amen.

Hiking In The Mountains*

Jesus came and touched them. "Get up," He said, "and don't be afraid." They looked up and saw no one but Jesus.
Matthew 17:7-8

Our lives are trails through time. Each of us walks our own trail, yet we can learn from each other's experiences. While on vacation in Rocky Mountain National Park one year, they noticed many parallels between hiking those trails and living a Christian life.

How impressive mountains are even when just driving through them. However, you can't fully experience joy and awe over God's creation unless you hike a mountain trail. Your feet may ache, but your eyes and ears make your spirit more aware that He *is* – and He is almighty!

Yet a danger looms on such hikes as on life's trail – the danger of forgetting. In thrilling to His creation power, we can forget what is more important: His love in Jesus as Savior. In daily life we can get so caught up in the pain or the rush of our activities that we forget even His power as well as Jesus.

The disciples on the mountaintop saw "no one but Jesus." Wherever we might be along life's trail, we need conscious faith in Jesus as the One Who died for our sins on Calvary's cross. Then we can relax in the love of our forgiving God, Who also promises to use His power to protect us daily.

Lord, help me today to keep Jesus, my Savior, continually in mind so that I will more faithfully serve You. Amen.

* *Edited versions of these June devotions were originally published in* Portals of Prayer, *August 1987.*

Theirs Is Nicer

Of course, there's a big profit in religion if we're satisfied. We didn't bring anything into the world, and we can't take anything out. If we have food and clothing, we should be satisfied. *1 Timothy 6:6-8*

In some campgrounds campsites are assigned when you arrive. The camper has no choice.

It's tempting then to grumble that "theirs is nicer" – even though mountain beauty fills the surrounding horizon.

How often on life's trail don't we also overlook what blessings we have, magnify our irritations, and lust after what others possess.

Yet the Lord has provided richly. "Food and clothing" is all we need, writes St. Paul; but we have these and so much more. Still better, we have forgiveness of sins because of the suffering and death of Jesus. He even paid for our complaining and coveting. How beautifully His blessings surround us!

In lifting our thoughts to these blessings, we recognize also that the Lord has acted with love and wisdom to place us where we are. We can accept and be thankful, then, for how He has blessed, especially in Jesus, in spite of what we dislike.

Lord, thank You for all you have given me, especially Jesus. Help me be content each day. Amen.

Foolish Little Bullies

"But God said to him, 'You fool, tonight you die. And what you've prepared – who will get it?' That's how it is when you store up goods for yourself and aren't rich toward God." *Luke 12:20-21*

Many Rocky Mountain Park campers hang up hummingbird feeders. Within minutes broad-tailed hummers buzz in for free food. Nearly as quickly one broad-tailed or a rufous will seem to become a selfish bully, attacking the others to keep them away.

What a foolish little bully! Others provide the food – all could share. But in apparent greed it flies itself into near exhaustion to keep it "mine". All in vain – for others always sneak in, and eventually the sugar water is gone.

"Mine!" Aren't we also tempted to be such selfish and foolish little bullies? By nature we plot and scheme to get and keep things "mine". So much energy we use – so much worry we have. How little we can enjoy things, when we are selfish. And in the end all will be gone anyway.

The fact is: what we have, the Lord has provided. Even better, through faith in Jesus, Who paid for our sins on the cross, He gives us blessings which will last forever.

Lord, thank You for Your blessings to me; help me not to be selfish but to share them with others who are in need. Amen.

Properly Equipped For The Trail

Finally, let the Lord and His mighty power make you strong. Put on God's whole armor, and you will be able to stand against the devil's tricky ways. *Ephesians 6:10-11*

To best enjoy a mountain hike you need to be properly equipped. Good hiking shoes are a must, also layers of clothing and a poncho to meet changing weather conditions – water, lunch, sunscreen, and a map are needed. Otherwise, your hike might be disappointing, even a disaster, instead of a joy.

On the trail of life we also need the proper equipment. Physical dangers are not the problem – "the tricks of the devil" are!

How often hasn't he ruined the joy of a day, not by an open attack, but by a sly trick. We spoke before we listened – we acted before we thought – we didn't realize what we were getting into.

Daily putting on "God's whole armor" prepares us for life's trail each day. The conscious reminder, "Jesus died for me", leads us to pray: "Help me, Lord, to live for You today." Reading His Word stirs our thoughts toward remembering His guidance throughout the day. Then we realize also that praying is not a fold-your-hands exercise, but a constant conversation with our Father all day so we can remain alert against the devil's tricks and for the opportunities to serve the Lord.

Thank You, Lord, that I can live this day with the power and protection You give by the love of Jesus in Your Word. Amen.

What Will The Weather Be?

You haven't been tempted more than you could expect. And you can trust God. He will not let you be tested more than you can stand. But when you are tested, He will also make a way out so that you can bear it. *1 Corinthians 10:13*

Will it rain? Will it snow? Will the sun shine through? The weather forecast alerts the mountain hiker to what might come. No 100% accuracy, but you get some idea what to prepare for. In Rocky Mountain Park almost without fail you must expect an early afternoon thundershower.

On the trail of life you know from God's Word what will come. He promises blessings. However, no one can escape the thundershowers, "rattlesnakes" of troubles and temptations.

Perhaps such storms will disrupt your life today. If not, what a sunny day you will have. Yet, if trouble or temptation thunder around you, still you always have a ray of spiritual sunshine, a "rainbow", to comfort and strengthen you. The God Who gave His Son for you still cares about you. He allows the storms, but He limits them. "He will not let you be tested more than you can stand" – and He is the One Who gives you the strength you need to "stand" by means of His Word and Holy Communion.

So, we set out on today's hike with confidence that the Lord will take us through whatever He allows to happen.

Lord God, thank You for Your promise to give me whatever help I need to remain faithful to You because of Jesus. Amen.

A Taste Of The New Creation

A wolf will live with a lamb; a leopard will lie down with a goat; a calf, a young lion, and a fattened animal will be together, and a little boy will lead them. *Isaiah 11:6*

Sometimes before a hike you decide to get up before dawn. In misty morning quiet you might see a herd of deer near your tent. Protected in Rocky Mountain Park, even a ten-point buck might wander by unafraid. You see its beauty, how tame it is – and a taste of the new creation is that morning's special blessing.

Why can't life be more like that? Why must we have such evil and fear, such struggle and fighting on life's trail? Tension invades even our family and congregation. We get so frustrated by it!

One day all will be different. In the new creation after Judgment Day righteousness will dwell, says *2 Peter 3*. In the new creation life will be as beautiful as the Lord originally made it.

That is our expectation. Not that we deserve to experience it; by our daily sinning we contribute to today's conflict. However, because Jesus entered this ruined world and took our sins upon Himself, we by faith in Him as Savior have forgiveness now and the joy of the new creation ahead.

Because He will give us this, we will try to bring a bit of His new creation peace onto life's trail today.

For the foretastes of the new creation and for Jesus only through Whom I can enter it, thank You, Lord. Amen.

Like A Colony Of Ants

You boast about the Law – are you breaking the Law and so dishonoring God? "You make the non-Jews slander God's name," as the Bible says. *Romans 2:23-24*

No matter where you camp or picnic, on mountain trail or at lakeside table, you probably will have ants. Such industrious creatures ants are. Each has a job to do – and each works hard at its task. Admirable, aren't they?

Usually not! Too often ants are an irritation, crawling over food, occasionally biting you, just being a nuisance!

Which view of an ant colony does your congregation resemble? What are you doing to give that impression about your congregation to others?

Obviously, a congregation should be like the hard-working ant colony. The Lord gives each congregation work to do and enough workers. When you use the abilities and time He gives you because you care about Jesus, Who gave His life to bring you into God's family, then you help your congregation also to bring glory to Him by your work together.

Too often, however, congregations irritate unbelievers as ants irritate us. Many refuse to hear the message of forgiveness because of the bickering, self-seeking, and lovelessness of members in their daily lives and even in the congregation.

When you clearly keep Jesus as the focus of your personal life and congregational activities, then your congregation will be more like the admirable colony and less like the irritating ants.

Help me, Lord, so that whatever I do today will bring glory, not shame, to Your Name. Help me for Jesus' sake. Amen.

Becoming Overly Dependent

Why do you sin against God's commandment for the sake of your own rules? ... God has said: ... But you say, ... For the sake of your rules you have set aside God's Word.
Matthew 15:3-6

"Do not feed the animals!" say the campground signs. Chipmunks and ground squirrels are so cute when they beg. Who can resist them? What will it hurt to give them bread or nuts? What happens is that they get too dependent on human feeders instead of finding a more balanced, natural diet.

We can get overly dependent on others along life's spiritual trail. It's tempting to follow the advice of the majority instead of the guidance of God. A friend might suggest something that is not quite honest or moral – even a pastor, because he also is a sinful human being, can say more – or less – than what God's Word actually teaches.

Not that we must be suspicious of what others tells us. But because we want to be faithful to the Lord Jesus, Who gave Himself on the cross for our forgiveness, we dare not blindly follow traditions or human advice. What others suggest, we will personally compare with God's Word. We will ask ourselves: "Is this really what God says?" Then we will know and by His help be better able to do what pleases Him.

Lord, help me today so that, no matter what anyone else might want, I will follow Your guidance because of Jesus. Amen.

The Map For Life's Trail

Your Word is a lamp for my feet and a light on my path.
Psalm 119:105

To begin a mountain hike without a map is foolish. Having one won't help either if you insist on following your own ideas instead of its directions. Even hikers who start out on a trail can get confused and lost.

So many people follow the trail of life without the map God has given, the Bible. Many have the map, but refuse to follow it, because they prefer their own ideas instead.

The Bible, God's inspired Word, most of all gives us the directions to eternal life. It guides us away from depending on our efforts to be good enough for God – no one ever can be. Then it shows us Jesus with His perfect life in our place, His suffering and death for us sinners, and His resurrection proof that He truly is the Savior. Through this message, if we pay attention to it, the Holy Spirit brings us to faith. Then He continues to work through the Bible to keep us in that faith and to guide us in daily living for the Lord.

He cannot work in us, however, if we won't use this map at all, or, if we use it but insist on following our own ideas instead of what He says.

Lord, help me so that I both hear and follow what You tell me about faith in Jesus and about daily Christian living. Amen.

On The Trail To Beauty

And He told all of them, "If you want to follow Me, deny yourself, take up your cross every day, and come with Me."
Luke 9:23

Why set out on a mountain trail if not to see beauty? A cascading waterfall, a spectacular view – God has made and given us great beauty to enjoy.

But people mess it up. How often doesn't litter and trash mar both trailside and beautiful scenes?

The trail of life leads to beauty also, both the beauty of eternal life and the beauty of God's blessings along the way.

If Jesus had not become the ugly sacrifice for our sins on the cross, our sinning would keep us from eternal life's beauty. By faith in Him, however, we count on seeing our "beautiful Savior."

Because He forgives us, we can also deal with the sins of others and of ourselves, which mar the beauty He intends until we reach eternity. By forgiving others, we in a sense "pick up the trash" of their sins. By faithful Christian living we bring more beauty into the lives of those with us on the trail through our kindness to them and our carefulness not to sin against them.

All this takes effort – it is part of the cross we are to take up daily. But His cross makes ours much easier to carry.

Lord, help me be Your willing follower today in whatever You want me to do, no matter how difficult. Amen.

Wildflower Beauty

A good man produces good things from the good stored in his heart, and an evil man produces evil from his evil stored there. What a person says with his mouth flows from his heart. *Luke 6:45*

Along most mountain trails you can't help but be impressed by the wildflower beauty. Delicate plants with brilliant colors might dot the rock cliff or cover an upland meadow. Wherever enough moisture and sun meet, a wildflower seems to grow. Each struggles to exist in mountain harshness, but its beauty must show or it will die.

Life for a Christian might not be beautiful, yet the Christian life will still be beautiful. We can be threatened by another's cruelty or trapped by harsh conditions where we live. But the beauty of kindness and compassion, of love and honesty, can still shine through us.

Such beautiful living can and will be seen in us because of the "good" the Holy Spirit has put into our hearts. That "good" is faith in Jesus. He endured the harshness of the cross and the punishment for our sins so we might live eternally.

Without the "good" of faith we would give in to the ugliness of sin around and in us. But because of God's forgiveness we can and will show more of the beautiful life He wants us to live as we live and work with others each day.

Lord, help me so that the beauty of kindness, honesty, and love is more evident in my life today. Amen.

Such A Variety Of Beauty

Men will do these things because they didn't get to know the Father or Me. But I told you this so that when it happens you'll remember I told you about it. I didn't tell you this at first, because I was with you. *John 16:3-4*

Why is there such a variety of beauty in the flowers and birds? Why should the colorful splash of the brilliant western tanager, the ceramic-like mushroom, the cascading song of the wren, or the many other beautiful flowers and birds exist?

Evolutionists claim to give totally natural explanations. But we recognize that these are evidences of the majesty and glory of God.

His greatest glory was revealed through the ugliness of the cross – there His love worked out our salvation by the suffering and death of Jesus so we can one day see God's visible glory. As we live now, He gives us hints of that eternal glory through the beauty He creates around us.

A mountain trail is not all beauty. Only now and then do you spot that flitting bird or delicate flower. All of living is not beautiful either. Often sin by us or by others makes life ugly. But God gives us moments of His created beauty, when sin's ugliness threatens us, so we will remember His beauty. Even better, we remember the daily beauty of His forgiveness through Jesus. Such remembering strengthens us to remain faithful to Him also on those days when we feel that life's trail is a weary trudge.

Thank You, Lord, for the beauty I sometimes see in birds and flowers. Thank You especially for Your daily forgiveness. Amen.

Each As It Is Able

Now, the Spirit shows Himself to each one to make him useful. *1 Corinthians 12:7*

The variety of beauty changes as one climbs a mountain trail. Plants of the valley can't exist at the mountaintop where others grow. Forest birds don't live about the tree line, but others do. Each lives in its own climate and does what it is able to do in its own unique way.

Each of us also is unique, especially as a Christian. You can't do everything someone else does. But God the Holy Spirit has given you abilities and opportunities to do what others can't. He gives these, however, not just to possess, but to make us "useful" in our congregation and to others around us.

One thing you cannot do. You cannot do enough to deserve God's forgiveness. Only Jesus had that unique ability as God and man in One Person. As man, He could and did obey the Law, suffer, and die. As God, He could and did do this for all of sinners. He did what only He could do so that we are now by faith in Him accepted, forgiven, and given eternal life.

Jesus is also why we will use our unique abilities, gifts, and opportunities to do what we are able to do for His glory and to be useful in His work.

Thank You, Lord, for making me a unique individual. Help me today to do what I can to serve You and others. Amen.

Tender, Fragile Power

I am not ashamed of the Gospel. It is God's power to save everyone who believes it, the Jew first and also the Greek.
Romans 1:16

Mushrooms are amazing! You can crush one to mush with your boot, they are so fragile; however, along the forest trail you see them pushing aside small rocks and downed branches as they grow. Such tender, fragile power mushrooms have!

The Gospel also seems so tender and fragile. What can mere words about Jesus' suffering and death for the sins of the world really do? How can words accomplish anything in the face of evil deeds around us and evil attitudes so easily within us?

Yet, it is "God's power". Of course, to be effective it must be the Scriptural Gospel about Jesus as Savior. Any "gospel" which emphasizes anything other than "Jesus Christ and Him crucified" (*1 Corinthians 2:2*) is false and powerless.

But when we clearly hear and think about the message of Jesus paying for our sins, then God's power works in us. Then His Holy Spirit keeps us in faith in spite of evil's attacks.

Also His Gospel power, as we think about it now, will comfort and strengthen us to serve Him faithfully today as we continue on life's trail.

Lord, thank You for the assurance that I am forgiven because of Jesus. Help me to live faithfully for You today. Amen.

A Deadly Beauty

In others the seed falls among thorns. They hear the Word, but the worries of the world, the deceitful pleasure of riches, and the desires for other things come in and choke the Word, and it produces nothing. *Mark 4:18-19*

One strikingly beautiful mushroom along Rocky Mountain Park trails is deadly. Eating a fly agaric mushroom can kill you.

"Things" can have a deadly beauty along life's trail. We need things to live, of course. God also provides things for us to enjoy. But too easily, urged on by appealing ads, we pile up so many things that we can begin to care more about them than about our Savior. How tempted we are to desire more and more "things" for ourselves at the expense of living fruitfully for the Lord by sharing with the needy.

As God, Jesus possesses all things. Yet He gave up everything to be the sacrifice for us who often put things ahead of Him.

Receiving His forgiveness through faith, we renew our Christian attitudes toward things. Although they are blessings, they aren't what makes life enjoyable. How we use things to help others and how we treat others in our daily contacts are fruits of faith to which God's Word calls us each day along life's trail.

Thank You, Lord, for how much You have given me. Help me to use my things and my life wisely for Your glory. Amen.

When The Way Gets Steep

For the joy that was set before Him He endured the cross, thinking nothing of its shame, and sat down at the right hand of God's throne. *Hebrews 12:2*

Hiking is easy, though tiring, when even a long trail climbs only gradually. Steep stretches, however, can quickly make one wonder: "Is this worth the effort?"

Most of life on our daily trail is probably not too difficult. At times it is easy to be a Christian, especially if others notice our kindnesses.

Sometimes the trail gets steep, however. Appealing temptations, faith made fun of, honesty unappreciated, or on-going unresolved conflicts can make us wonder whether it's worth remaining faithful. "If I'm trying, Lord, why don't You at least make it easier?"

Then we remember to look from current pressures to Jesus. How steep His way was to the cross, as He knew the waiting agony of the punishment for our sins. Yet He went on – because of the joy beyond the cross, the joy of welcoming believers into His eternal joy.

So we also will continue faithful – because of Jesus and the joy of forgiveness we have already, as well as the eternal joy yet to come. He will keep us going even if today's trail is steep.

Thank You, Lord, that even though there are steep times in living for You, You always give me sufficient strength to keep following You. Amen.

Off The Trail – Lost!

"Be happy with me. I found my lost sheep!" *Luke 15:6*

In the mountains an average hiker should never set out cross-country. Some think they can find their own way, but end up off the trail – lost! Most find their way back eventually – rescue parties find many – but some are never found.

One word for sin is "transgression", which can loosely be defined as "stepping off the trail". Once we sin, we are off God's trail, getting lost, with no way to find our own way back. Each time we sin, we need to be rescued.

Jesus is our rescuer. He left the glory of eternity to enter the wilderness of this world. He searched for us lost sinners by perfectly obeying what we disobey and laying down His life because of our sinning. This He did to rescue all people.

When we are brought to faith, then that rescue benefits us individually, for "by His grace you are saved through faith" (*Ephesians 2:8*). His work on Calvary also gives us the "rescue" of daily forgiveness.

Because He keeps forgiving us through faith, we keep coming back to and keep trying with His help to remain on the trail of following His will all day long.

Thank You, Lord, for daily forgiveness because of Jesus. Help me follow Your will faithfully all day long today. Amen.

Regular Rest Stops

Then Jesus came to Nazareth, where He had been raised. On the Sabbath He went into the synagogue as He used to do. *Luke 4:16*

More experienced mountain hikers appreciate regular rest stops. A few minutes every hour helps one relax, appreciate the new view, and regain energy for the trail ahead. To walk to the point of near exhaustion before resting will destroy the joy of the whole hike.

Along life's trail we also need regular rest stops – time with God's Word to relax in His forgiveness through Jesus, to realize His love and power, and to be strengthened for following His directions.

Most important is the weekly "rest stop" of public worship. God commands our coming to the preaching of the Gospel both because this shows our faith in Jesus as Savior and because we need it. Those who refuse public worship despise God as well as His Word.

To worship publicly each week, as Jesus did, is like overnight resting between hikes on a trail. However, we also need at least a few minutes daily with God's Word, as in these devotions, so that each day's obedience to Him might not be drudgery, but joy.

Help me, Lord, to willingly hear Your Word each worship day as well as each day of the week so I joyfully follow You on the trail of life You give me. Amen.

Refreshing Water Of Life

"If you knew what God is giving," Jesus answered her, "and Who it is that says to you, 'Give Me a drink,' you would have asked Him, and He would have given you living water." *John 4:10*

How refreshing the water of a mountain stream seems! But in Rocky Mountain Park all are warned not to drink natural, untreated water – you might get "giardiasis", a serious intestinal infection. How frustrating to see such clear, cool water ruined by human pollution!

The message of Jesus as Savior is the refreshing "water of life". Drained by the guilt of sinning, we find comfort only in what He did in our place. By taking our sins upon Himself and suffering God's punishment for sin, He earned life for us as God's child on earth and forever. That Gospel message satisfies our spiritual thirst, for it brings us forgiveness.

The pollution of human pride or self-centeredness, however, ruins that water of life. All who depend even a little on their own efforts to obey God no longer depend only on Jesus. All who add something to the Gospel to make it more exciting or humanly more appealing have turned to "another gospel" (*Galatians 1:8-9*) and away from eternal life.

Christ crucified for us sinners is the only message which keeps us full of faith and faithful.

Thank You, Lord God, for giving me the pure "water of life" in the Gospel of Christ crucified. Keep me trusting in Him alone always. Amen.

Safe Amid The Cascades Of Life

**Anyone who hears and does what I say is like a man who
had the sense to build his house on a rock. The rain poured
down, the torrents came, the winds blew, and they beat
against that house. But it didn't go down, because its
foundation was on the rock.** *Matthew 7:24-25*

Along the cascading streams in Rocky Mountain Park the
hiker will sometimes see an unusual little bird called the
"dipper". It not only flies – it also walks in and under the
rushing water in its search for food. Its nest is almost at the
waterline, so close that the baby birds are often splashed as they
stretch out their beaks to be fed. Yet the nest is safe – because
it is built on a rock.

Sometimes life seems to cascade down upon us. Events move
too quickly – sudden changes splash us like icy water – perhaps
even violence becomes a personal experience instead of merely
a news item. We wonder how we can bear it, whether we can
survive, what worse things the future will bring.

Especially then we need to remind ourselves of "the solid
Rock" on Whom we stand, Jesus. He underwent much more
than we could ever endure. He took upon Himself the violence
of God's punishment for our sinning. Only in Him do we have
eternal safety. Because of that fact we also know His personal
caring for us now. He has not promised a rose garden life
without thorns, but strength to endure whatever might happen to
us along the way.

*Thank You, Jesus, for Your promise to keep me safe in Your
care no matter what others might do to me. Amen.*

Stepping Aside For Others

Love is patient. Love is kind. Love isn't jealous. It doesn't brag or get conceited. It isn't indecent. It isn't selfish. It doesn't get angry. It doesn't plan to hurt anyone. It doesn't delight in evil but is happy with the truth. It bears everything, believes everything, hopes for everything, endures everything. *1 Corinthians 13:4-7*

Sometimes mountain trails have stretches so narrow that two hikers can hardly pass each other. Only as one stands still at the side can the other go by safely. If both insist on their own way, danger could turn into disaster.

Often on life's trail our desires might conflict with those of someone else. Who will let the other have his or her way? Too often neither gives in willingly – with disastrous results for that relationship in the future.

Jesus guides us in how to handle such situations. Humanly He prayed in Gethsemene for another way instead of Calvary, if possible. But He did not insist on His way. Instead He chose the way of the cross with its agony of suffering for us sinners.

Now, forgiven through faith in Him, we are able to forgive. Loved by Him, we also can love – not only God, but others as well. Part of that love for others is not to insist on our own way.

Of course, we must insist on God's way. When His Word clearly speaks, we must follow no matter how much conflict might result. But when today it is merely a matter of our way instead of theirs, then because of Jesus we can willingly step aside for the other to pass.

Help me, Jesus, to love others willingly today. Amen.

How Quickly Life Can Change

Humble yourselves, then, under God's mighty hand so that He may honor you at the right time. *1 Peter 5:6*

How quickly the weather can change in the mountains! A hike begun in magnificent sunshine can end in a soaking downpour. A thunderstorm can produce rain and hail, yet soon give way to a rainbow. Sudden lighting can bring tragedy into a beautiful day.

How quickly life can change, usually for the worse! A car accident, a heart attack, a doctor's terrifying diagnosis, a family member's personal disaster, a robbery – so suddenly our world can seem to fall apart.

Why, God? How could You let this happen? What have I done to deserve this? Such are the natural questions of our human hurting.

To which God usually gives no answer – except to say: humble yourself before Me and remember My caring for you through My Son on the cross.

Rarely can we figure out a "why" for what happens. But we always know "Who" is in control and uses His wisdom and power in a way to carry out His loving will for us. He didn't spare His Son. Jesus is, therefore, why we can be sure He still acts in love even when we can't understand.

Help me, Lord, to humbly accept the troubles You allow to come and to be confident of Your love in spite of them. Amen.

Guideposts Subscription Order

Mail this card to start or renew your own subscription, give a friend a gift—*or do both!* And we'll thank you with something special!

Send No Money — We'll Bill You Later

(Fold and detach at perforation and mail card below.)

☐ **1 YEAR $15.97** plus $.97 delivery
$19.94 Canadian/$28.94 Foreign

☐ **2 YEARS $25.97** plus $.97 delivery
$34.94 Canadian/$54.94 Foreign

YOUR NAME: (Please print)

Address _____ Apt. _____

City _____ State _____ ZIP _____

E-mail _____

Include my own subscription for: ☐ Regular ☐ Large Print (Intended for the visually impaired.) PREFERRED SUBSCRIBER

Send a gift and a gift card in my name for: ☐ 1 Year ☐ 2 Years

GIFT TO: (Please print)

Address _____ Apt. _____

City _____ State _____ ZIP _____

☐ Regular ☐ Large Print (Intended for the visually impaired.)

JL5211151J

guideposts.org/ins

GDP J15211DA7

(Fold and detach at perforation and mail card below.)

Preferred Subscriber Guarantee

1. We guarantee that you may cancel your subscription(s) at any time upon request and that you will receive a prompt refund on any unserved issues.

2. We guarantee to continue your gift subscription(s) at the then current rate for as long as you wish, without interruption, unless you instruct us to stop.

3. We guarantee if you include your own subscription we will also provide continuous service at the then current rate for as long as you wish.

4. Send no money now. As a Preferred Subscriber, a gift card will automatically be sent in your name every year (on receipt of payment) to the person named on the reverse side.

Don't miss an issue of inspiration! Order your own subscription or delight a friend with a gift subscription.

Guideposts

Poncho Protection

Be merciful to me, O God, be merciful to me because in You my life finds protection. I take cover in the shadow of Your wings till the threat of destruction passes by.
Psalm 57:1

Because thunderstorms come nearly every afternoon, the Rocky Mountain Park hiker needs some handy raingear. Slipping into a poncho makes it possible not only to stay dry, but even to keep on hiking in spite of the showers. Poncho protection can make the difference between having a miserable trek or an enjoyable hike in spite of the rain.

Is there a day when we don't need similar spiritual protection? Some days storms of evil lash at us through the cruelty of others or our own sinning. Other days the drizzle of sin unsettles us as unkind words of others hurt us or our own sinful thoughts disturb us.

God's "poncho protection" is primarily the Gospel good news of forgiveness through the sacrifice of Jesus for all sinners. But He shelters us also as we remember His promises to help us and His commandments to guide us.

Remembering these, we can continue on our daily trail with a confident, kind, and even joyful attitude. We know our Lord goes with us to protect and strengthen us no matter what might happen to us in this day or any day to come.

Lord, thank You for the protection and strength You promise to give me each day, especially when troubles strike. Amen.

All Ruined Unless Contained

The tongue is a small organ but can boast of big things. You know how just a spark will set a large forest on fire. The tongue is a fire. *James 3:5-6*

Occasionally a trail will pass through an area damaged by forest fire. Each fire started very small, but then spread to destroy more and more. Soon all the forest would be ruined unless the fire was contained and put out.

"The tongue is a fire." Such a little part of us, yet how destructive tongues can be. One word can hurt – but who stops with just one? Another and another strike out until what we say can become almost a vomit of angry evil or vicious gossip. Relationships can even be permanently ruined unless our tongues are contained.

But how to control the tongue? Some people consistently speak with kindness. Some talk about the good of others. Some are able to stop before saying too much that hurts. Why can't we all?

"No one can tame the tongue" (*James 3:8*). But the Lord can! "What you say flows from your hearts" (*Matthew 12:34*). As we let the message of God's forgiveness fill our hearts and thoughts, His love will work in us to make us more loving not only in deeds, but also in words. Our comfort and strength is that Jesus paid also for our sinful words.

Thank You, Lord, for forgiving all my sins. Help me today to speak only that which is good and kind and honest. Amen.

Even The Decaying Trees

We know that God works all things out for good for those who love God. *Romans 8:28*

Scattered in the forest along mountain trails lie the decaying hulks of downed trees. The passing hiker notices them, but doesn't always realize their value. Small animals and birds use them for shelter. Delicate plants grow on and around them. Gradually they enrich the ground for other trees to feed on. Even the decaying trees have their use.

As we follow life's trail, we hardly notice some incidents that happen. Other experiences are painful, forcing us to be aware of them, but without seeming to have any good purpose. Much in life can seem rather pointless.

But God reveals that in "all things" He is working for our good when we love Him because of Jesus, Who died and rose as our Savior.

That promise can be very comforting when painful things happen. But if He works in "all things", we can also look for good even in what might at first seem insignificant. We won't always understand "why" or realize the good He intends. However, if we try, we often will find unexpected meaning or blessing in what otherwise we might have taken for granted.

Lord, help me to appreciate more fully today how You work for good in all the things that happen in my life. Amen.

Now's The Time To Fish

As He was walking along the Sea of Galilee, He saw Simon and Simon's brother Andrew (who were fishermen) casting a net into the sea. "Come, follow Me," Jesus told them, "and I will make you fishers of men." *Mark 1:16-17*

Many mountain hikers will carry fishing equipment along in their packs. They don't fish in every stream or lake, because their hike would never reach its destination. But at certain places conditions seem right so they say: "Now's the time to fish", and out goes the line with a delicate fly to catch a mountain fish, if possible.

Jesus paid for the sins of everyone as well as ours. His Holy Spirit "catches" people, however, only as we put out the delicate "bait" of the Gospel message about forgiveness through faith in the Savior. We may not be very skilled; but, having enjoyed the "bait" ourselves, we can share it with others. Jesus expects us to be "fishers of men".

Yet the conditions aren't always right for this "fishing". We need to look for "the time to fish", but every conversation is not an evangelism opportunity. Making too much of a splash will only scare fish away.

Therefore, we need to be ready and, by our lives of Christian caring and helping, we need to make conditions good for His kind of "fishing". Then the Holy Spirit can use even our words to "catch" someone for eternal life through Jesus.

Lord, help me today to gently cast the "bait" of Your Gospel message, if a conversation seems to be "the time to fish". Amen.

Though Gnarled By Time And Trouble

Even though I live in the middle of trouble, You keep me alive. You stretch out Your hand against my angry enemies, and Your right hand saves me. The Lord accomplishes His purpose for me. *Psalm 138:7-8*

On a wind-swept ridge or near the tree line the mountain hiker finds many trees twisted and gnarled into all sorts of odd shapes, as they struggle to survive. No matter its appearance, however, each tree serves a purpose, providing food and shelter for birds or preventing erosion of the thin soil.

Time and trouble along life's trail can "bend us out of shape", physically or emotionally. Sickness or accident may gnarl our bodies and twist our attitudes. Sometimes we might wonder if it is all worth the struggle to go on.

Yet we know it is – just as we know that the agony of Jesus, which twisted His body on the cross, had purpose and value. By enduring it, He obeyed His Father and served us through suffering for our sins so we might have eternal life.

Because that grace comforts us, we will keep on serving Him as we are able. Perhaps our example of faithfulness in spite of limitations will encourage others to endure their burdens. Maybe because we are personally aware of how much a person can hurt, we can help others more sympathetically and effectively.

The Lord will use us no matter what our condition, if we let Him because of His grace in Jesus.

Help me, Lord, to serve You well even if I feel really bad today. Amen.

Looking At Life's Elevations

Now then, with all these witnesses around us like a cloud, let us get rid of every burden and the sin we easily fall into and with endurance run the race laid out before us, looking to Jesus, Who gives us our faith from start to finish. *Hebrews 12:1-2*

Standing near the mountaintop, the hiker easily sees how the mountainside changes with the elevation level. In the river-fed valley vegetation is lush with varied animal life and human activity. As one climbs, these thin out until one reaches the sparse tree line. Then come only scraggly shrubs and tundra until one reaches the bare mountain peak.

Life's elevations can seem similar, especially to those who have been many years on life's trail. Far back lies the busy growth of younger days. Life's activities changed as years went by. Near the end of the trail, life can even seem bleak.

Then life's hiker remembers! Life's peak is not merely an impressive mountain. The glory of eternity in God's presence above still is ahead – not because one was faithful, but because One earned it for us on His crucifixion mountain.

So even aged hikers continue faithfully on the trail of life. Perhaps they also remember that as the inviting peak and the hikers ahead enthused following hikers, so those beginning life's trail now are encouraged by the example of those who continue faithfully no matter how long the trail.

Lord, thank You for the example of faith those who have traveled the trail of life have given to me. Help me each day to be a good example to those coming after me. Amen.

At The Mountaintop!

How deep are God's riches, wisdom, and knowledge; how impossible it is to find out His decisions and trace His ways! ... Everything is from Him, by Him, and for Him. To Him be glory forever. Amen. *Romans 11:33,36*

What a glorious experience! To stand at a mountaintop and see His creation stretching out below, around, and still above you! Even if it's only a small, easily climbed peak, you can't help but be impressed by the beauty He has made. You also appreciate the strength He gave you to reach that viewpoint.

So much in life displays God's power. His creation is most obvious. Human accomplishments, whether to devise an artificial heart or put people into space, merely harness a little of His power and wisdom.

God's power also shows itself when we live as His children. We cannot obey Him by our own ability. Only as we receive His strength from His Word and Holy Communion can we follow His will at all.

Mostly, however, God's power revealed itself on that small hill of Calvary. In the crucifixion of Jesus He destroyed the power of sin, death, and the devil. There forgiveness was earned, not just for a few, but for the world. There He created the Gospel, which is "God's power to save", as it brings us to and keeps us in faith in Jesus (*Romans 1:16*).

O God, how great You are! Help me today to use Your strength in order to bring glory to You by my obedient living. Amen.

Back To The Plains Of Daily Life

When I remember You on my bed and think of You during the night – how You are my Help, how in the shadow of Your wings I shout happily, then my heart clings to You and Your right hand holds me up. *Psalm 63:6-8*

No matter how thrilled by the view, you can't live on the mountaintop – nor may you stay on vacation permanently. Soon you must go back to the plains of daily life with its everyday responsibilities. Memories of the mountain trail can, however, brighten your daily walk.

So it is with spiritual mountaintops, those special times of comfort and guidance, peace and strength God gives from time to time. How thrilling they are, whether during personal Bible study, public worship, or caring Christian fellowship.

But these are not the permanent realities of being a child of God on earth. As Jesus walked the trail of life obediently all the way to the cross, so God calls us to follow Him faithfully as we live each day.

Spiritual memories help. But our real power comes through His daily assurance, whether we feel it or not: "Jesus died for you! You are forgiven because of Him!"

In that forgiven joy we will keep on His trail, even in the plains and problems of daily life.

Thank You, Lord, for those special times You have given me. Thank You even more for Your daily assurance of forgiveness because of Jesus, my Savior. Amen.

Anticipating More Mountains*

"Be strong and courageous," David also told his son Solomon, "and do it. Don't be afraid or terrified, because the Lord God, my God, will be with you. He will not fail you or forsake you." *1 Chronicles 28:20*

Once thrilled by mountain trails, a person usually wants more such hikes and looks forward eagerly to another trip, whether back to a place previously enjoyed or to a new area enthusiastically described by someone else.

Of course, getting there might not be easy – there could be an accident or car trouble or bad weather or other problems. But we set out with anticipation, knowing where we are going.

On the trail of life we haven't seen our destination before; but we willingly go because the Lord has told us where the trail leads: to Himself forever – and He has given us the way: through Jesus Who died on the cross for us. Even more, we know we do not go alone; He goes with us, forgiving us as we depend on Jesus as Savior and guiding us as we use His Word.

So we set out on each day's trail with confidence and courage in spite of any troubles or temptations, "rattlesnakes", which might come.

Thank You, Lord, for promising to be with me wherever You take me on life's trail today or in the future, and so keep me confident and faithful whatever comes. Amen.

* *Edited versions of these July devotions were originally published in* **Portals of Prayer,** *August 1990.*

Planning For A Trip

You should say: "If the Lord is willing, we'll live and do this or that." *James 4:15*

When beginning a trip, you could just get into your car and start to drive wherever the roads might take you. Usually, however, it is better to do some advance planning – studying maps to know how to get where you want to go, gathering clothes and equipment for whatever you plan to do once you get there.

God's written Word is our map for the trail of life He gives us. In it He shows us the way: it isn't by our goodness that we will reach eternal life – the only way is through Jesus Who was good enough in our place and then was punished enough for all the sins of everyone. This is the message we need every day on our trail so that we don't lose the way.

His Word also is the equipment we need along our daily way. He gives us guidance to meet the challenges and opportunities that will come. He also gives us the spiritual strength we need to face these and remain faithful to Him. Here He comforts us by assuring us that we are in His keeping when the trail takes turns we don't expect or particularly enjoy.

So, just as one does not look at a map only at the beginning but throughout a trip, we keep using His Word daily on life's trail.

Thank You, Lord, for Your guiding Word; and help me remember that in whatever happens, You are truly guiding according to Your will. Amen.

Suddenly! What A View!

But the Lord made the heavens. Splendor and majesty are before Him; power and beauty are in His holy place.
Psalm 96:5-6

Sometimes you can drive and drive for miles in rather ordinary country, rolling fields or gentle hills or tall pines all around. Then at the crest of a hill or a bend of the road what a view! Mountains looming high! A waterfall across the valley! How suddenly the beauty of God's creation can impress you!

Life can plod along at times: same routine day after day, no excitement, boring. Even your spiritual life might seem to be in a rut: Bible reading just a duty, worship services only ordinary.

Then, suddenly! What a view! Perhaps someone compliments what you've done! Perhaps a Bible verse really strikes home! Perhaps the pastor's sermon is just what you needed! What a view! It gives you energy and enthusiasm again!

Does God lead us through the ordinary days so we will better appreciate the special times? Or does He plan to give us occasional special times so we will continue faithfully even though most days are just ordinary?

We can't always understand God's ways; but we know He always acts in His wisdom – His giving of Jesus as our Savior is proof enough of that; for what could be a more spectacular view of His love for us than Jesus crucified and risen?

Help me never doubt Your ways, Lord. And thank You for the special times of realizing Your presence that You give me. Amen.

A Patriotic Sky

Everyone should obey the government that is over him, because there is no government except that which is put there by God. *Romans 13:1*

For just a few minutes on one morning hike they saw a patriotic sky: some clouds in rosy glow from the rising sun, some still white, and the blue of the sky. God in His greatness made this appear briefly.

God in His wisdom has made the nations and the governments; but these appear only briefly in the course of history. Even our country will undoubtedly disappear eventually. For now, however, He has placed each of us under the government that controls where we live.

Therefore, we honor Him by how we submit to the government over us. We may work to change it, if we think it is not acting responsibly for the good of its citizens; but we also must act responsibly in such efforts.

No matter under what kind of government we live in this life, however, "we are citizens of heaven" (*Philippians 3:20*) so that our primary allegiance is to our Savior King. Because He died for us, we will live for Him.

Part of that living for Him is to be an excellent citizen of the country in which we live by paying taxes, giving respect, obeying the laws (as long as such do not force us to sin). Such citizenship shows that we are His.

Help me, eternal God, to be a good citizen in this country where You have placed me. Amen.

Too Concerned About The Trivial

But the Pharisee was surprised to see He didn't wash before the meal. *Luke 11:38*

Once while driving down a truly spectacular mountain valley, he got so tense and on edge because of all the curves that he said he never wanted to drive that way again.

Sometimes also on life's trail we can get so concerned about trivial things that we stop paying attention to what is really important.

In the congregation we may think more about a pastor's personality than his faithfulness. With others we may be troubled by some irritating habit so that we fail to appreciate the good someone is trying to do. We may begin to pride ourselves in some one way we serve the Lord and so turn from humble thankfulness for what He has done for us, sinners that we daily are. Churches may think more of their programs and buildings than about what is actually preached and taught.

But what is really important in the Lord's work? Most important is the good message of Jesus taking away the sins of the world so He could forgive those who depend on Him as Savior.

And then? Isn't it to help others come to faith in Jesus and encourage each other to live faithfully for Him no matter what our individual irritating ways might be?

Thank You, Lord, for using me in Your work in spite of how I irritate You and others by my sinning and by my particular ways. Help me be accepting of others even if their ways do irritate me at times. Amen.

Taking Real Beauty For Granted

Let us not stay away from our worship services, as some are regularly doing, but let us encourage one another, all the more because you see the day coming near. *Hebrews 10:25*

When first entering mountain country, one usually is greatly impressed by the beauty to be seen all around: immense nearby mountains, distant peaks, deep valleys, rushing streams. But after a while, these can be taken for granted, even becoming just ordinary for those who live there permanently.

Doesn't this sometimes happen in our worship life and even regarding God's message of forgiveness in Jesus? Worship week after week can seem to become ordinary. We hear the Gospel so often that we take it for granted.

When this happens, the devil quickly tempts us with: "You don't really need that this week, do you?"

But when we keep remembering our daily sinning, what could be more beautiful and comforting than the message of Jesus' suffering for us to take our sins away?

Therefore, we will not neglect or take for granted His message and hearing it in worship with fellow Christians. Not just by habit and not just because God commands it, but because of our need we will come to His Word each week. Only then can we leave our sins behind us through the announcement of His forgiveness and continue in peace on the trail of life with His guidance and help.

Thank You, Lord, for the beauty of the Gospel, which I hear preached in public worship. Amen.

The Eternal Divide

If you believe in Him, you're not condemned. But if you don't believe, you're already condemned because you don't believe in the name of God's only-begotten Son. *John 3:18*

A few miles north of Lake Louise in Canada is Continental Divide Creek; just past a picnic shelter this creek divides, half flowing west to the Pacific, half flowing east to the Atlantic.

An eternal spiritual divide faces all people, not just once in a lifetime, but daily. It is: "What do you think of Jesus?" Those who reject Him as Savior, thinking they don't need Him because of their own goodness, are heading toward damnation. Those who realize their sinfulness and see Him on the cross for them are on the way that leads to eternal life.

Daily we need to renew our faith in Jesus for eternal life, since the devil wants to destroy it and claim us again for hell. Pride and self-righteousness are his favorite weapons. This is why we need God's message daily in personal devotions: so that God can keep us in faith by the power of His Gospel message.

Daily we also need to be concerned about any individuals we know who do not depend on Jesus as Savior. We need to pray for them and share the Gospel with them, as we have the opportunity.

Keep me in faith today, Lord, and use me to help others come to depend on Jesus also. Amen.

Drifting Toward Disaster Unawares

"Even if they all turn against You," Peter answered Him, **"I'll never turn against You."** *Matthew 26:33*

A young family rented a Lake Louise canoe to enjoy the sunny day. Without realizing it, they drifted too close to the outlet creek and were caught in its current. People on the bank reached out to spare them from possible disaster.

Most people don't realize the eternal disaster they are drifting toward by going along with the ways of this world. Many church members also are unaware of this danger. Actually, none of us by nature would see it.

This is why Jesus came from eternity into our world: to reach out His arms on the cross in order to rescue us from the disaster of damnation. There is no other way except through Him, for we cannot save ourselves. The pressures of this evil world and of our own sinful selves are too much for us. But He came, and He reaches out by the message of His Word so that His Holy Spirit rescues us by bringing us to faith.

We can't rescue anyone else, especially not those who don't realize the danger they are in. But we can warn them; and we can be ready to reach out to them with loving help and the message of Jesus as Savior, when they do realize their danger.

Lord, help me to reach out lovingly and patiently to those who don't yet realize their danger. Amen.

Not Crosscountry, But The Trail

"I am the Way, the Truth, and the Life," Jesus answered him. "No one comes to the Father except by Me." *John 14:6*

When setting out on a hike, you could just go crosscountry – through the brush, straight up the mountainside - instead of following the trail with its time-consuming switchbacks. This would not be wise, of course. Not only would it be more strenuous and dangerous, but you could more easily become lost and definitely would cause additional harm to the fragile environment. It's best to stay on the trail.

Also in life it's best to stay on the trail which the Lord lays out for us. Instead of following our own ideas, we are safer ourselves and more helpful to others when we live His way, even if we don't always see how obeying Him will actually be better.

Especially must we remain on the trail to eternal life. Jesus is that way, come as God on earth so that He could obey all of God's commands perfectly in our place and then could pay for the sins of all people by His death on the cross. He has done it all.

If we try to change His way even a little to meet our ideas and desires, it would no longer be His way but ours, which would not lead to the Father but away from Him.

Lord, keep me on Your way today, both in faith and in living. Amen.

Some Rush And Some See

Look at the birds in the air. ... See how the flowers grow in the field. *Matthew 6:26,28*

Once on a trail they met some hikers whose main purpose seemed to be how quickly they could walk those miles. One wonders how much they actually saw as they rushed along. Oh, no one could miss the big views. But what about the little beauties God created: the wildflowers, the birds, the varieties of mushrooms?

Some people seem to be that way on the trail of life. They rush from one experience to another – they demand that everything be exciting.

But what about the little things of life? And what about the fact that life is not always exciting? And what about those times in life which are agonizing with pain or heartache?

That's when we need to appreciate the little beauties God gives us: the smile of a stranger, the listening ear of a friend, quiet conversation with a loved one, a delicate flower, a busy bird, a gentle rain, the sunset.

Exciting experiences can also be gifts from God; those are usually few and far between, however. But the little things are always here to encourage us, if we only take time to see them.

Most of all, Jesus is with us always, forgiving, comforting, guiding – our beautiful Savior.

Thank You, Lord, for the little beauties You have placed along my trail of life. Amen.

Easy In Sunshine, But In Rain?

"Lord, if it's You," Peter answered Him, "order me to come to You on the water." "Come," He said. So Peter got out of the boat, walked on the water, and went toward Jesus. But when he saw the wind, he was frightened and started to sink. "Lord, save me!" he cried. *Matthew 14:28-30*

What a joy to be out on the trail, when the sun is shining. It's easy then, even though the way may get steep, because of the beauty you see. But if clouds build up or raindrops begin, it soon is not so satisfying or enjoyable or easy. In fact, hiking in the rain can be "yuk"!

Is the trail of life any different? When the sun is shining or things are going the way we want, it's also easier to do what our Lord wants – to be patient and kind and helpful, even to those who are not pleasant to us.

But when rainy days come, whether weather-wise with one dreary day after another or otherwise with disappointments and troubles tearing at us, following our Lord's way is much more difficult. We are tempted at least to get fearful or selfish or rebellious – even though we know better and want to do better.

Peter's call, "Lord, save me!", is what we especially need to pray on such days. It already is our confession of faith in Him for forgiveness and eternal life, since He *died* for us. It also can be our plea for help when life for Him gets difficult, since He also *lived* for us and so knows exactly how to help.

Help me, Jesus, on life's rainy days. Amen.

Lightning – The Sudden Tragedy

**Or those eighteen the tower at Siloam fell on and killed –
do you think they must have been worse transgressors than
all the other people living in Jerusalem? I tell you, no.**
Luke 13:4-5

Rocky Mountain Park has no bears or snakes to harm or kill
you; but it does have lightning – which can strike almost
without warning. Lightning poses a life threat to any mountain
hiker.

Sudden tragedy can strike us any time on the trail of life: heart
attack, accident, criminal violence, natural calamity to name a
few.

And there really is no answer to our natural question of "why
did God let this happen to me?" Personal carelessness
sometimes is a factor, but usually not. God in His wisdom just
allows it – and sorrow, pain, even death can come *suddenly*.

Which means that faith in Jesus as our eternal Savior must be
our daily commitment – not only so we go to heaven if tragedy
kills us, but also so we have the comfort and strength we need if
tragedy causes only painful after-effects.

A hymn says: "we walk in danger all the way". But it also
says: we "walk with Jesus all the way". *He* is why we do not
have to walk fearfully, daily wondering what might happen to
us. He protects us so that not everything which could happen
does; and what He does allow, He has under control so we can
endure it by His help.

*Help me, Lord, to trust You no matter what You allow to
meet me on today's trail. Amen.*

July 13   Read: James 4

The Guide We Always Need

O Lord, help me know Your ways and teach me Your paths. Lead me in Your truth and teach me, because You are the God who saves me. *Psalm 25:4-5*

Sometimes the most enjoyable way to hike in the mountains is with a guide, perhaps a park ranger, who can explain and point out things you might otherwise miss. When hiking in wilderness areas, unless you are quite skilled, you need an experienced guide to get you in and out without getting lost.

Along life's trail we always need God's Word as our guide, not merely as a book, however, nor just as words that we carry around in our minds. He says we need His *preached* Word in public worship every week to remain faithful on His trail.

At times we are tempted to think we already know whatever we might hear in a sermon. But God has not commanded public worship merely so we just keep hearing *new* things. His purpose is for us to keep hearing and remembering and depending on the *true* things He has revealed, but which we so easily forget in the rush and the sinning of life each week.

He doesn't need us in public worship; we need His message of forgiving love through Jesus, Who had to die because of "the sinning of life each week", which we are guilty of. That's why we are to worship publicly, unless physically unable to do so, also this week.

Thank You, Lord, for using Your preached Word to guide me and keep me in faith in Jesus. Amen.

Like A Piece Of Hard Candy

I treasure in my heart what You say, so I won't sin against You. *Psalm 119:11*

While hiking a long trail, he found that having a piece of hard candy in his cheek seemed to keep his mouth and throat from getting dried out so quickly. It also gave some extra enjoyment from time to time with its sweet taste.

That made him think about the value of having Bible verses tucked away in one's memory to think about and be strengthened by as needed along life's trail.

That's how Jesus fought off the devil when He was especially tempted. The devil tempted, and Jesus replied: "It is written" (*Matthew 4:4*).

Even on the cross, as He suffered and died for us sinners, He quoted the Scriptures (*Matthew 27:46*) and remembered to fulfill its prophecies (*John 19:28*).

We need the public hearing of God's Word each week; but we also need to remember His Word so it can comfort or guide or even warn us during life's daily twists, turns, and temptations.

Perhaps today's text, if you memorized it, could be "like a piece of hard candy" for you sometime this week, since His Word of forgiveness does help us not sin against Him, if we only think of it when temptation comes.

Lord, help me to remember more of Your Word so I can think of it, as needed, as I live for You. Amen.

Always A New View?

A few days later the younger son gathered his possessions, left home for a distant country, and there squandered his property by wild living. *Luke 15:13*

If possible, they try to hike a circle trail not just up and back. Why not see a new view instead of what they already had seen?

On life's trail we are much tempted to keep looking for the new view, the "distant country", the different, the exciting. We quickly get bored with what is routine. We want change!

But much of life *is* routine – sometimes life even gets into "ruts" that *can't* be changed. What then? How do you manage to live joyfully for the Lord if you are imprisoned by the walls of your sickroom or feel trapped by your job or other circumstances?

God's promises of His presence (*Matthew 28:20*) and His planned purpose (*Romans 8:28*) can give us the attitude of accepting faithfulness which He wants in us, no matter what our situation is.

Since we aren't always so accepting but sometimes do get bored or rebellious, however, our real help is that Jesus paid for these failures also so that we can face each day fresh, forgiven, and trying to be faithful, even if nothing except the calendar date has changed.

Lord, keep me faithful today as I remember Your promises of presence, purpose, and forgiveness. Amen.

Work, But Worth It

Share hardships with me like a good soldier of Christ Jesus. *2 Timothy 2:3*

The hardest trail they ever hiked was Mt. Indefatigable Trail in Peter Lougheed Provincial Park, Alberta, Canada. The forest section usually seemed to rise at a 45 degree angle – the ridge section often was worse!

But, oh, was it worth it! Once on the ridge the views were spectacular – and got better the higher they went! Then near an alpine meadow was a spring gushing right out of the mountainside! Yes, "work, but worth it"!

Is the trail of life any different? Hardship comes in every life, but even more to us who are following Jesus. He tells us of our "cross" and of the "tribulation" we must bear. To be His means we must "crucify" our sinful nature so we do His will instead of the devil's. Being His isn't easy – it requires *work*!

Yet, it's *worth it*, isn't it? Because He did the work none of us could have done (completely paying the penalty of our sins before God), we are on the way to an eternal home better than can be imagined; and until we get there, we have not only His daily help, but at times even spectacular experiences of how He works in our lives better than we could have planned by ourselves.

Lord, help me keep doing what You want no matter how much work it sometimes is. Amen.

The Narrow Trail Of Faith

But the gate is small, and the way is narrow that leads to life, and only a few are finding it. *Matthew 7:14*

The ridge section of Mt. Indefatigable Trail not only is very narrow, but often has a wind which feels strong enough to blow you over the sheer cliff. Yet it's not really that dangerous, if you are careful to stay on the trail.

The trail to eternal life is very narrow. It leads *only* through the cross-shaped gate of our Lord Jesus, Who suffered and died because of all the times we humans have wandered off the trail God wants us to live. The trail to eternal life is the trail of faith in Jesus alone as Savior.

But the devil does not want us to receive the blessings Jesus has earned for us. So, all along the trail of life he sends the strong winds of temptation to self-righteousness on the one hand and to ungodly living on the other. Time after time he tries to destroy our faith in Jesus.

Which is why we dare not become careless regarding our faith. Instead we daily look to His cross to be reminded that He hung there for each of us individually. It is by His Gospel message that He keeps us on the trail of faith in spite of the devil's windy attacks.

His Gospel message also keeps us on the trail of life which shows that our faith is in Jesus alone.

Lord, keep me on the narrow trail of faith so I will follow Your trail of living today. Amen.

Out Of The Mountainside

They drank from the spiritual Rock that went with them, and that Rock was Christ. *1 Corinthians 10:4*

If you know where to look along Mt. Indefatigable Trail, you find a crystal-clear spring gushing right out of the mountainside. What a refreshing drink after a hot, strenuous climb! It's safe to drink, too, because it comes right out of a rock, not from a contaminated stream.

The trail of life gets exhausting, too. Not only the troubles of life which everyone experiences, but also the extra temptations which the devil blows at us make the work of living for God difficult and draining.

On those days when stresses pile up and even spiritual energy goes down, some human solutions do help. Even Jesus got away from the crowds at times; He also relaxed at suppers to which He was invited.

But the best help come directly from God. So Jesus spent time in worship and in prayer. And our real strengthening comes from Jesus, when we consciously turn to Him in worship and prayer to remember that He, as God's pure gift of love, is the "water of life" Who daily washes away our sins and so renews us for another day along the trail of life which He lays out before us.

When stresses pile up, Lord, refresh me by reminding me that You are forgiving and guiding me. Amen.

Rushing, Cascading Peace

I can lie down and sleep in peace, because You alone, O Lord, enable me to live without fear. *Psalm 4:8*

Why should waterfalls and cascading brooks be so fascinating? So easily we spend time by them, just watching and listening, then leave feeling refreshed and at peace. Why? It's only water, bouncing off the rocks.

Perhaps it is the combination of sound and movement that blots out whatever troubles us at the time. Inside we might be in turmoil with worrisome thoughts. But somehow God uses that splashing water to assure us: I'll keep you safe – I'll not let troubles get too much for you.

Especially He does that regarding the guilt of our sinning. Not only can't we deny our sin; sometimes we can't seem to get free of the guilt we feel regarding at least some of our sinning: How could I have done *that*? Can He actually forgive me for such a terrible deed? Why does it keep tormenting me?

That's when we need the "waterfall" of Jesus, our "water of life". We need His message over and over coming into our ears and being in our thoughts that He suffered and died even for *that* sinning. As we so listen and think, eventually we realize His rushing, cascading peace.

Help me, Lord, to believe the peace You have for me through Jesus having paid for **all** *my sins. Amen.*

Regular Water Stops

Anyone who drinks the water I'll give him will never get thirsty again. But the water I'll give him will be in him a spring of water bubbling up to everlasting life. *John 4:14*

Out on the trail you need to drink enough water. Probably it's best to pause for water at regular times, otherwise, it's too easy to get caught up in the scenery and forget long enough so as to get slightly dehydrated. Then you don't have the energy to enjoy the trail as you could; you also endanger yourself.

Jesus gives us the "water of life", the message of forgiveness of sins through faith in His death for us. We *need* nothing else to save us. There *is* nothing else!

Yet this "water" is not a once-in-your-lifetime experience. Just as having a water bottle along on a trail doesn't help unless you drink from it, so His message can't help us unless we keep receiving it. If we neglect it, we lose our spiritual energy and can even endanger our eternity (since faith in Jesus can be lost according to *Galatians 5:4* and other passages).

This is why God has commanded us to receive the "water of life" each week through the public preaching of His Word. As we regularly keep "drinking" from Him, we not only are better able to follow the trail of life He gives us, but also will have more joy in His blessings on it.

Thank You, Lord, for the strength and guidance You give through Your preached Word. Amen.

Delicate, Unexpected Beauty

The Pharisee who had invited Jesus saw this and said to himself, "If He were a prophet, He would know who is touching Him and what kind of woman she is. She's a sinner." *Luke 7:39*

The high alpine meadow was covered with delicate wildflowers! How unexpected to see dozens of varieties so high on that mountain! How could they survive such harsh conditions and be so beautiful? But there they were that summer day near the end of Mt. Indefatigable Trail.

And there she was, doing a beautiful thing for Jesus, in the Pharisee's house. But! How could such a "sinner" even be permitted to touch Him?

Perhaps you have wondered similar thoughts about someone who sinned publicly and now had returned to the church. True, we should be like the Prodigal Son's father (*Luke 15:11-24*); but in our sinfulness we sometimes are like the Pharisee.

That's when we especially need to remember the beauty of the Gospel and that, if its forgiveness can apply to *us*, then it also must apply to anyone who returns to faith in Jesus no matter what the sinning. Can another be a "sinner", but I am not?

And the beauty of the Gospel causes beautiful things to be done by those who come to faith in Jesus as Forgiver. That's why we walk His way, isn't it? That's how others also can change from ways of sin to the trail of life for Him.

Help me, Lord, to be humbly thankful for the changes You keep working in me so that I will encourage others as they also change through the power of Your forgiveness. Amen.

Can't Go Another Step!

Let us not get tired of doing good. At the right time we'll reap if we don't give up. *Galatians 6:9*

Sometimes trail's end can seem awfully far away. Perhaps it was the heat of the day or the steepness of the trail or just more miles than you had planned on, but it all turns out to be longer than expected. You're so tired that you think you can hardly go another step; but you can't quit until you get back to camp.

At times on the trail of life we get involved in a situation or responsibility that turns out to be much bigger or more difficult than we had originally foreseen. We are tired of it, especially if no end seems in sight. We would like to quit – let someone else do it!

Perhaps someone else can – and should! But often there is no one else. If we don't do it, it won't get done, no matter how worn down we feel. So, how to keep on – until it is done?

If we look at it selfishly ("eventually I'll be rewarded"), we'll probably get more tired and resentful. But if we remember that what good we do is service to Him Who did the greatest and the hardest good of all for us so we might receive the good of eternal life, then we can keep on faithfully and willingly even in spite of the exhaustion we might feel.

For the tiring tasks of today, Lord, give me the help I need so I do them well for Your sake. Amen.

Oh, My Aching Feet!

Even when you're old, I'll be the same, and when you're gray, I'll still carry you. I made you and will continue to bear you. I will carry you and save you. *Isaiah 46:4*

Back in camp at last many hikers experience an "aching feet" syndrome: tired feet want out of those boots and maybe even into cool water to recover from all those miles on the trail. But by the next day they are ready to go again.

Would that the aches and pains of aging would disappear so quickly! Usually, however, these keep "talking" day after day. As life's trail stretches on, the body the Lord has given you wears out, little by little. Perhaps for you it hasn't even taken all that many years to feel those on-going aches and the limitations which keep them company. These remind you that life's trail in this world will one day end.

But not yet! He has given you today's trail and His promise to "carry" you, as needed, while using you to do good to those He guides to cross your trail. You may not be able to do everything you once did for Him. But you still can serve Him today by your friendly attitude, by helpful kindnesses, by praying.

And He Who made you His not only by creating you, but especially by bringing you into His family through Jesus, promises: I'll help you live for Me today in spite of any aches and limitations.

Yes, Lord, help me do what I can for You this day, no matter how I might feel. Amen.

Clearer Than The Midnight Stars

As it is, we do not yet see everything put under Him. But we do see Jesus, Who for a little while was made lower than the angels, now crowned with glory and honor because He suffered death in order by God's grace to taste death for everyone. *Hebrews 2:8-9*

It got to be midnight, but they were still out on the foam pad, looking at the stars! They had never before seen them as clear and bright *and as many* as that night in the crisp thin air of that high mountain country! Spectacular!

Truly, "what is man that You should think of him?" (*Hebrews 2:6*) in comparison to those millions of stars and the rest of Your creation? Especially since we humans insist on polluting it by our modern ways of living and by our sinning, why should You care about us, Lord?

So, how blessed we are that You do! You made Your Son live down here with us, and, although unpolluted by sin (which is the cause of death), yet He did "taste death for everyone". How good to see Him as the way for us to live with You.

Yet, at times we hardly see Him. We get distracted by our own guilt – we get blinded by how others sin against us.

But shouldn't these facts of sin make us see Him ever more clearly? Isn't He our only hope, our only comfort, in this sin-stressed life?

We feel the effects of sin so painfully. "But we do see Jesus" – and we have peace.

Lord, help me see You clearly today no matter what might try to get in the way. Amen.

Kept In By Rain

Three times I begged the Lord to have it leave me alone, but He told me, "My grace is enough for you. When you are weak, My power is doing its best work." *2 Corinthians 12:8-9*

That day it just rained – and rained – and rained! You can hike in drizzle, but some days you are just kept in by rain.

And some lives are "kept in" by the "rain" of disability or constant pain or life-threatening illness. Perhaps this is your life at present. If not, it could very well yet so "rain" on you farther along on your trail of life.

From our sinful point of view it doesn't seem fair. Why, Lord, especially when others have lived far worse than I? True, we confess that because of our sinning "we justly deserve Your present and eternal punishment". Inwardly, however, how much do we really mean it? Don't we all think there should be "sunshine" on our trail every day? Some "drizzle" is unavoidable, but constant "rain"?

Yet when we "see Jesus", Who took all our deserved punishment on the cross, we know God isn't punishing us. In His grace because of His Son, He can't! The punishment is gone; only grace, forgiveness through Jesus, remains.

Which is enough to get a person through another day of "rain".

Lord, help me, whenever my trail is hard, to remember how hard the cross was for You in my place. Amen.

Why Did He Make Mosquitoes?

What a miserable man I am! Who will rescue me from the body that brings me to this death? Thank God – He does it through our Lord Jesus Christ! *Romans 7:24-25*

Some days out on the trail everything is just perfect: sunshine, blue sky, beautiful views. It couldn't be better!

Except for the mosquitoes, which so often come buzzing! Which makes one wonder: Why did He make mosquitoes? All they seem to do is hurt and irritate.

Perhaps by them He is telling us: No matter how good life can seem, don't love it too much – you aren't in heaven yet!

Most days we need no such reminder – life is no paradise. Occasionally, however, the trail gets easier, everything works out as we hoped: life is *good*!

And then He allows the "mosquito" of sin to "sting" us! Sometimes others do the damage – more often we ourselves are the culprits: we act selfishly or unthinkingly, and the day turns miserable.

God does not make us sin, but He doesn't prevent it either. Instead, He makes us aware that though we can't totally avoid it, we can finally escape it through the cross of Jesus. Forgiving us now, He is leading us to eternity where no sin will exist to mar our joy with Him.

Thank You, Lord, for today's forgiveness and for the coming perfect joy of eternity. Amen.

Don't Forget The Bird Book!

All Scripture is inspired by God and is useful for teaching, showing what is wrong, correcting and training in right living so that the man of God is ready and equipped for every good work. *2 Timothy 3:16-17*

One trail companion always good to take along is the bird book. One never knows which birds might flash into view, and most hikers are not expert enough to remember them all. Is anyone?

No one can remember all we need to know for the trail of life. That's why the Lord has provided His book, not just to possess, but to take along and use. Because of our sinful natures we aren't smart enough to identify all the sin He wants us to avoid and all the good He wants us to do. More importantly, by ourselves we can't figure out and then always remember the trail to Life itself: not by our doing, but only through the doing of Jesus, Who lived and died for us.

This is why just the bare Bible is not what He wants us to use all by itself. Just as an experienced "birder" can help you use a bird book better, so God has provided those who preach His Word in public worship so we can get all of His message.

Especially does the "preaching of His Word" keep us clear about the proper order: the Gospel gives us Life through Jesus so we can follow His guidance for living.

Use Your preached Word in me all through each week, Lord, to comfort and lead me on life's trail. Amen.

Soaring High And Free

Then God's peace, better than all our thinking, will guard your hearts and minds in Christ Jesus. *Philippians 4:7*

To see an eagle or a hawk soaring in the high mountains is quite a thrill. One might wish to be like that bird, soaring high and free! In reality, however, that bird with its telescopic eyesight is just searching for food.

On the trail of life we can think of God being like that soaring, searching bird. Not that He spies to pounce on us when we sin – He knew your sin and mine already before creation – that's why He planned and then sent His Son into time: so *He* would be struck by the punishment and we would escape safe and free. Instead, now He keeps us individually in His sight to see our needs. Then He shapes the trail ahead of us to provide whatever will truly help.

Peace with God is primarily that He forgives us for Jesus' sake. How He can *keep on* forgiving us day after day is beyond "all our thinking" – but He does!

That we are in His daily watchful sight adds to our peace, for we know He is protecting and guiding and helping better than we could plan for ourselves. This is why we go confidently on life's trail; in His care we are safe.

Lord, thanks for the peace You give me through Your daily forgiveness and protection. Amen.

Shadows Chasing Sunshine

Dear friends, don't be surprised that you're being tested by a fiery trial as though something strange were happening to you. *1 Peter 4:12*

From a high viewpoint on a breezy day it's rather interesting to watch the cloud shadows chasing the sunshine on the mountainside across the valley. Or is it the sunshine which chases the shadows away? Actually it is neither, instead, only sunshine and shadows.

Life's trail will have its "shadows"; we are not to be "surprised" at even painful trials which come because we follow our Savior. But should we think of them as "shadows chasing sunshine" or the other way around?

The more we think about the "shadows", the worse they will seem and the more reluctant we will be to risk their coming. That's how the devil tries to tempt us.

However, those "shadows" will be only fleeting if we concentrate on the "sunshine", the love of our Savior (Who willingly accepted our eternal suffering) and the blessings we do experience as we follow the trail He lays out for us, His brothers and sister.

So, though the "shadows" are not fun, we will endure them because of the "sunshine" that warms us: forgiveness and peace now with glory to come.

Help me, Lord, to keep seeing Your "sunshine" no matter how dark today's "shadow" might become. Amen.

A Peek At The Other Side

Then I saw a new heaven and a new earth, because the first heaven and the first earth had passed away. And there was no longer any sea. *Revelation 21:1*

One vacation in Banff National Park they climbed Sentinel Pass. They didn't have time to go down the other side, but what a view into Paradise Valley!

For us who depend on Jesus for forgiveness of our sins, the trail of life will one day lead into the real "paradise", being in His presence and after the resurrection of our bodies in His new creation.

Until then, however, we have only a "peek" into eternity and this through the Scriptures. Some people claim to have seen more during "life after life" experiences (even St. Paul perhaps did, *2 Corinthians 12:1-4*); but these are valid only if they agree with what God's written Word says, otherwise they are tricks of him who can even disguise himself as "an angel of light" (*2 Corinthians 11:14*). What God's Word describes is glorious enough to excite our expectations (also that of the entire creation, *Romans 8:18-21*) and increase our desire to enter it.

Which we will as we continue on the trail of faith through the power of God's Word working in us day by day.

For the promise of eternity and for Jesus, the way of entering it, thank You, Lord. Amen.

And The Trail Never Ends

I fought the good fight, I ran the race, I kept the faith. Now there is waiting for me the crown of righteousness which the Lord, the righteous Judge, will give me on that day, and not only me but all who love to see Him come again. *2 Timothy 4:7-8*

Where are you on the trail of Life? When did you begin? Not that either of these questions is really important. Some began as children, some later in life, no matter. Being on the trail and remaining on it until we enter the eternal day is all that really matters.

The trail, of course, is not our living – although our living shows we are on the trail. The trail is Jesus: "the Way, the Truth, the Life". Because He lived and suffered and died for us sinners and then rose again, we have the trail and have been put on it by the Holy Spirit causing our faith in Jesus as Savior.

This trail is, however, a one-day-at-a-time experience which never ends. After this life it will continue in service to God forever. Until then, we can't "take a day off" no matter how tempted, but daily are to consciously keep Jesus in mind as Savior so the Holy Spirit will keep us from stumbling off the trail and missing our eternal destination.

As we keep using His Word about Jesus, He will keep us on this trail of faith until we meet in His presence where no hindrances or sin will mar our living together for Him forever.

Keep me, Lord, on the trail of faith daily until I am with You forever. Amen.

Desert Lives Up To Its Name

I am weak enough to give up and am numb inside. I remember the days of long ago, think of all You have done, and meditate on what Your hands have made. I spread out my hands to You, longing for You like thirsty ground. *Psalm 143:4-6*

The "high desert" area of New Mexico doesn't really look like "desert"; instead of bare sand sparse grass, varieties of cactus, and other desert shrubs cover it. But at times it does live up to its name! In those years when rainfall is far less than usual even some cacti wither and die.

Some stretches of the trail of life truly turn into "desert". One stress, one trouble, one temptation after another wear us down into feeling spiritually numb. We hear the words about His love for us, but we don't feel His presence. Where are You, Lord? Why don't You help me out of this depression? Do You exist? Have you ever felt that way? Maybe some day you will.

Part of our comfort in such "desert" times is to know that a trusting relationship with God is not based on our feelings but on the fact of His Word as re-enforced by the fact of Baptism, when He called us by name as His, and the fact of Holy Communion, when He touches us personally with His Body and Blood. No matter how we presently *feel*, these facts assure us: He is – He is in control – He forgives – He will eventually bring us into peace and joy. As we remind ourselves over and over, even hour by hour: Jesus loves me and sacrificed Himself for my sins so I could get through this life into eternal life, our feelings will eventually catch up with these facts, and our "desert" will "bloom" again.

Lord, help me keep listening to Your Word so that I trust what You promise in spite of what I might feel. Amen.

When It's Hot, It's Hot!

When I kept silent, I wore out my limbs, groaning all day long. Day and night Your hand was heavy on me; my vitality was drained by the summer heat. *Psalm 32:3-4*

Whether in 90/90 southwest Missouri (90° temperature, 90% humidity) or 112/8 southwest New Mexico (112°, 8%), when it's hot, it's inescapably hot! Even fleeing to mountains or lake doesn't give escape from outside oppressive heat! Stepping into that outside steaming sauna or sweltering stove wears you out! Until you get into air-conditioned comfort!

Sometimes we are guilty of truly hurting someone, but don't want to admit it. We had our reasons for doing what we did – that person had it coming – I couldn't help myself – it wasn't really *so* wrong, was it? Of course, after a while we may succeed in pushing the incident out of our consciousness – until it springs up again, perhaps on a sleepless night. Such is the conscience at work – which can make living miserable, as that sin disrupts the family or destroys a friendship. Unbelievers can dull their conscience; but if we are trying to follow the Lord Jesus on the trail of life, He keeps pricking it, trying to make us uncomfortable until we admit both to Him and to that person the harm we've inflicted and our regret for having done so. For no sin is ever justified, that is, excusable.

But in that repentance we enter the cool comfort of His justifying us, that is, forgiving us, because He made up for what we did by what He did as He lived and died. Then we have peace.

Lord, keep me from hurting others today – and help me ask forgiveness from anyone I have hurt. Amen.

One Week Is Too Much

"Even if I have to die with You," Peter told Him, "I'll never deny You!" *Matthew 26:35*

Lilacs are a beautiful shrub – but they really can't stand much desert heat. One week without watering and they seriously wilt. With a good "drink" they usually perk up again, but on their own they can't survive.

Pride says: I can do it on my own! Peter said that: The others may be weak, but I'll even die with You, Lord, before I would deny You. And we know what happened! Three little questions, two by teenage girls, got him cursing and swearing that he never ever knew "Him" (*Luke 24:69-75*). That's what happens spiritually when a person depends on current commitment or past participation and thinks: I don't really need God's Word today. "Pride comes before…"

The "rattlesnake" of pride continually slithers along our trail of life. Not only does it tempt us toward thinking that worship this week isn't important "because I have my daily devotions", it also can lead us to say (to ourselves, if not out loud), when seeing the sinning of someone else: "I wouldn't ever do that!" Such pride already has us contradicting Jesus, just as Peter did.

But Jesus did not give up on Peter – with a look He called him back into His love. And Jesus looked out from the cross to see, already then, us in our downfalls of pride as well as all our other sinning; and He now says to us: I came to the cross so that I could accept you in spite of your sins.

Thank You, Lord, and keep me humbly depending on You by preventing me from ever thinking I don't need regular "drinking" from the water of life You give me through your Word and Holy Communion. Amen.

Inferno Forest Fires!

There is a way a man thinks is right, but it finally becomes the way of death. *Proverbs 14:12*

One especially hot and dry summer New Mexico had two inferno forest fires, both caused by unthinking following of well-meaning but impractical bureaucratic regulations. One began when a "prescribed burn" was set without regard to predicted high winds, which quickly fanned the fire out of control. The other happened when a dying tree fell onto a power line, which local officials had warned would happen if it were not safely cut down – regulations said the tree was outside the power line right of way so had to be left standing. Both of these fires resulted in tremendous loss of homes, property, harvestable timber, and wildlife habitat, because "regulations" were followed against common sense.

Of course, some loss was because people built homes only according to aesthetics without considering fire danger. Using wood shakes to roof a forest home looks beautiful but positively welcomes fire! Human ideas so often consider only short-term desires, not long-term dangers.

Especially spiritually! Every non-Christian religion seems right to those who practice it. But every one of them ends in eternal death, because they are all based on the human nature desire to save oneself, which can't be done. God's way is the only way – and His way is the gift of eternal life, which Jesus paid for by His life and death. Trusting in Jesus to save us, we also try to follow His directions for living, since human nature ideas about what is right are based on selfishness.

Help me today, Lord, to follow, not my ideas, but what You say is right. Amen.

Such Total Destruction!

The Lord's day will come like a thief. On that day the heavens will pass away with a roar, the elements will be destroyed by heat, and the earth and what was done on it will be exposed (*burned up*, KJV). Since all these things will be destroyed in this way, think how holy and godly you should live. *2 Peter 3:10-11*

Looking at a healthy forest, one can hardly imagine what total destruction a forest fire can wreak – such tall, beautiful trees reduced to ashes or bare burnt poles! That same fire can also turn a magnificent home into just a pile of rubble.

Do you think, looking at the world itself, that it can be destroyed even worse, completely returned to nothing? Yet that is exactly what God's Word tells us. Some Christians say in worship: "world without end". But Jesus specifically says that "heaven and earth will pass away" (*Matthew 24:35*). This creation came from nothing and will return to nothing – to be followed by God's new creation, of course (*Revelation 21:1*).

And we would similarly be destroyed because of our sinning if Jesus had not been our spiritual "firefighter", Who put out God's hot anger by smothering it with His blood on the cross so we could live in His new creation.

Now, until we arrive there, we are to live holy and godly lives here, which means: keeping from sinning and doing what is good, as best we can with His help – which does not contribute anything to our getting there, but is our thankful response to the eternal "fire protection" He has given us.

Lord, help me fight every "rattlesnake" of temptation and try to make "rainbows" of good today. Amen.

How Dry Is Dry?

I'm glad to be weak and mistreated, to suffer hardships, to be persecuted and hard pressed for Christ. You see, when I'm weak, then I'm strong. *2 Corinthians 12:10*

"Sure is dry", says someone whose area got only 12" of rain instead of its normal 24" during a summer. "Sure is dry", says a New Mexican when rains produce only 6" of moisture instead of the average 12" for the year. How dry is "dry"? It depends on your perspective, where you live, and what you are accustomed to.

When "dry" stretches on the trail of life oppress us, when we seem to accomplish nothing and when others make life more difficult by mistreating us because we try to be faithful to our Savior, how we weather them can depend much on how we evaluate and react to them. They can become "rattlesnakes" of self-pity or opportunities to trust Him more and see how He can use us in spite of or at times because of what we have to suffer.

When life goes too smoothly, we can become proud that what we do is due to our ability and ideas. So, by taking away easy successes, the Lord tries to remind us: not only is your eternal life not your accomplishment but the work of Jesus, so also anything you are able to do for Me is not by your power but by My strength. He also is calling us to trust Him that when we work without seeing positive results, He still is using us in His plan for the good of people. Sometimes He does let us know how He worked through us – but maybe we'll never understand until we are finally with Him and some others there will tell us how He reached them by what they saw and heard from us.

Lord, if my trail seems "dry" today, help me keep living Your way in trust that You are working even when I don't realize how. Amen.

Like A Hanging Dust Cloud

If your brother sins against you, go and point out his sin to him when you are alone with him. If he listens to you, you have won your brother. *Matthew 18:15*

The pickup roared by on a dry country road. Its plume of dust enveloped the walkers so they could hardly breathe. A slight breeze did gradually sweep away the choking grit. Still, a layer of irritating grime lay on the landscape until a good rain would wash everything clean.

When someone dear to us sins against us with sin that really hurts, it can choke our whole outlook on life. We might feel miserable at being betrayed, angry at being taken advantage of, and intent on getting even. In such a state we aren't pleasant to anyone around us.

Until the breath of God's Word reminds us: But I forgive you, though you hurt Me every day by each of your sins – I forgive you because of Jesus, Who hurt on the cross because of your sinning.

That gentle reminder enables us also to forgive, which means, to act with kindness to that person in spite of how he or she has hurt us.

Lingering memories, however, can still mar our attitude. That's why God wants us to gently talk to the one who hurt us to, if possible, wash away the past by the power of His forgiveness and in this way fully restore that relationship.

O Lord, help me talk with forgiveness to those who sin against me so we get over our hurts in order to live in peace and kindness. Amen.

Clouds Build To Block The View

Why am I so discouraged, and why am I in such turmoil? I must look to God for help, and praise Him as my Savior and my God. *Psalm 42:11*

Such a beautiful day when they began that hike with tremendous views of mountains all around! But then afternoon clouds gathered and built until, although they still could see spectacular valleys, the mountains were gone!

The trail of life doesn't have to be "dry" to be discouraging! Perhaps a "cloud" of serious illness or of personal conflict or of feeling cheated financially by someone you thought you could trust grabs so much of your attention that life doesn't seem worth living for the Lord. Sure, He still is giving everyday blessings all around, but even these seem dimmed by the turmoil swirling around inside of us. What's the use? Why try if this is what you get?

That's when we not only need to look to Him for help in that time of trouble, but also need to listen again to how He has best helped us. The "cloud" of sin had hidden God's love from us – the guilt of our sinning could not be stilled – there was no hope for us after death! From all this He has saved us.

So, when "clouds" begin to build in life, we must sing! Yes, sing songs of praise which remind us: "He is my Savior!"

Help me not to get discouraged today, Lord, since I know You've saved me from eternal despair. Amen.

Tantalizing Thunder Clouds

"When you see a cloud coming up in the west," Jesus said to the people, "you immediately say, 'There's going to be a heavy rain,' and so it rains." *Luke 12:54*

In most parts of the country thunderstorm clouds to the west mean rain is on its way. But not in New Mexico! Building clouds merely mean somewhere else might get moisture. Or perhaps your area will get "virga": although the clouds produce raindrops, the low humidity and heat of the desert evaporate them before they hit the ground.

Always temptation "rattlesnakes" promise more than the sin ever can deliver – which goes all the way back into the Garden of Eden: you'll get to be like God and know evil as well as good, said the tempter. And they did learn to know evil – by experience; but they did not become like God – instead they became afraid of God (*Genesis 3:1-10*). Sexual temptation offers thrills, but only temporary ones – gambling temptation offers big winnings, but only the operators always make money – getting even offers satisfaction for past hurts, but results in an on-going cycle of revenge – lying offers escape, but finally traps the liar. Every sin "rattlesnake" tantalizes with what will be – yet always fails to produce and would swallow us forever.

Except that Jesus used His cross to crush sin's hold on us sinners in order to free us from eternal death by His death.

Thank You for freeing me from what I deserve; give me clear thinking, Lord, and Your strength so that I don't give in to temptation today, no matter how attractive it seems. Amen.

Welcome Drops Of Relief

I was hungry and you gave Me something to eat; I was thirsty and you gave Me a drink. *Matthew 25:35*

Eventually it does rain, even on New Mexico's high desert, usually at first with little showers. In other areas people talk about how many inches of rain came that day – in New Mexico neighbors share how many hundredths they received! A real shower is better, but every little sprinkle is recorded and appreciated.

In thankful response for the eternal good Jesus did for us by rescuing us from being inescapably clamped in the trap of our sinning, we want to do great and significant things for our Savior. Yet that desire at least partly has the "rattlesnake" of pride poking its head into our motives with the desire to feel important by doing such things.

But He says that He sees and counts the seemingly insignificant deeds most of all, deeds such as a drink of water for someone thirsty, a sandwich for someone hungry, and all the other little deeds of kindness and helpful good to others. He knows these, because we are actually doing them to Him.

Perhaps He will give us opportunity to do something special for Him also. But mostly He wants us to be sure to give "welcome drops of relief" to those who are in need.

On my trail of life today, Lord, open my eyes to see and my actions to give also the little "rainbows" of good to people who need them. Amen.

Monsoonal Downpour!

(The rich man) said, "This is what I'll do; I'll tear down my barns and build bigger ones and store all my grain and goods in them. Then I'll say to myself, 'You have a lot of good things stored up for many years. Take life easy, eat, drink, and enjoy yourself.'" *Luke 12:18-19*

Eventually rains do come! Typically from mid-July to the end of September New Mexico experiences the "monsoon season", when the clouds can open with sometimes too much at once! Ribbons, curtains, and sheets of rain! Downpours! Which can present flooding problems, but which are worth it, since the high desert needs that moisture so desperately.

Although the Lord promises only enough on life's trail so we don't really ever have to worry (*Luke 12:22-32*), sometimes He gives so many blessings that a "rattlesnake" sneaks in among them, the "rattlesnake" which says: Just take care of yourself and those you care about. Which shows how we sinners totally need the abundance of God's loving forgiveness through Jesus to wash us clean of sin every day – everything we do has the dirt of sin contaminating it.

By comparison with most of the rest of the world, we all are rich, even if we have much less than those we call "rich". He has given so that we can enjoy these blessings, but also so we can share with people around the world whom we might never see, but who often need even the basics of life. Having much of this world's goods is no sin – but becoming a selfish slave to them kills spiritually.

Thank You, Lord, that You have blessed me abundantly – help me to share generously also through organizations which help people in other parts of the world. Amen.

Drought! Floods!

He makes His sun rise on the evil and the good and lets rain fall on the just and the unjust. *Matthew 5:45*

No rain for weeks! Reservoirs shrinking! Forests closed! Dust trailing vehicles like a fog!

Drought! Then within days: rain! And rain! And rain! And flooding! Some areas going from drought disaster to flood disaster in less than a month!

Lord! What are You doing? So might be our human complaint.

But He always knows what He is doing. Through the weather He calls people to remember Who is in charge. "Everybody talks about the weather, but" only He "can do anything about it." He wants us to remember to trust Him in all things, not just weather-related conditions.

Especially He wants us to trust Him regarding forgiveness of our sins. So easily we are tempted to think that God doesn't mind our sinning, because ours aren't as bad as how others sin. Or we think He overlooks the wrong we do because of how much good we do.

But like the weather, we actually can't do anything about how we've sinned; it's there, a fact. Only God can do and did do what had to be done about our sins. He did it through Jesus. He is the only One we can trust to take care of our sins before God.

Lord God, help me to trust You regarding the forgiveness of my sins, the weather, and whatever else You allow to happen along the trail of life. Amen.

Awesome Power Of A Flash Flood

Everyone who hears what I say but doesn't do it is like a man who was so foolish he built his house on sand. The rains poured down, the torrents came, the winds blew, and they beat against that house. And it went down with a big crash. *Matthew 7:26-27*

You have to see it to believe the awesome – and sudden – power of a flash flood! In New Mexico thunderstorm rainfall can be concentrated in a side arroyo which funnels the run-off into the main arroyo to form a 2' or more wall of water rushing down the channel. Below RnR's entry they sometimes see within 15 minutes a flood 4' deep and 100' across with water racing by faster than any human can run, since Alamosa Rio drops an average of 50' every mile! Uprooted cacti and downed branches float by with basketball-sized boulders clunking along under the surface! No person could stand up in, no vehicle could cross that raging water – as many inexperienced or foolish people have tragically discovered.

Nor can any person stand up to the awesome power of God's righteous wrath! Except for One! Jesus! God come to earth! He was big enough and strong enough to let the concentrated rage of eternal condemnation and punishment against all the sin of everyone pour down in one gigantic torrent to beat against Him while He was on the cross. Instead of being swept away, however, He suffered it all for us and survived it all for us. And, says God's Word, we also survive forever, as we let His cross shelter us – unless we should become spiritually foolish and try to cross His flood of punishment on our own!

Lord, thank You for making me trust in Jesus to save me from Your anger, which I know I deserve; keep me in this faith and help me show I have it this day and each day that You give me on my trail of life. Amen.

The Appetite Of A Flooding Creek

Be angry but don't sin. Don't let the sun go down on your anger.   Don't give the devil a chance to work.
Ephesians 4:26-27

A flooding creek develops a healthy "appetite" as it keeps running. Not only the initial wall, but the on-going rush of water gradually eats away at protective dikes, stream-side roadways, and especially driveway approaches – the longer it lasts (which might be hours, although Alamosa Rio at times has run bank-to-bank for days), the more it destroys.

Our human anger is not sin in itself – it just automatically happens, just as God immediately gets angry at our sinning. But what we say or do because of our anger almost always is sin as it hurts others. And the longer our anger smolders within us, the more spiritually destructive it becomes – unless we guard against it with the power of God's forgiveness to us!

Why should we remember God forgiving us when someone else has done the sinning? Because, as we remember and thank Him for having forgiven us because of Jesus, He gives us the ability and gradually the desire to forgive that hurtful person – which really is the only way to truly put out the fire of our anger even if that other person does not apologize or change.

Which forgiving benefits us the most; after all, anger held on to hurts oneself with all sorts of "rattlesnake" strikes, especially since very often the other people don't remember or even care what they did which hurt us. The sooner we let go of our anger, the quicker we can continue peacefully on our trail of life.

When I get angry today, Lord, help me to forgive quickly so I have inner peace even if I still feel the hurt. Amen.

The Ugly Mud Of Flood

"Which of those three, do you think, was a neighbor to the man who had fallen into the hands of the robbers?" "The one who was kind enough to help him," he said. "Go and do as he did," Jesus told him. *Luke 10:36-37*

What a mess a flood can leave! Mud all over! In the house – across the roads – covering the yard! Ugly! Heart-wrenching enough to see things ruined and to miss things lost, and then the clean-up staring at you! Nothing to do except get started! And to feel so grateful if a neighbor whose property wasn't flooded stops by to help you out!

"Who is my neighbor?" the man had asked (*Luke 10:29*). Any person who is in need was Jesus' parable reply – and you are a neighbor, when you help.

Which is His basic command for us on the trail of life: help those in need – which is what "love" is. Physically (the mud of flood or other needs), emotionally (the mud of hurt feelings or other sorrows), spiritually (the mud of doubt or of guilt by assuring that person of God's available forgiveness through Jesus) – do what you are able to do, when He guides you near someone who is hurting.

Which we try to do, not primarily because we are so commanded, but because of Him Who was the only One Who could and did help us with the mud of sin. He "helped" us? No, He did it all, washing us clean in God's sight, not with clear water, but through His red blood, poured out for us on His cross.

Help me try to be a helping neighbor, Lord, to anyone I meet or walk with on today's trail of life. Amen.

With Just Minutes To Spare

Then he said, "Jesus, remember me when You come into Your kingdom." "I tell you the truth," Jesus said to him, "today you will be with Me in Paradise." *Luke 23:42-43*

Within ten minutes of crossing Alamosa Rio and entering their RnR, the thunderstorm rained so hard that a flood came that quickly.

One man on a Good Friday cross had a spiritual close call. In the early morning he joined in ridiculing Jesus (*Mark 15:32*); but after a few hours he realized Jesus was the One to trust in, not to despise. Very possibly you know someone – perhaps a neighbor, a relative, a friend, maybe even your spouse or grown child – who has no use for Jesus. You have tried to share your faith with this person you care about without seeing any positive response. He or she doesn't care, doesn't want to be bothered with religious talk. What more can you possibly do?

First, we are not to give up: as long as the Lord lets that person live physically, He might make that person also come to life spiritually. Therefore, we should pray that the Lord will so guide on that person's life trail that he or she will realize help, Jesus' eternal help, is needed. But mostly we will live our faith, showing the difference that trusting in Jesus makes for one's life. Maybe nothing will happen for years – and maybe, we must recognize, faith will never come. But maybe later in life the message that Jesus suffered and died for all sinners will become good news for that sinner, just as it is for us.

Lord, I think now of this particular person, _____, and ask Your working through me or through someone else so that this one I care about does come to trust You for eternal life as I do. Amen.

Running The Arroyo

"It is also written," Jesus answered him, "Don't test the Lord Your God." *Matthew 4:7*

They were hot, tired, and hurting; had waited half an hour already; and the flash flood was lessening. He thought: we can make it across, so he gunned the pickup while she closed her eyes and held her breath! Just as they touched the other side, he felt the rear end of the pickup start to float, but their momentum carried them to safety. Which is when he said: Sometimes the Lord is kind to foolish people – but I think He is also saying right now: Don't try that again!

Perhaps you've also done something foolish, taken an unnecessary chance and just barely escaped. Perhaps it wasn't physical danger, but instead a spiritual one, that is, you gave in to an attractive temptation – and got away with it – in the sense that no one who knew you ever found out! Except for the Lord, of course! And He didn't strike you dead, though you deserved it, but He forgave you because Jesus died for that sin also. Yet, He also is saying: Go, and sin no more (*John 8:11* KJV) – don't think that I just let you "get away with" "secret sins" – they also cost me My Son – does He matter to you?

And so, when that stealthy "rattlesnake" approaches you or me, when we are all alone or are anonymous as far as those around us are concerned, we will ask His help to turn from the wrong, not in fear of what He could do to us, but with loving thanks for what He already has done for us through Jesus.

Lord, You know what a struggle I sometimes have with some particular temptations; give me Your strength so that for Jesus' sake I do not give in to them today or whenever they attack me. Amen.

Rattlesnakes!

I'm afraid that as the snake by its trickery seduced Eve, your minds may somehow be corrupted and you may lose your simple and pure loyalty to Christ. *2 Corinthians 11:3*

Did you know that rattlesnakes are truly Americans? In all the world they live naturally only on the American land mass (North, Central, and South). Nine of the 15 or more species found in the United States can be encountered in New Mexico, four of which have been seen on RnR (although one only because a flash flood deposited it at the gate). Unfortunately, most people seem to think that "the only good rattlesnake is a dead rattlesnake". But since they usually prey on mice and other rodents, rattlesnakes have their value.

The "rattlesnakes" of temptation and trouble (which can produce temptation) also have value for us. Yes, these are first of all dangerous; just as every rattlesnake bite can hurt or even kill, so even a "little (temptation) bite" can fester into spiritual death – it is possible to lose one's faith in Jesus as Savior. However, when we recognize that danger and thankfully receive the "anti-venom treatment" of forgiveness through Jesus, we are strengthened to be more spiritually alert against temptation and become more aware that we need His help through using His Word and receiving Holy Communion to keep our "simple and pure loyalty to Christ."

Thank You, Lord, for forgiving me already for the temptations I will give in to today; guide me so I face each one seriously and use Your help to reject as many as I can, because I want to remain loyal to You. Amen.

Why Afraid Of Rattlesnakes?

Keep a clear head and watch! Your enemy, the devil, is prowling around like a roaring lion, looking for someone to devour. Be strong in your faith and resist him. *1 Peter 5:8-9*

Most people do seem to recoil in almost irrational fear at merely the mention of rattlesnakes. But why? Records indicate that less than 10% of people die from being bitten by a rattlesnake – contrast that with the coral snake about which the saying goes: "black and yellow kill a fellow". Also, the reason it rattles is because it doesn't want to bite you: go away, you're too big to eat; it strikes only defensively, not aggressively like the cottonmouth snake.

The spiritual "rattlesnake" of temptation, however, gives *no warning* of its deadliness, *wants* to hurt, tries to *kill* – it is to be avoided, not fooled around with. Martin Luther supposedly said: You can't stop a bird from flying over your head, but you can keep it from building a nest in your hair. Yet so often some temptations, especially sexual although also revengeful ones, we don't immediately "resist", but think about them.

Which is why Jesus "was tempted in every way just as we are, only without sin" (*Hebrews 4:16*) – He resisted perfectly, because we don't; this was part of His work of saving us by being our Substitute.

Still, we are to "keep a clear head and watch … and resist", because the Lord wants to lead us safely past the "rattlesnakes".

Help me today, Lord, to turn away from all temptations, before any become especially appealing to me. Amen.

Rainbows!

After you have suffered a little while, the God of all grace, Who called you in Christ Jesus to share His everlasting glory, will make you perfect, firm, and strong. *1 Peter 5:10*

Although you might see a rainbow reflected off a distant shower, the most brilliant ones appear after you've been rained on, as the sunlight refracts into the full spectrum of visible color. All daytime rain showers produce rainbows. Yet we don't always see them, because either we aren't looking or we aren't observing from the right direction. Still it is true: if there is no rain, there is no 'bow.

On the trail of life every good thing we receive is a "rainbow" blessing from the Lord. But we don't always recognize them as such, because sometimes we aren't looking at them from His direction – instead so often we take the good for granted as we think too much about the bad, such as, the "polluted air" instead of His gift of air, the "cancer-causing sun" not the warming sun.

God *promises* "rainbows", however, after every "storm" in life, especially after we suffer opposition when following His way. Usually in this life we do experience the "rainbow" of health after illness, peace after conflict, rest after tension. Yet if we don't, we are comforted and strengthened to endure whatever we suffer by the assurance that "in Christ Jesus", Who lived and suffered and died for us, we will finally enjoy the "rainbow" of "His everlasting glory".

Help me see the "rainbows" You give me today, Lord; and help me always keep in mind the "eternal rainbow" You will finally give me because of Jesus. Amen.

Rattlesnakes Can Become Rainbows

I am Joseph, your brother; you sold me into Egypt. And now, don't feel sad or angry about your selling me here; God sent me ahead of you to save lives. *Genesis 45:4-5*

They had planned to go into town early, but the "rattlesnake" of a jammed pickup door delayed them; then down at the gate, as they were finally leaving, they met the new neighbors and pleasantly got acquainted with them – a small "rattlesnake" turned into a nice little "rainbow" for all of them.

Usually when we hear God's promise to work in all things "for good" (*Romans 8:28*), we wonder what good will come to us out of a "rattlesnake". But sometimes God's plan is for good to others through what we experience. Consider Joseph and his brothers: they sold him into slavery, but that resulted in his keeping them and the Egyptian people from starvation. Consider even more the experience of Jesus as He came to the end of His life on earth: what a "rattlesnake" attacked Him, but what a "rainbow" for us sinners His cross became!

So, we can be comforted during troubles by trusting that God will eventually bring some good to us after them; and we might also be even further encouraged if we will remind ourselves that God might be using us in our troubles to make a "rainbow" for someone else. Examples could be: the extreme of participating in a clinical trial which results in your death, but which prolongs the lives of countless others or the more ordinary of becoming part of a support group for others who experience what you went through. Which "rainbow" for them becomes a *double* "rainbow" in that it also blesses you.

Lord, help me willingly endure whatever trouble might afflict me today in the knowledge that You might eventually help others through what I experience. Amen.

Rattlesnake On The Doorstep

It is like a man running away from a lion, and a bear attacks him. Then he comes into the house and leans with his hand on the wall, and a snake bites him. *Amos 5:19*

She had gone outside in the night; as she returned, she heard that adrenalin-producing buzz of a rattlesnake, and there it was, coiled on the doorstep! Had she stepped over it going out or had it slithered to that spot as she was coming back? Either way, there it was: dangerously, unexpectedly, so close to the house!

Every day on the trail of life has its temptations and troubles – we just have to expect them. The ones we often don't expect are those close to home. Perhaps a comment is made in an unkind, unthinking way or a chore is neglected or a foolish purchase is made or a TV show is selected which offends – these are actually rather little things, yet they can hurt.

And sometimes big things explode at home: a sexual affair – an unmarried pregnancy – dishonest business practices exposed – violent arguments! Which are especially devastating because of being unexpected!

No matter the "size" of such "rattlesnakes" forgiveness is essential if loving family living is to be restored. The "bigger" the "rattlesnake" the harder to forgive, of course. However, we can, difficult as it is, as we remember daily our own being forgiven all our sins because of Jesus. Such on-going forgiving takes real effort, but He helps us so to follow His way.

Guard me and those I care about, Lord, so that we don't make "rattlesnakes" between us today or any day. Amen.

The Rattlesnake Of Cancer

As He came to a village, ten lepers came toward Him. They stopped at a distance and called out, "Jesus, Master, have pity on us!" *Luke 17:12-13*

Cancer! Most people naturally react to that diagnosis with even more dread than when seeing and hearing a rattlesnake! For cancer seems to be a death sentence! Of course, death will come sooner or later for us all, but having cancer makes it seem very definitely sooner rather than later – and probably very painful, too.

Because of medical advances in recent years, however, some medical people classify cancer as now being a major, but not necessarily fatal, illness with many possibilities for cure or at least control – depending on the type of cancer. Treatments are not always pleasant and can cause major changes in one's pattern of living – just ask someone who has experienced chemotherapy or major cancer surgery.

Death is not the worst thing for us who trust in Jesus. He went through it for our sins to give us life with Him forever. Yet, the Lord has provided life-extending treatments so He can continue to still use us on earth in His plan to bring others to faith; so, we do not view living and dying as a matter of mere quantity of time, but of quality in serving Him.

Therefore, we will use the days He gives us for Him, until He finally says: Come home!

Lord, help me cope with any cancer I do or will have; and also help me be an understanding friend to those who now are suffering from it. Amen.

Worse Than Cancer!

In them there used to lie a crowd of people who were sick, blind, lame, and paralyzed. ... One man who was there had been sick 38 years. *John 5:3,5*

Cancer is a scary rattlesnake! But there are health conditions worse than cancer, debilitating diseases which linger on and on for years, gradually deteriorating one's body until death finally ends the physical pain and emotional frustration: Parkinson's disease, Lou Gehrig's disease, muscular dystrophy, AIDS, various genetic diseases such as Batten disease. Also there are devastating psychological diseases such as schizophrenia and chronic deep depression with its temptation to suicide. These and other incurable illnesses as well as full body paralysis and Alzheimer's disease tremendously burden the stricken individuals and those who care about them – the "rattlesnake" of hopelessness also lingers in the shadows of consciousness.

If you have this as your trail in life, the good news is that release from this imprisoned life for the freedom of eternal life is yours – not because of your suffering, but because Jesus suffered far worse than you can in your place under your load of sin. He also promises to help you endure what is and keep you in faith with hope, because He is stronger than the evil one who keeps threatening you (*1 John 4:4*).

If you know someone so afflicted, to be a comforting friend means to be an ordinary friend, sympathetic but not pitying, talking about everyday things of life, naturally speaking of the Lord with prayer but not being overly "religious", for your friend is still a *person*, not just a *sick* person.

Lord, give me the help I need today to endure whatever burden I have with clear trust in Your love for me and those I care about. Amen.

Varieties Of Apples

There is no Jew or Gentile, no slave or free person, no man or woman – you're all one in Christ Jesus. *Galatians 3:28*

The RnR orchard of 24 fruit trees includes ten varieties of apples – many more are available from local and mail order seed and nursery companies. Yet, even though each variety has its distinctive appearance and flavor, all are definitely *apples*.

How many varieties of people make up the human race? Yet with all their different appearances and cultural "flavors", all are just *people* with one essential common characteristic: *blood* – which can be interchanged regardless of race, creed, or color. Another universal trait is sin – every person has sinned – which makes every person try to "hide" from God by denial or excuse, but without success since God sees and knows and rejects (*Genesis 3*). Which makes that common characteristic of blood spiritually essential, for only by the sacrifice of Jesus' blood are sinners accepted by God to live in the coming eternal Paradise.

All people who depend on Jesus' blood are now *forgiven* sinners and belong to His kingdom on earth, the "one holy Christian and Apostolic Church" (*Apostles' Creed*) in spite of varying physical appearances, cultural differences, and denominational "tastes". Yet we are all the same in God's sight: *people – sinful* people *– forgiven* people. Which "sameness" we must remember as we think about and live with fellow believers in other denominations, in our particular church body, and in our specific congregation.

Lord, especially in Your Church help me ignore the differences I see, forgive the sinning I experience, and humbly appreciate the forgiveness others give me because we are Your forgiven people. Amen.

Year Of The Apple!

Here the saying is true: "One man sows, and another reaps." I sent you to reap where you had not worked before. Others have done the hard work, and you have succeeded them in their work. *John 4:37-38*

The RnR orchard had not been taken care of for years before they bought it and that first year of ownership they picked almost no fruit of any kind. But the next year! Apples almost beyond belief! The previous owner said it never before had produced so abundantly! Unprepared for and inexperienced in trying to sell apples, they gave them away and gave them away - including two pickup loads to an El Paso Hispanic mission. Part of their generosity also was based on this understanding: they had not planted, they had not fertilized; yes, they had pruned and regulated the irrigation water, but really God had just given! For He limited the frosts and provided the perfect growing conditions to make that "year of the apple" (which has never been repeated in such abundance since)!

God provides everything in life for us. We sometimes think we get because we work so hard. But Who gives us health to work, opportunity to work, and a country which provides such job opportunities (which neighboring Mexico doesn't have)? Even if you have no pay-producing work, He still is providing much for you; you're not starving, are you? God provides it all.

Even better, He has provided forgiveness for all our sins through the work of Jesus Who did everything commanded and then suffered and died because we can't and don't do what God commands; Jesus makes every year a "year of forgiveness" for us. Which makes us thankfully generous in sharing with others.

Thank You, Lord, for all You give me, especially forgiveness. Amen.

Year Of The Bear!

A cow will feed with a bear; their young ones will lie down together; a lion will eat straw like a cow. *Isaiah 11:7*

They saw strange manure piles one year, then claw marks on a tree – finally one dusk: a bear! Because it had been so dry that berries and other bear food was very sparse, that bear (never seemed to be more than one) trundled for 15 miles from the mountains to the RnR and neighboring orchards. Although dangerous, it never did any harm – except to pick off the ripest apples it could reach or climb to. That year (and it's been repeated once since then) the Lord provided enough for them – and also for the bear.

People who live "on the frontier" near mountains and wilderness know quite a bit about providing feed and habitat for wild creatures; true, some have exploited natural resources without regard to negative consequences for wildlife habitat or forest health. But the vast majority of those who live there are real environmentalists: if they don't care for the land, they will literally go broke – they also know that providing at least some feed for wildlife is just the "cost of doing business".

Eventually in God's new creation wildlife and people will live together without fear or fuss – He will provide for all. His Word does not promise that pets will enjoy life there – animals there will be also His "new creation". But for us sinners to get there requires what only Jesus can provide: paying the cost to make up for each sin – which He did on the cross. Now as we live in this creation, all "environmentalists" need to work together reasonably in finding ways to protect wildlife and habitat while still responsibly using the resources He has given.

Lord, help me never be an extremist in thinking – except to trust in Jesus as the only Savior. Amen.

The Next Day: Gone!

"Naked came I from my mother's womb, and naked will I return. The Lord gave and the Lord took away – the Lord's name be praised." In all this, Job didn't sin or accuse God of doing anything wrong. *Job 1:21-22*

The grape vine looked like it really would produce that year, all leafed out with tiny grape clusters emerging. But the next day when they looked, gone! During the night deer decided: what a wonderful salad bar! Well, maybe next year (except then the birds got the grapes!).

Small losses are disappointing, but nothing to really grieve over. How do we react, however, when much is lost? When flood or tornado or fire destroys much property? When sudden tragedy takes away spouse or child or close friend? When economic recession or financial corruption demolishes savings? All these losses happened on one day to a man named Job – who accepted "the Lord's will" without complaint or sin. How could he? Self-pity would surely engross us – along with rebellion against God! How could You do this to me, God, when I try so hard to obey You? Oh, how viciously the "rattlesnake" of self-righteousness (I deserve better) bites!

Yet God does not turn away from us, because Jesus is pleading for us: I understand how they feel, Father – and, remember, I've already paid for this sinning, too (*1 John 2:1-2*). So, like a father lets his child cry in his arms, God accepts us, not to wallow in sorrow, but to allow our immediate emotions to settle so we can see clearly: I've lost all these blessings, but I still have the "rainbows" Jesus gives.

Thank You, Lord, that You accept me in spite of my times of self-pity. Amen.

Cutting Us Down To Spiritual Health

To keep me from feeling proud because such wonderful things were revealed to me, a thorn was put into my flesh, Satan's messenger to plague me and keep me from feeling proud. *2 Corinthians 12:7*

Some years an apple tree gets so loaded with fruit that a strong wind will knock immature fruit off the branches or an overly-loaded one just breaks. This is how God prunes back a tree that has gotten too big so it can remain healthy.

The "rattlesnake" of spiritual pride with self-righteousness, its sister, usually strikes at us when we've accomplished something good for the Lord (*see what I've done, Lord*) or kept from doing something wrong (*I didn't give in that time, Lord*) – it's almost an automatic human reaction. Which we usually turn away from when we are reminded from His Word in reading or through preaching that all our other sins must keep us humbly dependent on Jesus alone to be good in God's sight when we are bad in reality. But sometimes pride begins to grow without our realizing it: we *say* we are sinful, while inwardly we add, *"but not really too bad"*.

That's why God sometimes uses illness in self or tragedy to others to humble us. On a hospital bed or at a sudden death funeral we are forced to admit: Death is coming for me also, because I sin (*Romans 5:12*) – I'm not good enough to escape it. My only hope is in Jesus Who did everything good and suffered for everything bad. This is how God can cut us down to the healthy size of trusting alone in Jesus so we will serve Him humbly and more faithfully.

Lord, keep me from getting proud of what I do for You – yet keep me living faithfully for You because of Jesus. Amen.

No Spray, Yet Almost No Worms

But be holy in all your ways, like the Holy One Who called you. It is written: "Be holy, because I am holy."
1 Peter 1:15-16

Not every orchard in Monticello Valley qualifies for "organic" certification, but although hardly any fruit tree sprays are used, very many apples have almost no worms. The reason is primarily that the valley is surrounded by high dry desert mesas on its sides with mountains at the upper end so few bugs or fruit diseases have invaded the area. It's not a perfect environment, but it is greatly protected.

As we use God's Word and especially concentrate on His message that Jesus came to protect us from the consequences of our sinning by having endured them in His own body on the cross, we are assured that we are safe for all eternity. God's Word also works in us as protection against temptation not only by teaching us what is good and right (which we don't fully know by ourselves), but also by giving us His presence and power to do what He commands. Yet we always have to admit that we let more than just a few "worms" of sin live in us and show themselves.

Daily, therefore, we turn to Jesus to admit our sinfulness, to be assured of His forgiveness, and to ask His help to "be holy", which is, to be godly in our daily living. Even though the more specific we are, the better He can help us, we always find that although we will eventually improve in one area of life, other of "our ways" will always remain to keep us humbly depending on Jesus, never on any "improvement".

Lord, You've called me to live Your way in all my ways – work in me also today so that Your way will better control what I do and say and think. Amen.

Taste Of A Tree-Ripened Peach

Taste and see how good the Lord is; happy is the man who takes refuge in Him. *Psalm 34:8*

You have never tasted a peach until you've tasted a fully tree-ripened peach! Of course, you have to beat the wasps to that peach, for they know just when it's at peak juicy flavor and will eat it to the pit, if you are a day late in picking!

We do not experience as much of the Lord's goodness in this life as He wants to give us unless we respond to Him sincerely on a day-to-day basis. Merely being a Sunday-go-church member, who pretty much leaves the "God-talk" at the church door, will give no strength for the week-long trail. Even reading the Bible and a devotion like this one daily without trying to let it influence our attitudes will not give us the guidance or comfort we need that day.

Not that we must be quoting Bible teachings in every conversation (which usually becomes more preaching to others than applying to self); instead we need to "take refuge in Him" throughout the day by trying to remember for ourselves what He has said about how to live for Him, how He promises to help us, and especially how Jesus is our best refuge as He keeps forgiving us every time we stumble in following Him. Such continual "tasting" of the Lord does not mean we will always have smiles on our faces or songs from our lips. God assures us that He is our "refuge", because the trail of life is at times difficult and painful. Yet inwardly we can have confidence in spite of stresses and sorrows, because we know we can rely on Him to guide us safely day after day until we experience the total fullness of His glory in eternity.

Lord, help me trust only in Jesus so I accept Your guidance and follow Your way until I see You face to face. Amen.

Why Work So Hard?

Whatever you do, work heartily as for the Lord and not for men, because you know the Lord will give you the inheritance as your reward.   Serve the Lord Christ.
Colossians 3:23-24

Labor Day is a strange American holiday: to honor the work people do, they don't work! Seems like a contradiction! The fact is that most people don't like to work – they want the paycheck, but they listen to the rattlesnake which says: do as little as you can to just get by – which often results in shoddy products or services which can be dangerous to others.

In contrast, the Lord tells us to do the best we can whatever our job – whether employer, employee, self-employed, volunteer, or unpaid chore-doer – as service to Him because of His blessings to us now and for eternity. These blessings are not paid to us on the basis of how hard we work; they are an "inheritance", given to us because Jesus worked so hard to bring us into God's family by replacing our defective deeds with His perfect obedience as well as His death on the cross.

Actually, God created us to work. Our bodies and our minds function better – and usually last longer – when we are physically and mentally active. We sleep better and enjoy life more when we know we have done a good job. And even if the work we have to do is dull and boring or unrewarding emotionally because others do not place much value on it, we still will be more satisfied when two motives guide us: do the best you can, and, do it as thanks to God for Jesus. After all, He has so guided that we now have this particular work at this particular time on our trail of life.

Thank You, Lord for the work You have given me to do; help me always do it well for the sake of Jesus. Amen.

Eventually The Habitat

If you don't do right, sin is crouching at your door and wants to get you. But you should control it. *Genesis 4:7*

His 10-year dream to turn the pasture area into a bird sanctuary habitat was being realized: field laser-leveled, side water gates installed, three kinds of grasses sown. But what did he get? A whole field of 12' tall sunflowers! Not the big, seed-bearing kind, but *wild* sunflowers with very small heads and little food value! Where did they come from? The tiny seeds had been lying dormant for years, as many wildflowers do, just waiting for the right conditions to occur. It was going to take a lot of work to control them so the Habitat would finally emerge.

Because of our sinful nature we have much "sin-dormancy" within us. Daily we sin; but anyone also can be tempted toward even doing evil – it's just waiting for opportunity to explode!

Nor can we prevent that just by ourselves – the Holy Spirit has to use His power to keep such evil "unsprouted". But we must be on guard to avoid conditions which weaken our defenses, such as: too much stress, too little sleep, irregular attendance at public worship, lessening personal use of God's Word with prayer. Forgiveness is always available, since Jesus died for every sin; but God commands us to recognize the lurking "rattlesnakes" and not give them chances to strike.

On the other hand, also "dormant" within us are abilities God wants to develop in us for the good of others as well as our own thankful joy. These require courage and willingness when we are asked to help or see circumstances where we could help.

Give me power to avoid "dormant" sin today, Lord, and courage to use the good abilities You have given me. Amen.

Once There Was Nothing

In the beginning God created the heavens and the earth. The earth was desolate and uninhabitable, and it was dark on the deep sea. *Genesis 1:1-2*

Once there was nothing but God.
Then came the light made by God,
The plants and the creatures and finally man:
All from God's creative hand.
        Once life was perfect for man,
        Obeying God's every command;
        Then came temptation and sin's ruination.
        All then was lost for man.
But God would not let go of man;
In love He sent His only Son,
Born in a stable so He would be able
To carry out God's saving plan.
        He lived without sin every day
        And took all the world's sin away
        To Calvary's cross to wipe out our loss
        Of life in eternity's day.
Not by the works that you do
Only through Jesus it's true
Are you forgiven and taken to heaven
As you trust Him Who died for you.
        Now we shall live for our God
        With guidance from His holy Word
        To show our thanksgiving
        Through all of our living
        Until we are home with our God.

Written and music composed in September of 1989 while moving from Rathdrum, Idaho, to Truth or Consequences, New Mexico.

Does Soap Prove Creation?

And God saw that everything He made was very good.
Genesis 1:31

Who discovered that soap works so well to clean away dirt? Soap is not a naturally occurring substance – it has to be made out of fat or oil plus an alkali component. But was it strictly by chance that combining those ingredients would produce a cleaning agent? Or did God provide them so someone would discover how to get rid of dirt better than with only water?

Or consider the healing process of a cut or scrape on your finger: is it merely chance that your skin automatically, unless hindered by dirt or infection, will begin to scab over and grow together, often without even leaving a scar? Think also about the four parts of the heart and the blood flow path through them necessary to keep us alive with energy – just chance?

No! "God saw that everything He made was very good" – it all worked well together – and for the most part still does in spite of the effects of sin.

No thing and no logic "prove" that God created the world. It is only "by faith we know (or, understand) that God made the world" out of nothing (*Hebrews 11:3*). That "faith" is faith in Jesus as Savior, Who died for all the sinning we human creatures have done. That "faith" teaches us: if we trust what He says about where we are going and why, we surely can trust what He says about how we got here.

Thank You, Lord, for creating such a working-together world and for giving Yourself to make up for how also my sinning has damaged it. Amen.

Unsatisfying Sweetness

Don't store up for yourselves treasures on earth, where moth and rust destroy them ... But store up for yourselves treasures in heaven, where no moth or rust destroys them ... Where your treasure is, there your heart will be. *Matthew 6:19-21*

Sugar and candy are enjoyable to eat – as long as they are little extras, not one's primary diet. Even so, they have an unsatisfying characteristic about them: usually they leave you wanting more, even though you don't need "more".

Most pleasure in life has a similar effect. Enjoying some "fun" is a blessing, which can temporarily take our minds off our troubles. Even Jesus took time for the pleasures of good banquet meals; being fully human, He knew how to laugh, too.

Too easily, however, life can become a pursuit of pleasure – at the expense of responsibility. Some churches try to make even worship "fun" – or "people won't come." But such a mix up of priorities proves to be unsatisfying. Each form of "fun" eventually wears out, so something different and more exciting has to be found. All of which focuses one's attention more and more on self with little thought given to look up to God for His forgiveness, which at most is taken for granted, or for His guidance, which is ignored if it isn't "fun". That way of life ends in eternal death.

Along our trail of life the Lord gives us smiles as well as seriousness, especially as we keep Jesus as our Savior foremost in our attitudes, for by depending on Him we have satisfaction in life now with eternal joy still coming.

Lord, help me remain serious about following You even while I enjoy some fun along the way today. Amen.

Salt Of The Earth

You are the salt of the world. If salt loses its taste, how will it be made salty again?   It is no longer good for anything but to be thrown out and trampled on by people.
Matthew 5:13

Salt traditionally has had two typical functions: to add flavor to food in present eating and to help preserve certain foods for future eating. In which way are we who follow Jesus "salt"?

Preservation of this sinful world is not within our ability no matter what we do. God has already set the day when He will destroy this creation – we call it Judgment Day (*Acts 17:31*), which no one can delay. So our mission as "salt" is to bring the "taste" of God's love to those we live with so they might want to join us on the trail of life which praises Him (*Matthew 5:16*). We do this as we act with kindness toward others, even toward those we don't like (*Matthew 5:44-48*). Such deeds will not make anyone into a believer in Jesus – only God's message about Jesus having died for all sinners can do that. But who will listen if those who say they have "heard" act no differently than everyone else? Lack of loving deeds makes unbelievers despise Jesus!

And such lack shows that the "hearer" has not "heard" at all, but is only pretending faith.

How easy it is to be nice to those who are nice to us – how difficult to even smile to those who oppose us, even though they have greater need for our Christian love. So we need to pray daily:

Lord, help me be kind to everyone, especially those who are not kind to me. Amen.

Yellow: God's Favorite Color?

See how the flowers grow in the field, and learn from them. They don't work and they don't spin. Yet, I tell you, even Solomon in all his glory didn't dress like one of these. *Matthew 6:28-29*

At least in southwestern New Mexico most wildflowers seem to be yellow – some years entire fields will be carpets of yellow. Is yellow God's favorite color? Also regarding human beings: is yellow God's favorite color? After all, more people in the world have skin with a yellow hue than those with white or black or red tones. But God has no "favorites" among people – He judges everyone the same: sinners, who are condemned to everlasting punishment except for those who receive forgiveness of their sins through faith in Jesus (*1 Peter 1:17-21*).

We also need to be "color blind" toward people. Not only are we all the same as human beings physically – except for skin appearance; we also are all the same morally: sinners – with only superficial differences as to type of sins; and we who trust in Jesus are also all the same spiritually: forgiven sinners – although given a great variety of abilities for serving our Savior.

As we enjoy the tremendous beauty the Lord gives us in the wildflowers, which are not all yellow, but also red and purple and nearly every other color, so should we celebrate all our fellow travelers on His trail of life. And toward those who have not come to faith in Jesus we also will avoid prejudice, because each person is merely another human being with blood the same color as ours and for whom Jesus also shed His red blood.

Lord, I have to admit my tendency toward prejudice against others; help me today – and each day – to be "color blind", since You made us all and died for us all. Amen.

So Soon Glory Fades

All people are grass, and all their beauty like a flower in the field. Grass dries up, and a flower withers, when the Lord's breath blows on it. Yes, the people are grass. *Isaiah 40:6-7*

Usually the high desert can seem quite bleak. But after a few monsoon rain showers wildflowers may spring up suddenly in glorious beauty. Then almost as suddenly they wither and are gone as unrelenting heat resumes.

On the trail of life glory and fame sometimes comes. Not much point in counting too much on such glory, however. So quickly it is gone. This year's champion will be replaced next season. The beauty queen's face will soon have wrinkles. The politician will eventually lose favor and be defeated. Finally death ends all earthly glory.

Except that death can lead to unending glory! When a person counts only on Jesus and His suffering and death as the only way to eternal life, then at death that person enters God's presence of unending glory and blessing. We don't know exact details, but that's His promise to us undeserving sinners.

Which is why, if He does give us some earthly glory, we will thank Him for it. But we will still be daily "flowers", as we try to brighten the lives of others, especially those in nursing homes or other limited circumstances, with deeds of kindness.

Thank You, Lord, that I can look forward to Your glory because of Jesus; help me show Your glory through deeds of kindness today. Amen.

Where Are They All Going?

Why are you spending money for what isn't bread and your earnings for what doesn't satisfy? ... Hear and come to Me. Listen and you will live! *Isaiah 55:2-3*

Seeing all the traffic, especially during vacation months, one might wonder: Where are they all going, all those people in all those cars? Of course, just as you have your reasons, so the occupants in each car have their own story, their own purposes for driving that day.

Sadly, most human activity is ultimately pointless, just a filling up of time – unless a person is following God's plan for life by trying to fulfill His purposes. And His purposes are, primarily, to do what is good and to help others come to know Jesus, Who gives life eternal meaning.

But what can we do of God's purposes for all those hurrying travelers? Most obvious: be a good, careful, courteous driver yourself – and pray for those who aren't. Perhaps also you could volunteer at one of those coffee rest stops sometimes set up on holiday weekends.

And what about friendly conversation with others when you stop at a rest stop or for lunch? If we look for opportunities, we might be able to include a gentle witness to Jesus with our comments, such as, "God keep you safe on your way – and keep you safe forever through Jesus." Casual conversation dare never turn into preaching; but can't we give someone at least a little something spiritual to think about?

Lord, give protection to all travelers, including myself, if I have to be on the highway today. Amen.

Miles And Miles Of Miles And Miles

As far as the rising of the sun is from its setting, so far has He put our sins away from Him. *Psalm 103:12*

Especially to vacationing people from more populated areas, certain parts of our country can seem awfully long and boring, just miles and miles of miles and miles. Whether it's North Dakota's massive cropland fields, Wyoming's rolling grasslands, or Arizona's shimmering desert, the distance can seem almost endless before the longed-for destination will be reached. Thinking too much about "there", however, can make one miss the uniqueness of "now", for there is much to appreciate in those vast open spaces, when one looks carefully. Yet, the distances are undeniable.

Distance can be a blessing, however. Sometimes we need the length of distance, whether space or time, to unwind from the stresses of life "back home" or the hurts of sin "back then". Then, too, is the blessing of "distance" that God has put between our sins and Himself. If He had kept our sins on us, where they truly belong, then we would be eternally separated from Him. But He separated our sins from us by placing them on Jesus to carry on His long, lonely path to the cross. There, by His suffering, He threw them so far away from us that God no longer pays any attention to them.

Both relieved and thankful, however, we pay attention to the guidance He gives us for the trail of life, part of which is to appreciate the blessings He does give even when our trail feels boring or bleak because of a little-changing routine or the loneliness of on-going illness.

If I feel bored today, Lord, open my eyes to appreciate the blessings You do give me, if nothing else, Your forgiveness. Amen.

Antelope Along The Highway

All the animals in the forest are Mine and the cattle on the hills by the thousand. I care for every bird in the hills, and everything stirring in the field is present before Me. *Psalm 50:10-11*

Occasionally by really looking for them, they've seen antelope along New Mexico and Colorado highways; in Wyoming, however, one hardly has to look! How enjoyable to see many of these inquisitive wild creatures so close! How thrilling it also was to spot a golden eagle almost at eye level as they drove down into a Montana valley – and roadrunners scooting across a New Mexico highway – and a scissor-tailed flycatcher sitting on a Texas roadside pole! Such can be the special blessings one might see along those miles and miles of miles and miles – even while giving adequate attention to one's driving responsibilities.

The Lord's creation still is beautiful in spite of human sin. Because of our sinning He really should not be kind to us, but He is! His greatest kindness is His grace, His love we don't deserve, given in Jesus on the cross because of our sins so that we can finally be brought into His new creation. He also is kind to let us now enjoy glimpses of His wild birds and animals, as we travel – or as we attract them to feeders at home. We don't really need these brief experiences, but they do give us pleasure.

We surely have a wonderful Lord! He comforts us in our greatest need through Jesus and so often also gives us little extras to enjoy.

Help me notice something today, Lord, which will make me think of Your on-going kindness to me. Amen.

Doesn't God Care?

O Lord, how long will You look on? Rescue...my precious life from these lions. *Psalm 35:17*

September 11, 2001 – a day that changed the world! Other parts of the world had experienced acts of terrorism for decades. Now it had happened on such a massive scale in the United States! The entire world was shocked – and sobered. If that could happen there, anything can happen anywhere! Terrorists have no respect for life; 9-11 proved that!

But where was God on 9-11? How could He let such an evil happen? Doesn't God care? The answer is: God cares. He cares so much that He had already killed His own Son to pay the spiritual reconstruction costs for not only the evil doers, but also for those killed or hurt by the evil doers. There are no "innocent bystanders" before God. Everyone sins and deserves to suffer and die, including you and me. So God in His caring had His Son suffer and die in our spiritual place so we could have life after this life, if we depend on Jesus as having suffered and died in our place.

But why doesn't He care enough to stop tragedies, whether terrorist atrocities or the personal tragedies such as a family destroyed by a drunk driver or a child sexually abused and killed or any murder victim? Why? Because He does not force anyone to do only good. He lets also us choose to do sin or even evil, which then hurts or kills others. He created people, not robots or puppets. So tragedy happens – and victims suffer. Comfort comes, however, in knowing that those who die in faith in Jesus are immediately received into God's eternal care.

Lord, keep me and my loved ones in faith in Jesus so that if a tragedy "rattlesnake"strikes us, we will be with you. Amen.

Detour!

They went through the region of Phrygia and Galatia because the Holy Spirit kept them from speaking the Word in the province of Asia. ... One night Paul saw a vision – a man from Macedonia was standing there and urging him, "Come over to Macedonia and help us!" *Acts 16:6,9*

Road detours are always irritating inconveniences, especially during a vacation trip – they slow you down, disrupt your schedule, may even ruin your plans for that day's drive. We know they are caused by road construction or repair or perhaps serious accident; still, when God allows one to affect us, we should also try to figure out if He has a particular reason for it. Is it to show us a part of His creation we would otherwise have bypassed? Or is it merely to teach us patience to accept what can't be avoided?

Detours on the trail of life also confront us. Not little changes in daily plans, but those times when we are prevented from doing what we had seriously hoped to do and already made efforts to accomplish. Then our reaction should not be a self-pitying "why?", but real effort to figure out a possible reason why God has right now said "no" or "not yet" to our longed for goal. What is He trying to teach us or in what different way is He trying to use us that we would not have known or done otherwise? With this attitude we might discover that what we considered "detour" was actually God's better plan for us.

Often, however, we try to force our way instead of following His "detour". We also make our sinful "detours" off His Way. That's why Jesus took His "detour" from His eternal glory to life in this world, which unavoidably led to the cross for us.

Lord, help me to avoid sin "detours" and willingly follow wherever You guide on my life's trail today. Amen.

Guardian Angel At Work!

He orders His angels to be with you and protect you everywhere you go. *Psalm 91:11*

The 50-mile detour on a narrow two-lane New Mexico highway was crowded with cars and trucks off of I-10. When the cars ahead forced them to stop, the semi behind seemed to be coming too fast, but with squealing brakes its driver managed to turn just enough to avoid their back left fender. At home the next day, however, he found a smudge of black paint! Truly a guardian angel had worked to prevent a totaled car and probable serious backlash injuries. So, His reason for that "detour" was to teach them about His protecting care?

Although God actually does the protecting, He sends His angels to "work out the details". Therefore, we dare not, as some seem to, think more about angels than God Himself. In fact, we cannot understand how angels work or why God orders protection in one "close call" but allows death in another. He is in control – His angels only obey His orders.

Except for His creation work God accomplishes His will through individuals. He did not just say: "everyone is forgiven" – He worked out our forgiveness through His Son, come to earth, suffering and dying. So He does not just say: "you are protected" – He works through angels to care for us. And He uses us, almost as human "angels", to help other people in their needs, spiritual as well as physical – these are His "orders" for us. These we willingly try to obey, because we are thankful for Jesus, Who saved us, and also for angels through whom He protects us.

Help me, Lord, to be an "angel", a "rainbow", a helper to someone who needs help from You through me today. Amen.

Spotting The Golden Arch

So let your light shine before people that they may see the good you do and praise your Father in heaven. *Matthew 6:16*

When it's lunchtime on a vacation trip, the quickest way to find fast food is to look for that "golden arch". MacDonald's may not serve the most health-enhancing food, but the company has used its visibility and its consistency of quality and standards to become the largest fast food chain in the world.

Our invisible Lord can only truly make Himself "seen" through the power of His Word, His message that Jesus is the Savior for sinners. Yet He has chosen to initially show Himself through us who already "see" Him through faith, because unbelievers will not want to "eat" His Word unless they see the results of "His food" in our lives, which are "the good (we) do". The more consistent we are in making His way visible by our good living, the more likely others will be willing to try "His food" also.

Yet we do not try to do good to impress others – we do good by helping others as "praise" to our heavenly Father because of the eternal good our Brother Jesus has done for us. Then at least some others who see or receive this good will eventually also join in praising Him with us.

Lord, help me do what is good today so others may become interested in seeing You also. Amen.

Which One To Choose?

I urge you, fellow Christians, to watch those who cause disagreements and make people fall by going against the teaching you learned. Turn away from them. Such men are not serving Christ, our Lord, but their own bellies and by their fine and flattering talk are deceiving innocent people. *Romans 16:17-18*

Obviously, there's more than one fast food chain – all very similar, yet each with its own style of menu. So, which one to choose, since all have to meet health standards? We each have our personal preferences so it really doesn't matter too much.

Along the trail of life, however, it will matter much which spiritual "restaurant" we "eat at", for not all who claim the name "Christian" or that "we use God's Word" actually meet God's eternal standards. Most "Christian" churches are just that: "Christian", truly proclaiming that Jesus is the only way for sinners to be accepted by God, even though they present this message in different styles.

But some no longer preach that good news or never did. Some teach that all religions worship the same god, only using different names – these are no longer "Christian" at all. Others have leaders who primarily want personal followers who give them much praise and money – their lavish lifestyles indicate this attitude; such are not "Christian" either. Individually we need to be sure that the church we attend does teach God's message, not merely human ideas. Fast food restaurants might give you temporary indigestion – a non-Christian church will give you eternal damnation.

Lord, bless the church I belong to, if it actually proclaims Your message; and if it doesn't, help me find one that does. Amen.

First Things First

Seek first God's kingdom and righteousness, and all these things will be given to you, too. *Matthew 6:33*

One vacation Sunday in Rocky Mountain Park they decided to go on a long morning hike and attend the public worship service scheduled for that evening. But a severe thunderstorm cancelled that service – from which they learned again to "put first things first". Better to hear God's good news first, even if perhaps a hike is rained out than the other way around – and usually the weather allows a hike, the next day anyway, if not that afternoon.

But does it really matter to miss one week of public worship? There's always next week, isn't there? That attitude, however, has been infected with the "rattlesnake's" bite. For next week the same excuse will sound just as good, if something else is appealing. By then, God has been relegated to second place – or further down our list of priorities – instead of being *first*! Each worship day thus becomes a decision day: Who or what is first in my life?

The Lord is first for us, isn't He? Not only do we owe Him our very created existence because He made us; also we belong to Him, since He freed us from the possession of the evil one by His Son, Jesus, washing us clean from our sins through the shedding of His blood for us on the cross.

And as an extra blessing, we have His promise, which we have experienced to be true: when we do put Him first, He gives us all we need plus more.

Help me every day, not only on worship days, to keep You first in my living, Lord. Amen.

Relentless, Pounding Surf

God is our Refuge and Strength, our very great Help in time of trouble. We're not afraid even when the earth quakes, the mountains topple into the seas; even when its waters roar and foam. *Psalm 46:1-3*

Along the Pacific coast the relentless, pounding surf can fascinate a vacationer, especially one from a desert area. The ceaseless, ever-changing waves can almost hypnotize the eyes – their continual roar can overpower the ears and mind to drown out troubling stresses. How enjoyable – and relaxing – to walk the beach, when the surf is "up".

When the "surf" of life is "up", however, when "rattlesnakes" of temptation and trouble seem to pound and crash without ceasing, that's anything but enjoyable or relaxing. Then we can just feel overwhelmed!

Except we have Someone to help us Who is greater than anything the "rattlesnakes" can pound against us. We have the One Who was not overcome by all the punishment against the sins we and everyone else have given in to. He took all God's righteous anger, soaked it up, and turned it into the calm sea of His forgiving peace.

Therefore, although we daily rely on Him for help, when the "rattlesnakes" seem relentless, we turn even more to Him for strength to endure and be faithful for that one day – and each day, one day at a time, as long as needed. And He holds us firm and safe!

Thank You for Your help, Lord, whatever stresses I will experience today. Amen.

Undertow And Offshore Currents

When the Son of Man comes, it will be like the time of Noah: They were eating and drinking, and men and women were marrying until the day Noah went into the ark, and the flood came and destroyed them all. *Luke 17:26-27*

Watching the ocean surf is exhilarating – being out in the water is fun: surf-boarding, body surfing, wading as smaller waves crash against you, swimming out beyond the breaking surf. Yet unseen dangers can threaten: undertow – that strong current below the surface which can make it difficult to get back to the beach; offshore currents which can drift swimmers out far beyond their abilities and strength to return. These "water rattlesnakes" strike when swimmers or surfers get caught up in their fun and don't pay attention to water conditions.

Most people get so caught up in the ordinary activities of life that they pay no attention to where they are spiritually. They say they believe in God, but there's too much to do to have time for His Word and His way. Which is why they are unprepared for the moment of death, and those alive then will be totally terrified when Jesus comes again on Judgment Day.

Our preparedness for death and Judgment Day is not a constant thinking about when these will occur or any certain amount of time we give to God; instead it is a continual trust in Jesus that He will take us safely into God's presence when they take place. By His resurrection, after having suffered for our sins, He assures us that He will. So, as we are engrossed in living, we need to keep Him in mind daily in private and weekly in public so we don't drift away from Him without realizing it.

Lord, throughout this day stay at least on the edges of my thoughts so I can also turn to You quickly for special help when troubles or temptations crash against me. Amen.

Dolphins, Whales, Sharks, And Man-Of-War

We shouldn't be babies any longer, tossed and driven by every windy thing that is taught, by the trickery of men and their clever scheming in error. Let us tell the truth with love and in every way grow up into Him Who is the Head – Christ. *Ephesians 4:14-15*

Some ocean inhabitants thrill us if we happen to glimpse them: dolphins, whales; some we definitely do not want to meet: sharks with their tearing teeth, a Portuguese man-of-war with its poisonous tentacles. Yet none of these care about us to give us pleasure or to do us harm – they are just doing what they need to do to survive.

Some people, on the other hand, do mean us harm. With tricks and schemes they try to cheat and hurt for their own advantage – there are all sorts of scams, religious as well as economic, which we need to be on guard against. Especially in the church we must watch out lest deceivers mislead us. Although some deliberately do so, some are unwittingly deceived themselves: they take some Bible verses without understanding the real meaning or because they want approval for their own ideas and then teach what is not God's truth, even though it might sound good to our sinful human natures.

Our test questions for every teaching we hear must be: Does this help me trust in Jesus as my only Savior? Does it help me follow Him better? Does it agree with all of God's Word? If you get "yes" for all three of these questions, then the teaching will help you "grow up into" Christ; if not, don't believe it – and try to correct the one teaching it.

Lord, guard me also today so that I don't get deceived by anyone or deceive myself because of a sinful desire. Amen.

The Steady Tides Of Life

As long as the earth stands, sowing and harvesting, cold and heat, summer and winter, day and night will not stop.
Genesis 8:22

All around the world you can count on exact tide times – storms may increase a tidal surge, but the time remains as regular as an atomic clock. So has God set the cycle of the seasons – again, storms may affect certain aspects of them (temperature extremes, moisture amounts), but the cycle continues. God has promised mankind so to care for His creation in this very set pattern – and so it is.

God has given us many other promises, which we also can count on. At times we might doubt one or more of them, because the details of what actually is happening doesn't meet our expectations. He promises the full forgiveness of our sins because of Jesus' suffering and death in our place, but our guilt feelings can make us wonder if He really does. He promises to work out everything for our good, but we can't imagine how some situations could possibly have any good in them. He promises to give us guidance for living, but we sometimes can't see what is the truly right thing to do in what confronts us. He promises to give us enough for living, but our money doesn't always seem to cover our apparent needs.

Can we be sure God does keep all His promises? The tides and the seasons say so, as do rainbows (*Genesis 9:13*). But mostly the resurrection of Jesus from the dead says: Yes, you can be sure of forgiveness through My Son, and so you can be sure of all My other promises also.

Help me, Lord, to trust Your promises, even if things happen today which tempt me to doubt You. Amen.

Like A Piece Of Driftwood

You besiege me from behind and in front and lay Your hand on me. Your knowledge is too wonderful for me, too high for me to reach. *Psalm 139:5-6*

Driftwood! Some ocean beaches have piles, while others have nearly none. Where does it all come from? Perhaps just up the coast or maybe from thousands of miles away. The driftwood itself has no control over its destination – it all depends on the winds and the ocean currents.

We each are to a large extent a piece of driftwood on the ocean of life. We do have some control over where we now live and the kind of person we are – we have made decisions about residence location and what we do day to day. Still, we had no control over what country or into which family we would be born or when in history we would live – that depended completely on God's will.

Also totally dependent on God's love is our having faith in Jesus. It feels to us as though we decide whether to believe or not; but since His Word says we by sinful nature are spiritually ignorant (*1 Corinthians 2:14*), dead (*Ephesians 2:1*), and even God-hating (*Romans 8:7*), we had no power to choose to believe; instead the Holy Spirit made us want to and then begin to believe (*1 Corinthians 12:3*). Now in faith we do have to struggle to choose to keep from sin and to do what is good. But even when we obey Him, the Holy Spirit caused us to do so (*Philippians 2:13*). Yet we are not puppets, for He cannot stop us from choosing to do wrong – which is not logically correct, but is Scripturally true, although beyond our understanding.

Lord, thank You for the faith in Jesus You have worked in me; help me live this faith as well as possible today. Amen.

September 22   Read: Exodus 11

Driftwood Beauty

When Simon Peter saw this, he fell down at Jesus' knees. "Leave me, Lord," he said. "I'm a sinful man." *Luke 5:8*

Some people walk by driftwood as just so many chunks of wood – others see a kind of beauty in particular pieces and with some imagination turn them into valuable works of art. It depends on the vision and the skill of the observer.

When the Lord looks at us, He should see only our sinfulness – by nature we cannot do anything perfectly good. But He has turned His eyes away from our sins to look at Jesus carrying them to the righteous punishment of the cross. Now when He looks back to us who trust in Jesus, He sees the beauty we now have in His forgiveness and how useful we can become in the work He still is doing on earth.

We also can look at each other with such God-like vision to see not just sinners, but forgiven sinners, whose usefulness we may not always recognize, but whose service to the Lord is valuable.

Nor should we refuse to let the Lord work through us to accomplish beautiful things for Him, when He gives us special opportunities of serving Him which we perhaps never imagined we possibly had the abilities to do.

Lord, as I think about my pastor and church leaders, help me overlook their human sinfulness so I will value the good they are trying to do for You. Amen.

Ocean-side Peace

**So that you and all the holy people can grasp how broad
and long and high and deep His love is, and know how
Christ loves us – more than we can know.** *Ephesians 3:18-19*

At least some, if not most, people feel great peace when
looking out across the ocean. All that water! Thousands and
thousands of miles between continents – thousands and
thousands of feet in depth in so many areas! How insignificant
we humans are, how petty our concerns compared to all that
water! Of course, after leaving the ocean-side, we have to
plunge back into the rush of human activity, but for a while at
least we had peace.

How insignificant, however, even the oceans are compared to
God's love. His power made and controls the whole universe,
sun and moon and stars and everything in between. But His
love, as shown in Jesus, surpasses even His power. For His
creation does not sin and never did – it always obeys Him. But
we, His human creatures, are rebels! We want our way, not His
– left to ourselves, we make up idols from our own
imaginations instead of worshipping Him. Yet He loves us!
All the multi-billions of us, who have and now and yet will live!

How insignificant we are, how petty our concerns, yet He
loves us. What sinners we are, yet He loves us and gave His
Son to keep us from drowning in our sins. What peace He so
gives us. Which calm peace is not something we leave at the
"ocean-side" of a church building; His peace goes with us along
our entire trail of life, if we keep remembering Jesus, Whose
suffering and death for us shows the vastness of His love for us.

*Lord, no matter how hectic today becomes, help me
remember Your continual love for me in Jesus so I have
inner peace in spite of the turmoil around me. Amen.*

Computerized Shoreline Map

You were told, O man, what is good and what the Lord wants from you: only to do what is right, love mercy, and live humbly with your God. *Micah 6:8*

Before the computer and satellite age, all our shoreline and marine maps were just approximations, sketches drawn from remembered visual observation. These were generally adequate for then. But now computers convert satellite images into maps which can be continually enlarged until even a person on a beach can be located, if not identified – the broad picture becomes the precise photo.

The Bible, God's Word, gives the whole broad picture of Who God is and how He has dealt with us humans. Its greatest message is how He focused His attention on all sin and then concentrated all that sin onto One Person, Jesus, His Son sent to earth. Then He further condensed that sin into one place at one particular time so He could punish it. Now He switches His attention to focus on us individually to give us the forgiveness Jesus made possible for all people. So, the broad picture of His love becomes the precise photo of our being forgiven.

The Bible also gives us the broad picture of His guidance for us: "do what is right, love mercy, live humbly". But He also sharpens the focus by giving us His definite commands as summarized in the Ten Commandments. Finally He gives us the precise word to keep in mind so we can decide on specific actions: "love", not as feeling, but as doing what is good. The more we use God's Word, the more He will guide us not only to better know, but also to better follow His way.

Thank You for giving us the Bible, Lord; help me use it faithfully so I remain in faith and follow Your will better each day. Amen.

Where Did The Creek Go?

In another the seed falls on rocky ground. He's one who
welcomes the Word with joy as soon as he hears it, but it
doesn't take root in him. He believes for a while, but as
soon as the Word brings him trouble or persecution, he falls
away. *Matthew 13:20-21*

Just below the Gila Cliff Dwellers caves in New Mexico runs
a small creek; you cross it on the trail up to the caves, but it's
nowhere to be seen when you complete that circle trail – it just
disappears into its gravel bed. Once flowing – then gone!

Can a person lose faith in Jesus as Savior?   According to
Jesus the answer is: yes! A person can "welcome" the message
that Jesus did everything necessary to free people from eternal
punishment for their sinning, actually believe it for a while, but
then give it up. He mentions the "rattlesnakes" of trouble and
persecution as being the cause, and later adds worry and
pleasures as contributing factors.

Soberly we need to hear this warning and spiritually evaluate
ourselves. If we truly keep "first things first", we will be safe-
guarded. But how easily worry about troubles and preference
for pleasure can begin to fill our lives so that when persecution
(opposition to our Christian faith or living) attacks, we could
give up that faith as not worth it. Once flowing – then gone!

So we need to regularly and squarely examine our attitudes,
remember the eternal value Jesus is for us, and pray the Lord's
protection. Recognizing the danger that we could lose our faith
will keep us depending more fully on His strength so we won't.

*Lord, at times I do struggle about faith – keep me trusting in
Jesus for just one day at a time so no day ever comes when I
consciously or unconsciously give up my faith in Him. Amen.*

September 26   Read: Exodus 15

Enjoying An Opportunity

The Lord is my Shepherd – I have everything I need. He makes me lie down in fresh green pastures and leads me to water where I can rest. He restores my life. *Psalm 23:1-3*

It had been a long hot hike in Glacier Park. Then she enjoyed the opportunity of soaking her feet in the cool waters above Ptarmigan Falls. Ahh, comfort for the feet with spectacular scenery all around to relax the eyes! He, however, skipped the foot wash and was satisfied with the views.

The Lord gives us many opportunities to relax and enjoy His blessings, no matter how hurried – or how routine – our trail of life might be. Some are easily appreciated: perhaps a visit with family or friends, perhaps a vacation, perhaps a night out for entertainment. Other times, especially when we feel trapped in unyielding responsibilities or confined by sickness, we have to recognize and appreciate smaller blessings: a compliment for work done, an ice cream cone perhaps, the sight of a beautiful bird, the hug of a child. These, too, are gifts from God to refresh us.

Most comforting, of course, is the Lord Himself, our Shepherd, our Good Shepherd, Who has given His life that we might live forever. If we had every other blessing, but not Him, what good would those be?

And so, even if we should at times seem to have absolutely no other times of enjoyment, when we lie down at night, we can rest assured that He is with us to lead us along the trail of life until we are in the perfect "pasture" of eternal life.

Lord, no matter how stressed or bored I might get today, help me see the little blessings You give me and especially help me remember that You are my best blessing. Amen.

Regret For Missed Opportunity

But one thing I do: I forget what is behind, reach for what is ahead, and with my eyes on the mark I go after the heavenly prize to which God has called us in Christ Jesus. *Philippians 3:13-14*

It would have been almost a perfect photo along that trail: blooming bear grass in the foreground, snow-capped peaks across the trail. Something wasn't quite right, however, and "There'll be a better one later". But there never was – so he had a bit of regret for missing that opportunity.

Most likely we have missed opportunities along the trail of life: something is offered – perhaps a job or someone's love or a good deal on a purchase, but we had reasons for declining – and then later wish we hadn't. Not that it does any good! One can't go back – and also can't know whether that chance would actually have worked out as well as we now think. So we have to let it go and deal as wisely as we can with the opportunities that now come to us.

Same way with sins – not having missed the chance to sin, but that we took it and did sin – and now still feel regret and guilt and perhaps even shame: why did I ever do that? How could I? Which brings us to the opportunity of re-appreciating what Jesus has done for us. The reason why He took the opportunity to come into the world and to His cross was because He knew before we ever existed how we would sin and, therefore, how we would need what only He could do: make up for our sin. Now He assures us: I've forgotten about that sin along with all your sins, so you can also. Just concentrate on living for Me now the best you can with My help.

Help me live today for You, Lord, without letting the past trouble me, since You have forgiven me. Amen.

September 28   Read: Exodus 17

Cowbirds: Cowards Or Courageous

All day long my enemies hound me, as many fight against me. O Most High, when I'm afraid, I put my trust in You.
Psalm 56:2-3

Two kinds of cowbirds can be seen in southern New Mexico: the brown-headed, whose range extends throughout most of the United States, and the bronzed, which lives mostly along the Mexican border. The brown-headed is a coward – just a clap will chase it quickly from feeding; the bronzed is more courageous – that clap might make it ruffle its feathers or flap into the air a foot or so, but it quickly keeps on eating.

When facing the "rattlesnakes" of trouble or opposition, we ought to be like the bronzed, but so easily we act like the brown-headed. It's almost unavoidable to be stunned somewhat if we are diagnosed with cancer or if someone viciously opposes us. Will we, however, "go to pieces" with worry or retreat from doing what is good because some don't like us? That would be the brown-headed response. Or will we be like the bronzed cowbird, just keep on, "ruffled" a bit, but trusting that the Lord is in control and will help us endure whatever is threatening.

Even though we do sometimes give in to our worries and fears, we can count on God's forgiveness, because Jesus never gave in to the devil's opposition, but completed His mission of rescuing us for eternity. And in that confidence we can also turn to the Lord for His help when any "rattlesnakes" attack.

Lord, give me courage to be faithful to You today, no matter what might come. Amen.

Two Flashing Beauties

The whole group of believers was one in heart and soul. And no one called anything he had his own, but they shared everything. With great power the apostles told the truth that the Lord Jesus had risen, and much good will rested on all of them. *Acts 4:32-33*

Within fifteen minutes on one New Mexico Black Range trail they saw two somewhat localized flashing beauties they had never before seen: a red-faced warbler and a painted redstart. What a special thrill!

At times the Lord gives His local church a special thrill: perhaps a number of new families join the congregation – perhaps the pastor's sermon really gives encouragement to everyone because it is so fitting in a time of stress – perhaps someone who long had turned away from faith returns in repentance with thanksgiving for the Lord's forgiveness – perhaps the Lord says "yes" to their prayers so an ill person receives quick healing. How exciting such times are! And how tempted we are because of our human natures to think that such blessings are what build up the church.

The Gospel, however, is the only real power to bring people to faith and keep us in faith (*Romans 1:16*), the message that Jesus, Who was put to death in the plan of God to wipe out the consequences of sin, "temporal and eternal punishment", rose from that death as proof He completed that plan. This message unites a congregation ("one in heart and soul") and guides it to do good ("they shared everything"). Thrills are temporary blessings – the Gospel message strengthens permanently.

Thank You, Lord, for special blessings in my life and especially for the best blessing, the assurance that Jesus is my Savior. Amen.

September 30   Read: Exodus 19

A Vee Of Geese

But we who are strong must be patient with the weaknesses of the weak and not just to please ourselves. Every one of us should please his neighbor for his good, to help him grow. *Romans 15:1-2*

During these fall weeks those along the flyways of our country will see "vees" of geese high in the sky. This formation apparently allows these large birds to fly further each day of migration, because each bird is partly "dragged along" by the speed of the goose in front of it. The lead goose has the most tiring task and so will drop back after a while for another strong flyer to take the lead. Each goose contributes to helping the others reach their winter's destination.

In a congregation not everyone has the same depth of commitment or breadth of understanding about faith in Jesus as Savior: some are just learning, others are well-seasoned – some have more struggles, others have weathered such storms. Therefore, the Lord calls His people to help each other spiritually as well as physically according to how each might need help. Which might vary from day to day since we never know what economic or health "rattlesnake" might devastate one of us so that someone "strong" today might need much comfort tomorrow. Also spiritual "rattlesnakes" can threaten anyone so that doubt can arise and need patient encouragement. Even Jesus needed help at times in His life for us. In the Garden of Gethsemene He asked the disciples for prayerful support and prayed to His Father for help (*Matthew 26:37-29*); He also was strengthened by an angel (*Luke 22:48*). Then He was able to carry out His task of saving us sinners. To give and to accept help is why He places us into our congregation.

Use me to help others in my congregation, Lord, and help me through them when I need encouragement. Amen.

Spectacular Fall Color!

He has made everything beautiful in its time. He also has put a sense of eternity in their hearts. *Ecclesiastes 3:11*

In the New England states during the first weeks of October many people go "leaf peeping". They drive the countryside to see the spectacular fall color. Tree leaves there almost glow with brilliance. Most areas of our country also have a fall display of beauty. Why? Scientists can describe how the leaf colors come, but can anyone really explain why? Why some trees, not others? Why such a variety of color? Why also do we humans thrill to such beauty? After all, those are just dead leaves about to fall.

Yet, God has put into us an appreciation of color and beauty as part of what makes us human. Female birds apparently are attracted to feather colors, but that's only a matter of reproduction – stronger colors mean a stronger mate. We, however, just appreciate beauty for its own sake. God made us this way.

And God has given us so much beauty in His creation to enjoy and be refreshed by. For spectacular fall color or any creation beauty renews us; for a while it takes our minds away from the "rattlesnakes" on life's trail. Also, if we let it, such beauty can give us some idea about the perfect beauty of eternal life to come.

Which beautiful life we will receive because of Jesus, Who wasn't beautiful in His suffering on the cross, but Who through that cross became the "beautiful Savior".

Thank You, Lord, for beauty now and yet to come. Amen.

Striptease Trees!

No creature can hide from Him. Everything is uncovered before the eyes of Him to Whom we must give account. *Hebrews 4:13*

Consider the fruitless mulberry tree! True, its pollen can be so bad that some cities have banned planting it. But it gives such deep shade that even the temperatures of the desert southwest are cooled significantly and Bermuda grass doesn't grow under it. How dense those leaves are! Until the first hard frost! Then almost overnight it does a striptease with nearly all its leaves dropped, leaving it quite bare. In a short time also the leaves dry out so much that they crumble into dust.

Consider how similar we are before God. When others see our kind deeds and successful accomplishments, they might think we are not just decent, but even quite good people, surely acceptable to God.

He, however, sees our reality. To Him our good deeds are just so much dust, nothing compared to our sinning. Why? Because, being without sin, He demands perfection, sinlessness.

Which is how Jesus lived: sinless! perfect! That's how He satisfied God's holy demand. Then He took our sins on Himself to His cross to satisfy God's justice. When we now let His perfect sacrifice cover us, God accepts us.

As we do not trust in the "leaves" of what we do, but in the reality of what Jesus did for us, our lives will be "rainbows" before God and for others.

Thank You, God, for accepting me because of Jesus, even though You know exactly how sinful I am. Amen.

All Those Leaves!

He won't keep thinking how short his life is, because God makes him work hard with a happy heart. *Ecclesiastes 5:20*

Fall leaves can be beautiful, but then they fall! And all those leaves have to be raked up and disposed of! What a chore! Of course, all those leaves can be fun for kids to play in or for making a fire to bake potatoes in or for adding to the compost pile. But it's a chore we've got to do (unless a strong wind blows them to the neighbor's yard).

All those leaves! Just one of the many chores on life's trail! So many responsibilities we have! So much hard work we can't escape, if we are going to accomplish anything in life.

In contrast, God gives us eternal life. We cannot earn the blessings of life forever, because each sin increases our debt before God – daily we keep getting farther from Him, not closer, if we try to come to Him by ourselves. Therefore, God decided to give us what we cannot ever earn. Still, a gift has to be paid for. But the giver does the paying, not the receiver. So God paid for the gift of eternal life, not with gold or silver, but by the holy, precious blood and innocent suffering and death of Jesus, God Himself come to earth.

He gives – we receive. And we show thanks also by willingly doing the chores of life.

Help me remember, Lord, what You are giving me, as I do the necessary chores of life. Amen.

To Burn Or To Compost

It is permissible for us to do anything, but not everything is beneficial. It is permissible for us to do anything, but not everything encourages growth. No one should look for his own good, but rather for the good of the other person.
1 Corinthians 10:23-24

Once all those leaves have been raked, the choice must be made whether to compost or burn them – or, in urban areas, send them to the landfill. Not a major decision to make, still, which is best in your situation?

Although we all have some big decisions to make, primarily a whole string of little ones await us on each day's trail. Some are truly "tiny" in their importance (which breakfast cereal to eat); many are so routine that they are no longer "decisions" but habits (always smiling "hello" to fellow workers or the supermarket checker); yet more of them than we sometimes like to admit do require specific thought instead of just selfish reaction: will I take time to listen to a neighbor's troubles? should I try to zip through the almost red light? must I be completely honest in reporting income and/or expenses? Then, too, is the decision about any temptation that hisses or entices.

Our guiding principle next to God's standard of right and wrong is: will what I do be helpful to others who might be affected? Although this should be our basic intention, this is not our consistent action. Which is why we cannot go a day without humbly thanking the Lord for Jesus, Who always did what was helpful for us, most of all, as He made up for our sinful decisions on the cross.

Lord, help me be conscious throughout this day of how Jesus helped me so that I will more consistently do what is helpful for others. Amen.

Staring At The Flames

Create a clean heart for me, O God, and give me a steady new spirit. *Psalm 51:10*

When he was young, burning the leaves was fun. First came the exuberance of jumping into the leaf pile, then anticipation of hot potatoes, placed at the bottom of the pile to roast, and finally the fascination of watching the leaves burn and disintegrate. Which also brought about an interesting effect: staring at the flames and feeling the heat on his face made time seem to stand still and gave a sense of being almost a different person. Which effect disappeared as quickly as did the flames and the heat.

When we "stare into" the "flames of God's love", which we see in Jesus' sacrifice of Himself on the cross, we do see "time stand still", in the sense that the sins of all time were "raked together" into one pile and "burned up" by His suffering love. The effect of such "staring" (hearing and considering the good news of that "fire") is first of all faith: depending alone on Jesus for forgiveness ("a clean heart"); the second inseparable effect is: being a different person ("a steady spirit"). The Holy Spirit enables us to fight the "rattlesnake" of temptation and to be the "rainbow" of doing what is good and helpful.

Since, however, the "old person" still makes its presence known each day, the only way our "different person" will remain is as we keep "staring" at God's love in Jesus.

Help me act today, Lord, more like the "different person" You've made me rather than the "old person" who still wants to control me. Amen.

A Single Coal Will Die

After he had been instructed in the Lord's way, he spoke with a glowing enthusiasm and taught correctly about Jesus but knew only John's baptism. ... When Priscilla and Aquila heard him, they took him with them and explained God's way to him more accurately. *Acts 18:25-26*

No matter how fiercely it is burning, a single coal will soon die – it needs to be with other coals to burn completely to ashes.

No matter how glowingly enthusiastic a person's faith might be, it will die if that person willfully separates him/herself from others who have faith in Jesus. Like cancer victims or alcoholics, each follower of Jesus needs the "support group" of fellow followers to keep each other remembering: our common "disease" is sin – our "health" comes only from Jesus.

At times, however, we can get upset with or offended by those fellow sinners and think we don't need them, because, after all, "I have Jesus – so I don't need anybody else, especially people like them!"

But if we should let that "rattlesnake" bite us, its deadly venom of self-righteousness has already killed us, for we would be depending on our own "goodness" (by comparison with others) instead of only on Jesus' suffering and death for us.

Circumstances on some trails of life might prevent individual believers from "walking with" other followers of Jesus. Yet, in all except extreme situations the one who trusts not at all in self but only in Jesus will always be in one of His "support groups", both to support and to be supported by fellow forgiven sinners.

Help me, Lord, to be a humble and patient member of my congregation, my "forgiven sinners support group". Amen.

Even A Fire Needs Food

What should you do, then, my fellow Christians? When you meet, every one is ready with a song, something to teach, some truth from God, another language, or an explanation. Do it all to help one another grow. *1 Corinthians 14:26*

Firefighters know that every fire needs three ingredients to keep burning: heat, oxygen, and fuel. Freeze the heat with water, smother the oxygen with foam, or remove all nearby fuel, and the fire will go out. Actually, all three are "food for a fire".

The "fire" of faith, even in the "support group" of a congregation, also needs the "food" God gives so it does not "go out" in individuals or in the whole group. Such "food" God gives us through His Word as it is heard in worship, read in Bible study, felt in Baptism, and seen in Holy Communion. To absent oneself from this "food" is to begin to die individually.

Even a congregation, however, can die if the "food" it receives is contaminated by those who insist on their own human ideas instead of proclaiming only what God has revealed in His inspired Word, the Bible, for faith in Jesus as Savior and for guidance in living.   To let human thinking or popular opinion control what is to be believed and followed is to invite the "rattlesnake" of eternal death to begin working.   The message of Jesus as the only Savior must never be "poisoned" by any other message, and the guidance of God for the trail of life dare never be overruled by sinful desires.

Use me, Lord, to make sure that only what Your Word has revealed will be proclaimed and followed in my congregation and also by myself. Amen.

Campfire Conversation

Pleasant is a friend giving helpful suggestions from his heart. *Proverbs 27:9*

Out on an overnight hike or just on an evening outing a campfire provides heat, cooked food, and opportunity for conversation. There's something about being with family or friends away from the busyness and noise of daily life that promotes enjoyable and helpful talk. Usually it's all light-hearted and encouraging; but sometimes what is said can become serious sharing of advice and helpful insights.

Most of our conversations along the trail of life are not too serious – a large number are even rather trivial. Yet also these are important builders of love and trust in the family and with friends as long as they are positive, not degrading.

When such love and trust are established and strengthened, then God often guides someone concerned about what might be coming in life to want helpful and sincere suggestions. Not that we can tell anyone else exactly how to live their lives – and sometimes a person wants only a listening ear. But, when suitable, we can give ideas to consider, Bible verses which might apply, assurance that God guides for good in all things, and, above all, encouragement to keep depending on Jesus for the forgiveness we all need wherever the trail of life leads.

Guide my words, Lord, when You do give me opportunities to encourage others. Amen.

Toasted Marshmallows

I can do everything through Him Who gives me the strength. But it was kind of you to share my troubles. *Philippians 4:13-14*

After the roasted hot dogs on a stick, baked beans from the pot, or other campfire food, often a special treat might be toasted marshmallows, browned to gold, although some like the delicious contrast between outside cinder and inside runny mellow. Toasted marshmallows also give younger ones the chance to give an "umm, good" to parent or other relative. Toasted marshmallows are completely unnecessary – but they sure are good!

The Lord says He never allows any "rattlesnake" trouble that a person cannot endure; so St. Paul said he could do everything required with the Lord's strength. Still, he appreciated the extra help the Philippians sent to him.

Sometimes strength from the Lord comes through those who give a person major help. But little extras – perhaps a smile, a compliment, a thank you, flowers or a plant sent to a sickroom – usually will also give a person encouragement in their troubles and may be just what was needed that day. Such "toasted marshmallows" are satisfying to give as well as to receive. Someone has said: "It's just nice to make nice."

Jesus gave us not major "help", but all we need regarding our sinning: forgiveness. And He also gives us so many little gifts of help through us and to us.

Help me be at least a "little rainbow" to someone today, Lord. Amen.

Half Hot! Half Not!

**I know what you are doing, that you aren't cold or hot! I
wish you were cold or hot. But now that you are lukewarm
and not hot or cold, I'm going to spit you out of My mouth.**
Revelation 3:15-16

One problem with campfires on very cold nights: one side of
you gets hot – the other side stays cold. Of course, you can
change positions often enough so you aren't totally
uncomfortable, but most of the time you're not even completely
lukewarm!

"Lukewarm" is rejected by God! But what is "lukewarm"?
One example is when a church member, even a pastor, puts on a
show of following the Lord in public, but doesn't live faithfully
in his or her family – which has destroyed the eternal life of
many children who cannot accept the hypocrisy.

For that's what "half hot – half not" is: hypocrisy – pretending
faith through public words, but refusing to live the Lord's way
at home or where no one knows the person. Such people have
no faith in Jesus and are "spit out" by Him.

Of course, no one can live perfectly at home or in public –
that's why we turn daily to Jesus for assurance of forgiveness –
and also for His help to walk the way of faith more fully with
those nearer to us as well as in front of those who don't know us
so well or at all.

*Help me live faithfully every day, Lord, especially with my
family and relatives. Amen.*

So Quickly Cold

"Man, I don't know what you are talking about," Peter said. Just then, while he was still speaking, a rooster crowed. Then the Lord turned and looked at Peter, and Peter remembered the Lord telling him, "Before the rooster crows today, you will deny Me three times." So he went outside and cried bitterly. *Luke 22:60-62*

Doesn't take long to get cold, when you move away from the fire on a cold night – or on a trail when you pass from bright sunshine into windy shade.

Peter was trying to keep warm by a fire, but the coals of unbelief crowded around him so close that his pride melted into denying Jesus, Who had warned him it would happen! As can easily happen also to us, if we have primarily unbelieving friends. Of course, our pride thinks: "Maybe I can help rescue them from their unbelief" – and some spouses have so succeeded (*1 Peter 3:1-2*). But unless you faithfully let the Lord give you courage through His Word each day privately and each week publicly to refuse to do the wrong your friends want and to influence them to do what is good and then to speak to them plainly about Jesus, probably you need to find new, Christian friends.

It's not easy, however, to leave old friends, and sometimes we slip, when we are with them. Jesus does not ever forget about or give up on us; instead He calls daily to us through His good news: And for this I suffered, too. Which assurance keeps us or brings us back to following Him.

Guide me, Lord, to decide which friends to keep, which ones to leave, and which new ones to make so I will not drift, either slowly or quickly, from following You. Amen.

Light In The Darkness

The people sitting in the dark will see a great Light. For those sitting in the land of the shadow of death a Light will rise. *Matthew 4:16*

On a moonless night a small flashlight beam can be seen from some distance away. That speck of light has no value for you, however, unless it gives you assurance that someone else is out there. You need "the great light" of the sun, if you are going to go to that person.

And we need "the great Light of the Son" to get through this life on the narrow trail of faith, "the Light of the Son", shining on us from that day on the cross, when all the darkness of sin descended on Him to be destroyed by His victorious love.

His Light, however, shines not just for us, who have now seen it, but also for sinners in all countries of the world. We might think: What can my little "flashlight" – for even if I gave thousands for missions or became a foreign missionary myself, it would still be "little" – what can I accomplish in such overwhelming darkness?

Yet He is the Light and His message provides the "candlepower", and He says: Do what you can, as you are able, because I came also for them.

Lord, make me generous also for foreign mission support – and bless Your message which especially foreign missionaries are sharing. Amen.

Just A Sliver Of Moon

You are the light of the world. A town can't be hidden when it's built on a hill. And you don't light a lamp and put it under a bucket but on the lampstand, where it gives light to everyone in the house. *Matthew 5:14-15*

On the high desert of New Mexico even just a sliver of moon will give enough light to cast a shadow and let you walk a nighttime trail – if it's wide enough. But in a city even a full moon can't give light to help anyone – unless shining into a dark room.

Jesus is "the Light" *for* the world's forgiveness. We who follow Him, however, weak and sinful as we are, are, He says, "the light *of* the world", meaning: people in the world cannot immediately see Him – their darkness of unbelief blinds them to His message. But they can see us and how we reflect "His light" into this sinful world by our living. As their eyes see this reflection, the Holy Spirit can then open their ears to the good news that Jesus also came to be their Savior.

So, we dare not be content to be mere "slivers" of "His light", but want to "shine" as brightly as we can with "rainbows" of good deeds, for we want as many others as possible to see and hear of and depend on Him, just as we do.

Today, Lord, help me do the best I can under Your guidance and with Your strength so that some others might be willing see and to hear You as their "Light" for eternity. Amen.

Life: A Short-Lived Mist

You don't know about tomorrow. What is your life? You're a mist, seen for a while, then vanishing. *James 4:14*

The high desert of New Mexico rarely has morning fog in contrast to that almost morning ritual in other parts of the country. Morning mist seems to have little value (although the costal redwoods of northern California depend on it for growth) and mostly is a temporary inconvenience.

The trail of life is not an inconvenience, but it truly is temporary. When we were kids, the month between Thanksgiving and Christmas seemed forever – now that month feels like only a week, for "the older you get, the quicker time flies". Before 40 we think life will just go on and on – at 60 one thinks: Where has all the time gone? Seems like only yesterday that I was young! Of course, inside – in one's outlook – that sixty-year-old still *feels* like that young kid – it's just the body with its aches and pains that tells you: But you aren't a kid any more.

So quickly life speeds past – so soon we will be gone – how true that life itself is "short-lived".

However! This life is not all there is to our existence! We are not "temporary"! The Lord has made us to live forever! And He has provided the trail of eternal life, which we enter through the "door" of Jesus' having paid for our sins on the cross.

Thank You, Lord, for life – now and into eternity. Amen.

Life: The River Of No Return?

If the dead don't rise, Christ didn't rise. But if Christ didn't rise, your faith can't help you, and you are still in your sins. Then also those who have gone to their rest in Christ have perished. If Christ is our hope only for this life, we should be pitied more than any other people.
1 Corinthians 15:16-19

In east central Idaho flows the Salmon River, "The River of No Return", so called according to folklore because the early miners who floated down it knew there was no return by boat up through its raging rapids.

Obviously, life is a "river of no return" – or is it? In one sense, yes – because we cannot go back to relive childhood or last year or even yesterday – "no return"! But in another sense we will "return" – to live again in resurrected, recreated bodies.

The first reason why Jesus rose from the dead was to prove that He is truly the Savior from sin; if He had not risen, we would have no reason to depend on Him and would have to find a different way to be forgiven. But the second reason why He rose is to assure us that we also will rise bodily from death. God created our bodies not merely as temporary tents for this creation, but to live in, changed and glorified, eternally in His new creation.

The facts are: we cannot go back in life on this earth, but we will come back for bodily life on the re-created earth after Judgment Day.

Thank You, Lord, for forgiving my past and for promising me a blessed eternal future because of Jesus. Amen.

Aches, Pains, And More

Think of your Creator, while you're still young and vigorous – before the days of trouble come and the years catch up with you when you will say "I have no pleasure anymore". *Ecclesiastes 12:1*

Apples will stay nearly fresh for many months – their skins protect them, although not permanently. Cut into one, and it will start turning brown within minutes.

Our bodies are no longer protected by God's creation perfection; sin has "cut into us" so that we "start to die from the first minute we are born" with our increasing aches and pains reminding us of that inevitable destination.

All because of sin! Not as though "sin x" produces "ache y"! Nor is it the weight of all those birthday candles which wear us out. It's sin, our sinning and the fact that sin entered this world when Adam and Eve first sinned.

However, Jesus also entered this world. He, the sinless One, could have lived here forever. But He chose to die so that we could live, free from the effects of sin. His perfect life and His suffering and death give us the assurance of life beyond our current deteriorating existence.

Lord, help me not to think too much about my aches and pains, but to live the best I can in spite of them. Amen.

Lifting Weights At Your Age?

Training the body helps a little, but godliness helps in every way, having a promise of life here and hereafter.
1 Timothy 4:8

Younger men and women can really get involved with weight lifting and fitness training – it makes them feel better with more energy for living. Studies have also shown that such programs benefit senior citizens, too, even to the point of lessening some of those inevitable "aches and pains". The fact is that God created our bodies for physical activity; and so, if we don't get sufficient exercise in our normal course of activities, a schedule for "training the body" is wise to follow – in spite of its limitations: it does help the body stay productive, but it doesn't spare us from aging and eventual death.

In contrast, "godliness" helps us live better now and leads us into eternal life. "Godliness"? Can't be "godly" unless we depend on Him Who was "God on earth", Jesus. Can't depend on Him, however, only for forgiveness of our sins – actually depending on Him results in following Him. We are not forgiven so we can do what *we* please, but so we will be able to better do what pleases *Him*! "Godliness", therefore, means following Him by faith on the trail of life.

"Godliness" does not get us into eternal life – only Jesus does that through having used His body as sacrifice for our sins. He is why we try to live increasingly "godly", faithful, obedient lives – including taking as good care of our physical bodies as we reasonably can.

I need Your blessing, Lord, as I try to take care of my body; help me especially to follow Your way of godly living with my body as well as my mind. Amen.

Now I Lay Me Down To Sleep

Even though I walk in a very dark valley (*"valley of the shadow of death"*, KJV), I fear no harm because You are with me. *Psalm 23:4*

The traditional children's prayer, "Now I lay me down to sleep", perhaps is not that helpful for children – it may make them think they might die in their sleep any night. Perhaps that's why at least one certain adult still doesn't like to go to sleep at night.

But that prayer is very fitting as one lies down to the sleep of anesthesia before a surgical procedure, for statistics show that every surgery, no matter how minor, does carry some risk of "if I should die before I wake". And that prayer is very comforting before surgery, for one would not pray, "I pray Thee, Lord, my soul to take", in doubt, as an agonizing "maybe yes, maybe no" – instead one prays with confidence: "and this I ask for Jesus' sake".

If we approached God alone, just on our own, His decision would not be "maybe", but a definite "no!" However, we do not come to God alone; as Psalm 23 says: "You are with me" – which means, not only to help us endure the "rattlesnake" troubles of life, but especially as we approach God's judgment. Especially at that moment He Who died for our sins is with us so that God will say: "Yes! Forgiven! Enter My life forever!"

No one likes the prospect of surgery. But He is "with us" then, too, if that must be on our trail of life.

Give courage and comfort, Lord, to those facing surgery today or soon, especially this person whom I care about _____ - as well as to me, if such will soon be my "bed". Amen.

Spiritual Heart Surgery

Let the peace of Christ, to which you were called as one body, be in your hearts to decide things for you. And be thankful. *Colossians 3:15*

Surgical procedures have so progressed that what once was spectacular, now seems almost routine – such as open heart surgery – which even pales in significance (except for the one who benefits from it) when compared to a heart transplant. All such heart surgery gives the person "a new lease on life"; however, that life probably will not change much from how the person lived previously.

To change one's way of life, to follow Jesus instead of self on the trail of life, spiritual "heart surgery" is required – not, however, just a "bypass improvement", but a whole new "heart" attitude, controlled by the peace which Jesus gives us.

"A new heart", of course, is an illustration to help us picture what the Holy Spirit does in us through the "peace of Christ", which is not symbol, but reality. Jesus worked out peace between us rebels and God. Once sin had invaded us humans, we had no ability or even desire to submit to God's rule – we just wanted our own way! So Jesus suctioned our sinning onto Himself, offered Himself as "peace offering", and so achieved "peace", forgiveness and acceptance for us.

"Peace" also means: end of war attacks, working together. When His peace message enters us by faith, He gradually controls our decisions more and more so we are thankful – for the peace He gives, for the living at peace with God which we enjoy, and for the ability to better live at peace with others.

Continue what You've begun, Lord, so that Your love will more fully guide my decisions today. Amen.

Simple Plus Short Equals Sweet

The Lord comforts His people and is merciful to His own who are suffering. *Isaiah 49:13*

When people are sick, the Lord does want us to visit and comfort them (*Matthew 25:36*). But in order to truly "comfort" someone, wisdom must be used to recognize what the ill person needs at the time, for there is a difference.

Someone long-term ill and lonely would probably appreciate a longer visit with plenty of chitchat. A guiding factor then would not be so much "how are you doing?" as "what others are doing" (remembering, of course, the difference between actual "news" and judgmental "gossip"). Even then, however, one must be careful not to tire the other out.

But when someone is truly *hurting* sick, especially just after surgery, then wisdom says: "simple (*sympathy*) plus short (*five or ten minutes maximum*) equals sweet (*comfort*)." Pain has drained the ill one, who doesn't need long-winded visitors (including pastors) who drive "drained" into "exhausted"! Which you can remember if you've ever been in the bed during a visiting situation.

Jesus truly helps us according to our need. For our need because of sin, He had to visit earth long enough to go to the cross. For our living needs He provides "enough", yet requires our efforts. For our comfort needs He works through fellow sinners, especially those who use wisdom in recognizing what we might need in each particular situation.

Lord, guide me to be a comfort to someone today – but not a further burden. Amen.

I Will Die!

I don't count my life worth anything. I just want to finish running my race and doing the work the Lord Jesus entrusted to me, declaring the good news of God's grace. *Acts 20:24*

None of us really thinks we are going to die. Oh, we all know in our heads that death is inevitable. But in our selves, our inner being, we can't imagine no longer being alive in this world. "Heaven", yes, because of Jesus – but not to be alive here? That just doesn't seem possible!

Until something forces us to face that harsh reality. Perhaps a car accident injury – which could have been death; perhaps the sudden death of a loved one by heart attack or stroke; perhaps the diagnosis of cancer; perhaps something as trivial as one's 40th birthday. Then, as someone has said: "The imminence of one's death is unpredictable at present, but its inevitability can't be ignored". Then what?

One expects: I've claimed faith in Jesus all these years, so death will merely open the door to eternal life. But since "faith" is "faith", meaning, unproved trust (what is proved requires no "belief" or "faith", but is fact), one's reaction might be disappointing. Yet not to be surprised; the "rattlesnake" of doubt does lurk close by each of us.

So our comfort – and our courage – in facing the fact of "my dying" is: I'm a sinner, that's fact – I can't by myself quiet my conscience about my guilt, that's fact – the message of Jesus does give me peace, that's fact – so I'll just trust His promises, that's faith – and still do what I can for Him, that's my goal.

Thanks for assuring me, Lord, that You love and forgive me no matter my sometimes doubts and my daily sins. Amen.

But I'm Still Me!

By speaking very boldly I will now as always glorify Christ in my body by living or by dying since for me to live is Christ, and to die is gain. *Philippians 1:20-21*

Sometimes it seems that when a person is very sick or definitely dying, others can begin to talk about that person as though he or she wasn't really there. Or, they only talk about the illness and "how are you doing today?". To which the person inwardly shouts (but is too polite to say it out loud): Yes, I'm sick! Yes, I'm dying! But I'm still *me*! I still care about the same people – and about the same activities as I always did. Please talk to me as a person, not as only a *sick* person! I'm not just a "sickee"; I'm still me! True, some individuals do think only about their dying condition and how meaningless much of their interests in life have been – but most do not, for they know they are still living – at least for the time being.

Which teaches us two things especially: first, when visiting, we need to think more about the person than about that person's illness or death; second, we need to be encouraging when the person still wants to do what has been a life activity or interest – too often some are well-meaning but wrong when so quickly they respond: I don't think you can manage that – which means they want to run the dying – or aging – person's life according to their desires instead of allowing that person the dignity of living his or her own life.

As long as the Lord gives life, He expects it to be *lived*. And also the sick or dying person wants to *live*, not just exist. Only then can the person also continue to thank the Lord with deeds as well as words for Jesus' gift of salvation.

Lord, help me today so I do not try to impose my will on others, but instead encourage them to do Your will. Amen.

Final Yard And Garden Chores

I think it's right, as long as I'm in the tent of this body, to refresh your memory because I know I'm soon going to lay aside my tent; our Lord Jesus Christ has told me. And I will do my best to see to it that you will have a constant reminder of these things after I'm gone. *2 Peter 1:13-15*

Toward late fall, before winter sets in, are always final yard and garden chores that need to be done: leaves to rake, garden tools to store, that final lawn mowing, as well as various winter preparation projects on the house.

Toward the end of this life, whether one knows it because of age or illness, are also some final chores that should be attempted, if not fully completed.

First is to encourage your loved ones in the Christian faith. A parent or grandparent or friend can tremendously influence that child, grandchild, or friend by quietly sharing how trust in Jesus right now helps in facing the end of life – and how it helped live life in the past for Him. No "sermon" needed, just sincere sharing.

Second is that one's will include a Christian preamble, a statement of the faith which comforted, strengthened, and guided you in life.

Then, a third "chore" might be, even long before death seems to be approaching, to list your favorite Bible verses and hymns which could be used at your funeral; for these would be a tremendous witness and comfort to those who gather to thank God for how He worked in your life.

Lord, help me live in such a way that others will be encouraged to have the same faith in Jesus as I have. Amen.

Written In Stucco Instead Of Concrete

I want you to know, fellow Christians, so far I have been kept from coming to you, but I often planned to come. *Romans 1:13*

Stucco is a weaker form of concrete: cement with sand without any small rock. It does a good job of sealing a wall for a long time, but isn't as strong as solid concrete: eventually it can weather away and can be easily chipped away, if required. Which gave them a saying regarding plans they made: "written in stucco instead of concrete", meaning: this is what we really want to do, but something might happen to change these plans, so we will adjust to those changed circumstances. The Scriptural way of saying this is: "if the Lord allows".

God's people on the trail of life have always had to have that attitude, primarily because our view of the trail is limited by what we might reasonably expect, and we don't have His vision of all that will be involved. On tomorrow's trail might be accident, natural disaster, or unexpected opportunity; these can change everything we had planned. So, we make our plans, but we don't set our expectations on them too much, for only He knows now what will come then.

And we trust Him however He might guide because His plan was set in eternal concrete and never could change: His plan for our forgiveness. Even before creation He knew we humans would sin so He already then planned for Jesus to suffer and die for all sin so sinners could enter eternity with Him. Why did He create what He knew would be a failure? His reply is: Here is My Son, punished in your place, so you could enter My place.

Because You carried out Your plan for my eternal benefit, Lord, help me willingly accept changes in whatever I plan so I will better carry out the plan You now have for me. Amen.

It Could Be Worse!

"You may do what you like with him," the Lord told Satan. "Only spare his life." *Job 2:6*

Their outing took them along a forest road in the Black Range of southwestern New Mexico which was so "unimproved" that at about the halfway point he said: "Might as well go on, because it couldn't possibly be worse than what we've been on." But it was! However, it did finally lead into the pleasant Mimbres valley.

Most of the time the trail of life isn't too difficult: a few boulders to skirt, some minor washouts to pick your way through, not even too many "rattlesnakes" to elude. But then come some rough stretches! Perhaps spiritual "rattlesnakes" raising serious questions of doubt or guilt – perhaps emotional ones of family heartache or community conflict with bitter personal attacks – perhaps physical ones of illness, accident, or financial loss. As the "rattlesnakes" keep coming, we might try to encourage ourselves: It surely can't get any worse! But it can – as the man Job experienced.

Yet no matter how rough the trail we do have comfort in knowing that our God is in control. Why He has led us into this we may never know; but that He has set limits to how rough it gets we do know, for so has He promised.

The trail of life for Jesus was so rough, so sin-strewn, that only He could travel it – which He did in our place so that, rough as our trail might get, finally we will come to His pleasant place of eternal blessing.

Give me courage, Lord, to endure any rough spots which might be on my trail of life today. Amen.

With A Mental Melody

Be filled with the Spirit as you speak psalms, hymns, and songs to one another, and with your hearts sing and make music to the Lord, always thanking God the Father for everything in the name of our Lord Jesus Christ. *Ephesians 5:18-20*

Music, as one of God's special gifts, very definitely can affect our moods as we live. Some music stirs us, some comforts, some saddens, and some just entertains. Usually music is a multi-person activity: music maker with audience – which is why the Lord is pleased to use music in our worship of Him – not that He is our "audience", since He knows before hand what we will speak or sing, but in singing to Him, we are also sharing messages from His Word with one another, which helps us remain thankful for Jesus, our Savior and Leader.

Which is why we will also benefit if we sing or at least hum to ourselves, inwardly even if not audibly, especially when on the rough sections of life's trail. The "audience" for our music-making will be ourselves – the effect of it will be comfort and courage, not from the music itself, but from the message of that music which keeps us remembering God's having loved us in Jesus on the cross and God's loving us still through His daily presence to help us enjoy the "rainbows" or endure whatever "rattlesnakes" He is allowing to come.

May I sing a mental melody today, Lord, so I am reminded of Your loving care and presence wherever You lead me. Amen.

No One Would Know

Slaves, obey your earthly masters in everything. Don't serve them only when they are watching you, as if you meant only to please them, but sincerely because you respect the Lord. *Colossians 3:22*

The sign says: Do not remove any flora or fauna from the park – which means: don't take even a souvenir stone from that area. The fishing regulations say: daily catch and bag limit of no more than two trout at least 13" long. The speed limit says: 65mph. But no one else is in sight – who would know if you took that rock or kept that not quite long enough fish or added an extra 15mph on the speedometer? You would know – and the Lord would know! Actually, He even knows our desire for that rock, fish, or quicker trip – as He knows every sin of everyone.

Which is why already in eternity He planned how to cover up what we do wrong so that He would not have to keep knowing our sinning – which is what Jesus accomplished on the cross. He removed our sins from us and from God's memory so He can look at us individually, as we have faith in Jesus, as though we had not even sinned (this is called "justification by faith").

So now, do we in a sense "take advantage of" God's "memory lapse" and just do what we can humanly get away with? Or, do we respect and love Him because of Jesus and do what is right even when no one else will know?

Lord, thank You for forgiving those times when I have done what I could get away with; help me do what is right and so serve You even if no one else other than You and me would ever know. Amen.

Not A Level Spot Anywhere

Certainly there's no one so righteous on earth that he only does good and never sins. *Ecclesiastes 7:20*

Most are not this way, of course, but at some mountain campsites there just isn't a level spot on which to pitch your tent for your sleeping bag: slope of the ridge, jutting rocks, poking underbrush – you might push pine needles together or even gravel to make yourself reasonably comfortable, but by itself there's not a level spot anywhere.

If God were searching to find a person "on the level" with Him upon whom He could lay His blessings directly, He would find absolutely no one. No matter how good anyone ever has been, no one (other than Jesus) "only does good and never sins". All of us are guilty, each in our own way of sinning, so every single one of us fails His search for goodness.

Therefore, He had to undertake a spiritual "bed preparation" job. Jesus had to come to "fill in" the holes of the good we fail to do by His perfect obeying in life and to "chip off" the outcroppings of our sinning by the hammer of His cross death. Now, as we admit we are completely undeserving in ourselves, He covers us with His holiness and presents us to the Father for acceptance into eternal blessing.

For which we thank Him by trying to be faithful to Him as we now live each day.

Help me be faithful to You today, Lord, because I am so thankful You have accepted me because of Jesus. Amen.

Everyone A Believer?

A fool says in his heart, "There is no God." They do corrupt and detestable things. *Psalm 14:1*

Standing on the rim of the Grand Canyon, a person could say: See what a river can do, given a few million years – or a person could say: See what God did by means of Noah's flood in just one year. Which statement is correct? Neither can be proven – each is a belief.

Same holds true regarding belief in God Himself! Either a person *believes* God exists or a person *believes* He doesn't! Neither *belief* can be proven – actually, a matter no longer is "belief" if it is "proven" (one does not "believe" two plus two equals four – that's just fact). So, which belief should one choose regarding God's existence or not? And why choose one or the other?

God's Word says that only "a fool" – that means, only a person who doesn't fully use his or her reasoning process – *believes* "there is no God". God's Word also gives the reason why that "fool" makes that choice: because that person prefers a life of sin – no "god" will tell me what to do!

We who *believe* in God's existence, however, look at the world all around us and conclude: Someone had to be behind this – it couldn't have been merely chance! We who *believe* in God's existence also look at our sinning, the guilt we know, and the peace we have through the message that Jesus paid for our sins, and we joyfully exclaim: And He cares about me! Yet our "belief" is not a result of our mental conclusions – faith comes by the work of God the Holy Spirit.

Use me today, if possible, Lord, to help someone believe Your existence – and Your love in Jesus. Amen.

Why Pick Up That Rock?

Here's another picture of the kingdom of heaven: A dealer was looking for fine pearls. When he found a very expensive pearl, he went and sold everything he had and bought it.
Matthew 13:45-46

As he walked along a dry arroyo, he suddenly bent down to pick up a small stone. But why pick up that one and not the one right next to it? It was something in that particular stone, some quality, which appealed to his concept of beauty or value. Even if he might later have only said: I decided to bring this stone home to put on the bookshelf, the stone itself is what made him do it.

When we come to faith in Jesus as our "very expensive pearl", as our admission price into eternal life, it feels to us like it was our own personal decision. In a backward way this is true – in the sense that we can decide *not* to depend on Jesus. But if we "decide" to believe, that happens only because the value we see in what He did by His life and death on earth for us causes us to believe. We can decide to reject – we can only receive what He gives. So, our "decision" is appearance – His causing it is the reality.

However, we will not remain in this faith unless we keep looking at Jesus to see His value, not as in occasionally glancing at a pretty stone on a shelf, but as in daily holding Him in the hands of our mind to appreciate the "rainbow" that He is for us.

How precious You are for me, Lord; help me show how much I value You by how I live today. Amen.

On Being Friends, Not Enemies

So whenever we have a chance, let us do good to everyone but especially to the household of believers. *Galatians 6:10*

October 31 is, of course, Halloween. But Protestant Christians celebrate it also as the day when Martin Luther in 1517 unintentionally began what is called the "Reformation". The aim of his protest was only to turn the western Christian church away from certain errors of doctrine and church practice in order to bring it back to what the Bible actually taught. But the final result was division of the church into the variety of Christian denominations which we have today. With division came conflict and competition so that Christians of different denominations often acted like enemies.

Some think the church can and should be just one big happy family no matter the differences in doctrines. Such would be only a pretend unity of appearances which would not please God nor satisfy His children. Conflicting doctrines cannot be ignored.

However, since the Lord commands Christians to do good to and live with kindness toward all people, surely we who trust that Jesus is the only way to receive forgiveness of our sins and eternal life can act with kindness as friends instead of enemies no matter our differences.

Help me, Lord, to live in kindness toward all others, especially toward those who have faith in Jesus as the only Savior. Amen.

Thanksgiving: Eating or Praying or Living?

Through Jesus let us always bring to God a sacrifice of praise, that is, the fruit of our lips, praising His name. And don't forget to do good and to share; such sacrifices please God. *Hebrews 13:15-16*

Thanksgiving Day, whether the end of November in the United States or the middle of October in Canada, so easily becomes mostly a day of eating – "Turkey Day", say some – with little thought of thanks at all. How sad, because giving thanks is what this day is meant for.

But for how long can one say "thank You", especially when the turkey, the mashed potatoes and gravy, the squash and other vegetables are waiting and cooling? And how many thanks are spoken while relatives are talking, kids are playing, or sports are being watched? Thanksgiving Day surely is to be enjoyed; but it also should include more than short (or even "long") prayers.

Thanksgiving Day really needs to be a day in which we pledge ourselves again to thanksliving, showing that we do appreciate the "rainbows" God gives us in life in spite of any "rattlesnakes" which He also allows.

Sometimes those "rattlesnakes" can look so large that we hardly see any "rainbows" – unless we think more specifically about the very best blessing God has given us, the "rainbow" which shined out of a dark day over Jerusalem, the "rainbow" of a Man, Who was God on earth and Who brought us God's light and forgiveness through His suffering and death.

Thank You for blessing me, Lord, especially through Jesus. Help me show my thanks by my living. Amen.

The Hills of Home

In My Father's house there are many rooms. If it were not so, I would have told you, because I go to prepare a place for you. *John 14:2*

Within six weeks after moving to New Mexico, they were "enchanted"; finally they felt "at home". And every time they come to the hills of their retirement property, they still get that "home" feeling: relaxed, content, peace.

Perhaps you also are blessed with that feeling where you live. Others may wonder what you see in such an old house or just an apartment or in rather desolate surroundings, but somehow it pleases you as being "home".

On the other hand, perhaps you have to live somewhere that definitely is *not* "home": a health care center – a geographical location you don't like – a neighborhood with people you don't enjoy. A person doesn't have to be physically "homeless" to *feel* "homeless".

Still, whether blessed with that "home" feeling or not, we can look forward to a heavenly home, bought and paid for by Jesus as He lived among the hills of Palestine and died on the hill of Calvary. Now, He has said, He is preparing that home for all who depend on Him to take them there.

Being assured of that "home", we can accept, perhaps enjoy, or else endure where we live now until we live there.

Lord, thanks that being at home with You will be even better than any home I might have now. Amen.

Their Dream House

You are my Rock and my Fortress; for the honor of Your name lead me and guide me. *Psalm 31:3*

To accomplish anything in life you have to dream. But dreams don't "just happen" – you have to spend much time and effort to fulfill your dream, whether to have a happy family life, be a sports champion, become a community leader, run your own business, or lose weight. Their dream was a house, owner-built, out among those "hills of home".

But we must be careful with our dreams. They can become all-consuming (think how long it takes to build a house or the practice time required to become a champion), and they might be just plain selfish ("I want this for *me!*"). Also, we can get so wrapped up in what we want that we minimize or totally forget what God's will might be for us in life.

Why want His will at all? After all, it's my dream and my life, isn't it?

But since He is the One Who gives us life and even allows us to "dream" and since He not only blesses and protects us daily, but also has accomplished not a "dream" but His *plan* through the hard work of Jesus so we could have life forever (which will be far better than we can dream or imagine), this is why we need to pray today and each day:

Lead me and guide me, Lord, in all that I try to accomplish this day on the trail of life You have given me. Amen.

To Make a Dream Come True

If you want to follow Me, deny yourself, take up your cross, and come with Me. *Matthew 16:24*

To make a dream come true, you can't just begin. Three preliminary steps have to be taken first: research (reading about your intended goal, talking with someone who has already achieved it or a similar goal), resources (deciding whether you will have the time, money, and energy to do it), and determination (willingness to devote those resources and to endure the inevitable hardships that will come). These steps are necessary whether your dream is to build a house by yourself, plan an extended vacation, plant a garden, develop a healthier life-style, or reach any goal you aim for.

On the path of life which follows Jesus toward the goal of eternal life, especially determination is vital. Using His cross, He has blazed the trail to eternal life. Using His Word and Holy Communion, He gives us all the resources we need for following Him. But it requires determination to "deny yourself (and) take up your cross (to) come with" Him day by day. His trail has "rainbows", but more "rattlesnakes" than other "trails", because the devil and his allies want to knock us off the eternal life trail.

But if we use the "rattlesnake" crosses which come to us to remind us of His cross for us, He will strengthen us not only to continue in our determination, but to endure those crosses patiently and at times even joyfully, for we know that He will not let the devil overcome us.

Lord, help me willingly follow You no matter what cross might come. Amen.

He Knows Better Than We

We have a High Priest Who can sympathize with our weaknesses. He was tempted in every way just as we are, only without sin. So let us come boldly to God's throne of grace to receive mercy and find grace to help us when we need it. *Hebrews 4:15-16*

No matter how much research you do, if you are going to build a house, you probably should get an architect or someone skilled in building homes to advise you. He or she knows better than you which "rattlesnake" problems to avoid so you end up with a house you enjoy.

When "building" our lives throughout the year, we need to continually turn to the One Who knows better than we what life is all about. He knows, because He created everything, including us. He knows also, because He lived among us to experience especially the "rattlesnakes" of temptation and trouble in life. He knows even better how to give us eternal life, because He died in our place so we might live with Him.

So we need to hear His guidance for living through daily Bible reading and weekly listening to His preached Word, as well as asking His help daily to put it into practice.

Even more we listen to His assurance of love and forgiveness so we don't despair when we fail to follow His "plan" fully.

Lord, guide me today to "build" Your way. Amen.

Preparing the House Site

A voice will be calling in the wilderness: Prepare the way for the Lord, make the paths straight for Him. Every ravine will be filled; every mountain will be cut down. *Luke 3:4-5*

Their only possible house site was the rocky side of a ridge. A bulldozer did the rough leveling, but a backhoe with front bucket had to finish up. Only then was the house site ready for the construction to come.

Our *heart* sites must be prepared so the Lord can claim us and use us. First comes the bulldozer of His Law to knock down our mountain of pride ("I'm good enough! I'll do enough by myself!") by demanding: You *must be* **perfect!** Hearing that absolute requirement honestly, however, can only plunge us into a ravine of despair ("I can't! I'm too guilty! There's no hope for me!").

So He then dumps a bucket load of His grace on us, His message which says: Because you can't is why I did! On My cross for you!

Once a house site is prepared, only a weather catastrophe can ruin it. Our *heart* site, however, must be continually prepared, because the "rattlesnake" temptations to pride and to despair continually strike at us. That's why He keeps using His Law to humble us and His message of grace ("I've already taken care of all your sins") to comfort us. In that humbled comfort He then is able to use us in His spiritual building, the Church.

Lord, keep me humble and comforted daily so that You can use me effectively in the work of Your Church. Amen.

Make It Level!

**I will instruct you and teach you the way you should go.
I'll advise you, keeping My eye on you.** *Psalm 32:8*

After a house site has been roughly leveled by the heavy
machines, a transit (construction scope) is used to make sure the
forms for the footings and foundation walls are absolutely level.
This instrument, a small telescope on a swivel, in effect spots
where the ground level is high or low so corrections can be
made.   Otherwise, the builder will have on-going, irritating
extra work to make up for the unevenness.

Spiritually: our *heart* site keeps being leveled by God's Law
and Gospel. Yet we never are "absolutely level": the wrongs we
still do and the good we fail to do irritate others and ourselves.
If we could only do better!

Specific Bible verses can help, both to remove temptation and
sin (think of Jesus against the devil, *Matthew 4:1-11*) and to add
those good deeds we so often ignore.

"I will instruct you and teach you," says the Lord. This would
depress us as just more we can't obey, if He had not added the
promise: "I will (be) keeping My eye on you", for His are not
I'm-going-to-catch-you eyes (He knew each of our sins when
He took them to the cross), but His are the gracious eyes of
forgiving love and merciful strength.   And He gives us these
"eyes" through those specific Bible verses of "don't" and "do",
when we keep in mind Who is so "advising" us.

*Help me learn and remember Bible verses, Lord, so I can
hear Your guidance, comfort, and strength daily. Amen.*

Get It Square!

You also are being built as living stones into a spiritual temple, to be holy priests who bring spiritual sacrifices that God gladly accepts through Jesus Christ. The Bible says: "I am laying in Zion a Cornerstone .... and if you believe in Him, you'll never be disappointed." *1 Peter 2:5-6*

If the exterior foundation dimensions are not square, not only must the builder have to continually compensate, but the structure will not be as strong and will not look as good as desired. Same is true for interior rooms – if not square, nothing will fit easily.

To get a building square, the algebra formula for a right angle is used: 3 – 4 – 5: if one side is 3' and the other is 4' and the distance from the two ends is 5', you have a square corner (the longer the distances, the more accurate, however); each corner can be so "squared" to be sure of having a square house.

In Bible times a perfectly square cornerstone was used instead; sighting along each side made for a square structure.

No one can be part of God's building ("temple", the Church) except by continually keeping the Cornerstone, Jesus, in sight as the only way out of our sinfulness into His eternal presence.

Once "in", we cannot be "dead weight", but have His work to do. Which work is not so much what takes place on church property (necessary as that is), but what we do on the daily trail of life (see *Romans 12:1-2*). Yet, even this, since it never is "perfectly square", is accepted by God only because of Jesus.

Keep me in Your building, Lord, and help me as I try to do Your work today. Amen.

Overwhelmed!

I always keep the Lord before me. With Him at my right hand, I can't fail. *Psalm 16:8*

Sometime in the owner-built building process, that owner gets an overwhelmed reaction. Perhaps it's just after the house site is all prepared and he thinks about how much there will be to do and how long it's going to take and how much it's going to cost! An old-time saying might help: "Hard by the yard, a cinch by the inch". In other words, if you just go at it one step at a time, each step won't be that hard or long or costly, and finally it will all get done.

At times on the trail of life that "overwhelmed" feeling also comes. Perhaps it's when an unchristian person keeps opposing us or when a particular temptation keeps attacking. We also can feel overwhelmed by job requirements or the demands of selfish or needy people. A young mother might feel it with a croupy baby – an addict when struggling to live God's way instead of the devil's. Will this never end? Can I endure it without giving in or giving up?

Yet all we have to live is one day at a time; surely we can use His power to remain faithful until the end of this day.

Not really – if we try to do it by ourselves. But "with Him at my right hand", that is, as we consciously remember He is with us always, as He promised, forgiving and helping, He will keep us from failing.

Lord, thanks for always being with me, because I never know when an awfully big "rattlesnake" might come onto my trail. Amen.

Digging the Trenches

**"You have heard it was said: 'Don't commit adultery.'
But I tell you, anyone who looks at a woman to lust after her
has already committed adultery with her."** *Matthew 5:27-28*

Unless you have exposed bedrock, building just on the house
site surface makes for an unstable structure - trenches must be
dug for foundation footings and walls - only with concrete
anchored in the ground can a house withstand wind and rain.

When we listen to God's commands, our sinful pride prefers
to look just at the "surface statements", the "letter of the Law";
examples: I've never murdered anyone or had a sexual affair, so
at least I've obeyed those commandments!

But Jesus digs beneath our surface appearances. He expands
every commandment to include thoughts and words as well as
deeds. In this way God's Law cuts deeply into our lives to
force us to face the desperate reality of our sin separation from
God. Only then do we look away from our self-supposed
"obedience" to see the One Who perfectly obeyed every
command and so was the innocent sacrifice for us sinners.

With such repentant faith, instead of despairing with guilt, we
are thankfully determined that with His help we will more and
more obey Him in word and thought as well as in deed.

*Lord, thank You for having sacrificed Yourself for me,
sinner that I am. Help me to obey You better each day, not
only in deed, but also in thought and word. Amen.*

Pouring the Footings

When the storm has passed, the wicked man vanishes; but the righteous person has an everlasting foundation. *Proverbs 10:25*

Pouring the footings is the first actual construction step in building a house. These concrete footings must be below the frost line and at least twice as wide as the foundation walls (depending on soil composition). The purpose of footings is to better distribute the weight of the house, which rests on the foundation walls, so it doesn't sink or shift.

How much does sin weigh? More than any individual can carry and still stand before God. Sin's weight would sink each of us into hell!

And the weight of every sin by every person from every year of all time? Nothing could bear that weight!

But Someone did! Jesus took on Himself the load of all sin. He was "below the frost line" of sin – sin never touched Him by His own doing. And being also God as well as human, He was "wider" than all sin so He could carry it all to the cross where He made it all disappear from God's sight by suffering the punishment all that sin deserved, that *we* deserved.

Now we can stand "righteous" (forgiven) before God to live forever in His service – but only because of Jesus, on Whom we "rest".

Lord, thank You for the peace I have, because You took also my sins to the cross. Help me today to do as much good as I can instead of sin. Amen.

Building the Foundation Walls

You are built on the foundation of the apostles and prophets, and Christ Jesus Himself is the Cornerstone. In Him the whole building is fitted together and grows to be a holy temple in the Lord. *Ephesians 2:20-21*

Once the footings have hardened adequately, the foundation walls can be constructed. These might be concrete poured into forms or concrete blocks with the cores filled with concrete.

By faith, we rest on Jesus as our "everlasting foundation". Yet, we do not know Jesus directly – we know Him only through the writings of "the apostles and prophets", that is, through God's inspired Word, the Bible. Although the Bible teaches us many things, including how God commands us to live, primarily its purpose is to "make you wise and save you through faith in Christ Jesus" (*2 Timothy 3:15*).

Many use the Bible to try to predict the future or to turn its message into only a catalog of demands from God of what to do and not do. But all of Scripture points to Jesus as Savior. Even the demands from God are, yes, to guide us, but their real purpose is, to make us realize we need a Savior, because we can't fully obey those demands.

So we need to keep the message of the apostles and prophets straight and true by asking first: how does this Bible verse help me to better see Jesus as my Savior; then after that we ask: and how does He also want to guide me through this Bible verse. Following God's set of "building plans" in this way makes us "grow to be a holy temple in the Lord."

Thank You, Lord, for your saving and guiding Word. Amen.

Inside Strength

Don't live like the world, but let yourselves be transformed by a renewing of your minds so you can test and be sure what God wants. *Romans 12:2*

To strengthen concrete you must place rebar (reinforcing bars) in the footings and reinforcing mesh in the floor slab. This steel helps keep the concrete from cracking or even breaking apart due to the house weight and, sometimes, frost or moisture conditions. That inner strength is needed for any larger concrete pour.

On the trail of life the Lord calls us to turn from unbelieving ways to follow Him. But we cannot do this by our own strength, since our sinful nature tempts us to want what the world says, and people around us pressure us to leave Him to join them in doing what displeases Him (many TV commercials boldly glamorize selfishness and ungodly living).

So we need an inner strength which only He can give – which He does give through the message of His Word, both as we read or hear it and as we receive it in Holy Communion. We need that strength to keep renewing our minds about what He wants (to daily forgive us because of Jesus and to guide us) and then to begin to and continue to do what pleases Him.

His strength actually comes to us as we think clearly about Jesus and how He used all His strength to walk His path to the cross for us. Remembering that, we will remain in faith and live faithfully no matter how the world around us might beckon.

I need Your strength, Lord, to keep my mind on Your love and my life on Your path. Amen.

Before Your Pour

On the first day of the Festival of Bread Without Yeast the disciples came to Jesus. "Where do You want us to get things ready for You to eat the Passover?" they asked. *Matthew 26:17*

Before you pour concrete for the floor slab, you had better have all the preparations completed: reinforcing mesh and moisture barrier in place, plumbing roughed in (water pipes, drains), whatever duct work is needed. After the pour will be too late.

God's strength comes to us especially through public worship services. True, we receive His strength also when we personally read His Word; but in that we are limited to only the understanding we ourselves might have. This is why He commanded His people to worship together publicly – so we will consider how someone else understands His Word and so we can receive His special help in Holy Communion (as the Old Testament believers received in their Passover observances).

We will get more of His help, however, if we prepare ourselves by thinking of how we've wandered from His path in the week past and by asking His protection so we aren't distracted from His message by the personalities of others or by our own daydreaming. Then He can more effectively work in us the peace of His forgiveness because of Jesus and the strength we need for the coming week's path.

Lord, help me receive as much as I can from You as I attend public worship each week. Amen.

With the Help of Friends

Children, let us not love only in words or in talk, but let us put our love into action and make it real. *1 John 3:18*

They had so much help from friends that they almost had to say: we helped our friends build our house. Not really, of course, but it so seemed at times. Helping! That's what a friend does, if possible.

All along the trail of life the Lord expects us to help others who are in need. The kind of love Jesus commanded is love not as feeling, but love that acts to do what is right and good and helpful, even if no positive feelings are present. For we are called not just to love, to help, our friends and those who help or are kind to us – it's easy even to make time to help them. But, as Jesus explained in the story of the Good Samaritan (*Luke 10:25-37*), another person's actual need is what determines whom we are to help.

Not that we always can – you can't give CPR to a person who isn't breathing, if you never learned that technique. Nor must we respond to everyone who only claims to "need" something, but actually only "wants" it. But when there is need and we are able, then we are to help, even those who have hurt us.

Of course, we don't always want to so help others. But didn't Jesus help us, though we daily still hurt Him by our sinning? He is why we can be "rainbows of helping" not only to people we like, but even to those who might be "rattlesnakes".

Thank You, Lord, for having helped me eternally by Your cross; guide me to willingly help the needy people You might place along my path today. Amen.

Anything to Make It Easier

Live worthy of the Lord, aiming to please Him in every way as you produce every kind of good work and grow in the knowledge of God. *Colossians 1:10*

When building, a person looks for anything that will get the job done easier – which is why tools were developed: the wheelbarrow, the hammer, the cordless drill. In all of life we look for shortcuts or ways to more easily do what has to be done. The computer is more efficient than the typewriter, a cell phone is more convenient than a telephone, a backhoe is quicker than pickax and shovel.

In some situations, however, nothing can make the required task easier or quicker: a child needs the loving concern of a parent for years, a spouse needs expressions of caring daily, an athlete needs the discipline of hard practices all season long.

The path of life on which the Lord has placed us allows no easy or quick ways either. To keep depending only on Jesus as Savior is a struggle because of those who oppose Him. To try to "please Him in every way" is challenging because our sinful nature wants its way instead of His. To keep on producing "every kind of good work" can be very tiring. No "tools" can make these easier – just: "live worthy of the Lord".

Ahh, that's why we stay on the path without trying to "cut corners". We are following *Him*, Who refused to take any easy way, but obeyed every command and paid for every sin for us.

Lord, help me try to be faithful today in every way so that I might better please You. Amen.

A House of Straw?

All people are like grass, and all their glory like the flower in the grass. The grass withers, and the flower drops off; but the Word of the Lord lives forever. *1 Peter 1:24-25*

They built a straw bale house – and were teased whether some "wolf" might not blow it down or burn it up!

But once those bales on a concrete stem wall are covered both sides and top with stucco, that house is solid and can withstand fire as well as wind (and also insects and fungus, which can't get into the "hermetically sealed" bales) better than any "stick-built" house.

Would that our lives and deeds would be as long lasting! Instead, so quickly the years take their toll and death comes and what we have accomplished will so quickly be forgotten. Truly we are no better than blades of grass in human history.

Which would surely cause us to despair if it were not for the message of God's Word, which "lives forever". It tells us that though our daily sinning makes us as rough and dusty in His sight as deteriorating straw bales, because He encases us completely with the work of Jesus, He will make us live *forever* with Him!

Lord, although I know that what I do will not really last, help me be the best "straw bale" I can be for You each day You give me life. Amen.

The Necessary Framework

They had spiritual leaders elected for them in each church. And with prayer and fasting they entrusted them to the Lord in Whom they believed. *Acts 14:23*

A straw bale house can be built without any framing at all, the walls held in place by cable tension. Most choose, however, to first build a post and beam framework with the bales then used to form the walls, because this seems easier and stronger.

Some followers of Jesus think they can stay on His path just alone as an individual – which has to be done if no other Christians live in the area.

But otherwise, God has directed that His people enjoy a "rainbow" together, the necessary framework of a local congregation: believers united under the care of a pastor, who will help them remain faithful to the Lord.

We all, including the pastor, need this help, because the "rattlesnake" of self-righteousness is always coiled to strike at us. So easily we compare ourselves quite favorably to others, especially "church people" who show they aren't in heaven yet, but remain sinners.

But who isn't? That's why God commands us to receive the preaching of His Word every week so each of us keeps admitting: "I need His forgiveness just like everyone else" – and so together we keep rejoicing: "and we have it because of Jesus."

Lord, help me most of all to see my own need for Jesus – and thank You for the pastor whom You have given to help me see both: my need, my Jesus. Amen.

Pinned Together By His Love

Let Christ's Word live richly in you as you teach and warn one another, using every kind of wisdom.   With thankful hearts sing psalms, hymns, and spiritual songs to God. *Colossians 3:16*

Straw bales stacked six or seven high have little stability – a child could push them over. They must be pinned together with rebar down the center and stucco wire attached on both sides to be sturdy, although it's only when the stucco is finally applied that they become solid.

Piled together in a congregation, we followers of Jesus often show our sinful nature instability. Sometimes we talk without thinking or push our point of view without listening to others or get easily offended because of tiredness. And if a sermon should challenge one of our ways of thinking or living that we hold dear, we may react angrily.

How much worse it would be, if we were not "pinned together" by God's love through His preached message of forgiveness through Jesus. He is why we keep coming together.

Yet His message becomes more effective as we realize that also we are His messengers to each other. Our singing of hymns and our worship service responses are not meant so much for God's ears as for ours, since He knows what's in our hearts before we open our mouths. By what we sing and say in worship we teach and warn and encourage each other to follow Jesus with one another as well as in daily life.

Lord, help me listen and take to heart and try to practice what I sing and say and hear as I worship. Amen.

A Roof Over Our Heads

How precious is Your kindness, O God. People come for shelter under the shadow of Your wings. *Psalm 36:7*

That summer the New Mexico rainy season began just one week before they completed the roof under which the straw bales were to be sheltered. How relieved they were when they finally got a roof over their heads – and those bales!

God promises to shelter us on the trail of life. But "storms" can't be avoided: accidents happen, illness strikes, bereavement comes, conflicts develop, a job layoff ruins our financial outlook – and we get "soaked"! That's when the "rattlesnake" might hiss: can you trust God, Who lets this happen to you?

Of course, God's promise is based on the life fact that storms *do* come – only in eternal life will we have none. Here on earth His "shelter" is that: He is in control, He will help us endure, He will bring a "rainbow" eventually.

But why believe this when cold, painful facts make us miserable?

Because of His kindness to us sinners through Jesus! How kind that on His cross He spread His arms to shelter us from the hopelessness of eternal misery! Since He did that, we can be sure He will provide all the "shelter" we need in this life.

Lord, help me trust Your promises, even when a "storm" makes me "shiver", so that I face life more confidently no matter what is happening. Amen.

The Beauty of Stucco

God does not see as man sees, because a man looks at the outward appearance, but the Lord looks into the heart.
1 Samuel 16:7

Stucco! Finally getting the straw walls covered with stucco was a major construction milestone; now the bales were fully protected from the elements. And how pleased they were with its hand-applied appearance. Most stuccoed buildings look machine-sprayed; but theirs had "character" (so they said to themselves to excuse their amateur abilities).

How much we depend on appearances for ourselves (cosmetics are a multi-billion dollar industry) and in others (first impressions are usually based on a person's looks).

Appearances, however, don't matter to God! He looks through any outward show to see what's going on inside our hearts, the selfish motives, the lusting thoughts, the self-centeredness, the pretending. We may be able to deceive others, but we can't fool God! He sees just how sinful we are!

He also sees how valuable we are, worth the precious blood of His Son to wash us clean in His sight. This is why we try to present a pleasing appearance to others, not as cover up, but because we know we are now pleasing enough to God so that He uses us as His representatives in His work of bringing others to Jesus, too.

Lord, thanks that though You know what I really am, You love me anyway and are willing to use me to help other sinners see how You love them also. Amen.

A Time to Laugh

There is an appointed time for everything and a right time for everything we want to do under the sun ... a time to cry and a time to laugh, a time to mourn and a time to dance. *Ecclesiastes 3:1,4*

One friend who helped them all through the building process would always laugh when a mistake was made, whether by himself or by them.   Not a sneering laugh, but a "so it happened, but we'll correct it" laugh, which encouraged them to realize that a mistake should not be taken too seriously, instead: "for every problem there is a solution".

Which attitude we can have even about the problem of our spiritual mistakes, our sins. That problem is nothing to laugh at by itself, for sinning would mean the unending problem of eternal separation from God in punishment.

But God Himself has provided the solution so we can relax in peace; His solution transfers our sinning onto His Son so He could then give us His innocence leading to eternal life.

With that solution taken care of He makes us able to laugh – or at least smile – even in the midst of tears, since we know that eventually He will help us find "rainbow" solutions.

He also wants us to laugh and smile and celebrate along life's trail, whenever possible, for this makes following Him easier.

Lord, when the consequences of my mistakes or when other problems weigh on me, enable me to at least smile in the confidence that You will always provide the help I need to solve or endure them. Amen.

Moving In At Last!

So it is my judgment that we should not trouble these non-Jews who are turning to God but write them to keep away from unclean things of idols and from sexual sin and not to eat anything strangled or any blood. *Acts 15:19-20*

Finally, moving in day! The fulfillment of their dream! Yet not necessarily without stress! For any change requires adapting to new conditions through trial and error to find the most comfortable new way.

The early church learned that also. When the Lord finally made them realize that His work was to save non-Jews as well as Jews, they had to adapt their thinking and find a way so there wouldn't be unnecessary clashes over no longer required regulations with which they were quite comfortable.

Through the centuries God's people have had to similarly adapt to the needs of people from different cultural backgrounds who had come to faith. Language change was the most obvious: God could speak His Word in Latin as well as in Greek, in German and in English and in Swahili as well.

Such change continues today. Yet only outward appearances dare be changed, not the message of Jesus as the only Savior. Also, the needs of longer time members have to be considered as well as those of newer ones so that all are helped in their following of Jesus.

Lord, help me to be willing to change in my church ways when this is necessary to help others see You more clearly. Amen.

We've Barely Begun!

In view of that, try very hard to add to your faith moral excellence, to moral excellence knowledge, to knowledge self-control, to self-control endurance, to endurance godliness, to godliness brotherly kindness, to brotherly kindness love. If you have these and they grow more and more, they keep you from being useless and unproductive in the knowledge of our Lord Jesus Christ. *2 Peter 1:5-8*

The major construction was sufficiently completed for them to move in! But in a way they had barely begun; there were all those finishing details yet: cabinets, doors, moldings. Would this house ever be absolutely, completely done?

As we follow Jesus on the trail of life, we may answer both "yes" and "no": when He at last welcomes us "home", He will finally complete our new life for eternity. But until then we will never get done "growing" into the person He wants us to be.

Looking at the list of "improvements" in our text, some might think: after I've attained the first quality, then I'll work on the second, etc. Two problems: one, we can't complete these by our own power or in this life; two, the Lord wants us to work on all of them at the same time.

So, although we have to consciously make the effort, we rely on Him to keep working changes in us through His Word so we become more and more like Jesus, Whom we follow because He has rescued us from the useless and unproductive life of sin by having lived and died for us.

Lord, help me each day to keep in mind these changes that You want to grow in me. Amen.

The Family Makes the Home

He took them up into his home and gave them a meal. He and everyone in his home were very happy to have found faith in God. *Acts 16:34*

Although a follower of Jesus may by choice or circumstances enjoy "home" all alone, for most people "home" involves family. Things are pleasant and useful to have, but people, not things, primarily make the home. And "home" is happiest when the family is united in faith in the one and only true God, the Triune God, Whom we know through faith in Jesus, the Savior.

Such family faith has to be lived to be real and to make happiness, however. Claiming faith with words but not showing it in daily deeds eventually destroys family happiness.

But when we openly admit our sinning and our struggles with the "rattlesnakes" of life while celebrating the "rainbows" as God's gifts to us, especially His forgiveness, all in the family are more likely to hold on to faith and live it joyfully.

If a family member does not have faith in Jesus, the others need to be even more faithful in their lives and especially pray for the unbeliever as well as from time to time seriously talk about the blessings God gives us through faith.

Perhaps God even gives us family so we can practice our faith with those dear to us as preparation for showing it publicly.

Lord, help me live my faith in Jesus especially at home as well as in public. Amen.

The Marriage Trail

Then the Lord God said, "It isn't good for the man to be alone. I will make him a helper such as he needs." *Genesis 2:18*

Yet God Himself through the Scriptures (see *1 Corinthians 7*) teaches that marriage isn't for everyone. Some of His people by choice or by circumstances do follow Him faithfully without being married.

Necessary to remember because of the sex-addicted world we live in, however, is that such faithfulness means no unmarried sexual relations, since God condemns such evil as unbelieving rebellion against Him (*1 Corinthians 6:9-10*); also, sexual relations are an extra "rainbow", blessed by Him in marriage, but are not really essential for personal fulfillment, as many unmarried and as married people in special circumstances have found out.

To experience God's lifelong "rainbow", marriage trail partners need to keep remembering: first, God is the One Who guided them to be mutual helpers (for not only the already created "man", but also the that-day-to-be-created "woman" needed a life helper); second, "helping" always means "submitting to one another" by each according to the other's need; third, such helping submission can only be continued "as you respect Christ" (*Ephesians 5:21*), Who, though equal to Him, submitted Himself to His Father's requirements because of our need for forgiveness (please read *Ephesians 5:21-28*).

Lord, please help all marriage partners to be faithful helpers to each other. Amen.

Will This Marriage Survive?

Similarly, you married women, submit to your husbands. Then even if some of them refuse to listen to the Word, you will win them, without talking about it, by the way you live as wives, when they see how you fear God and are pure in your lives ... In the same way, you husbands, live with your wives with understanding. *1 Peter 3:1-3,7*

Someone has said: "If you can build a house together without getting divorced, you have a strong marriage." Why? Because many construction decisions uncover strong conflicting preferences which are intensified by work weariness.

Conflict "rattlesnakes" are unavoidable on the marriage trail, for each intimately knows exactly how to hurt the other – and sometimes each does, which can make one or both so angry that their united following can seem irreparably destroyed.

Yet, God does not abandon those whom He has joined together. He supplies all the help needed for them to continue to be helpers to each other, if they will just let Him help them. And His help says: Always both are sinners – always both need forgiveness – and always both, being forgiven through Jesus, can also be forgiving so they can keep on helping.

The happiest marriage trail partners are those who follow Jesus together. But if only one does, by example of faithful following that one might bring the other to follow Jesus also so that God's "marriage rainbow" will finally lead to the "eternal rainbow" for both.

Lord, guide the troubled marriage partners I know so they will use Your help to become joyful helpers again. Amen.

As Time Goes By

Our people should learn to be busy with good works to help real needs and not waste their lives. *Titus 3:14*

Home, marriage, family can become pure selfishness: *ours!* to take care of *us* (and our grandchildren, when the Lord so blesses)! His purpose in giving us these "rainbows", however, is not so we waste our lives just on ourselves, but so we also will be "busy with good works" among neighbors and others. As has been said: "In marriage the two together can do more than the sum total of what each individually could have accomplished."

A balance must be achieved, of course, since you can't really help others if your own needs are not sufficiently taken care of. But the love of Jesus, Who left His heavenly home to meet our need to escape the deadly trap of all our sinning, will draw us out of ourselves to see where we can help others. Why else has He made you live in your present neighborhood?

Our church home is meant to be even more of an island refuge apart from the struggles of life among so many "rattlesnakes", not merely as "escape", but especially as His strengthening power so that, refreshed through the assurance of His forgiveness and protection, we return to our daily trail to help others in their physical and their spiritual needs.

Guide me, Lord, so I make time today and every day to help others – including family, neighbors, and others – while still taking care of my own needs. Amen.

Then There Was One

Sarah lived to be 127 and died ... Abraham went in to mourn and weep for Sarah. *Genesis 23:1-2*

Suddenly! The trail of life almost seems to disappear! Whether by accident, heart attack, or even after lingering illness, suddenly! Gone! One cannot really prepare for that grief of separation, no matter how expected! The one left behind feels lost! With not only devastating grief, but often also with anger, even against God! No! How could he (or: she) leave me so alone? How could He allow this?

Nor do the usually spoken words of comfort ease the sorrow very much at first, words about blessing now for the one gone with reunion to come for the one remaining, even the true words about eternal life not because of one's "good life" (which the survivor knows was not completely "good"), but because of One's *perfect* life, the One Who experienced death so we could go *through* death to eternal life.

Tears do come, bitter tears, lonely tears, angry tears; for He did not make tears only to wash irritations from the eye, but also to ease hurts out of the heart so that our numbness would eventually have room to be comforted by those words.

To cry, to listen, this is how He helps us get around the landslide of grief, whether caused by the separation of death, the abandonment of divorce, or the greater pain of mourning a child (for children just aren't expected to die before their parents).

Lord, help me lend a gentle shoulder to cry on to anyone who needs it. Amen.

The Memories Live On

O Lord, listen to my prayer, and let my cry for help come before You. Don't hide Your face from me when I'm in trouble; turn Your ear to me; when I call, answer me quickly. My days vanish like smoke, and my limbs burn as on a hearth. My heart is parched and withered like grass – I forget to eat my food. As I groan my bones cling to my flesh. I have become like an owl in the desert, like a night-owl among ruins; I'm always awake, like a bird alone on a roof. *Psalm 102:1-7*

How lonely life can be when your dear one is gone! The gaping hole of bereavement grief begins to close, as months and years go by. But some days it seems as big as the day it happened! A sound, a scent brings life "before" rushing back into *now*! The house seems so empty – the bed so cold. How can I keep on alone? I'll never forget!

Nor should you! The Lord still keeps you on the trail of life, and He is the One still giving you the "rainbow" of memories of the one you loved to still be thankful for.

He may give you another "rainbow" trail partner – or He may not – according to how He has carved out your trail. But he promises that He will walk with you, wherever He guides. He is as close as the whisper of your heart, the trickle of your tear.

For He is the everywhere present God, Who in His saving love condensed Himself into the One Who entered the trail of life so He might be with us whatever comes now and in forever.

Lord, help me serve You by being a friend to someone who is alone. Amen.

When It's Time to Leave

Even when I get old and gray, don't forsake me, O God, until I tell this age what Your arm has done; and tell all who come about Your mighty action that Your righteousness reaches to heaven, O God. *Psalm 71:18-19*

Eventually, unavoidably, the time comes when you no longer can manage: your strength can't handle the chores around the house – perhaps your memory also gets too forgetful – you have to leave "home". Your deteriorating condition might be due to illness, if not age. What good am I then? Why doesn't the Lord just take me home to be with Him?

Because He still has work for you to do for Him on this life's trail! Partly it is to give others the opportunity to "be busy with good works to help (your) real needs and not waste their lives"(*Titus 3:4*). To be a humble receiver is just as much serving Him as being a willing giver.

Mostly, however, He still enables you to be a "giver", a teller of His love as you have experienced it, especially His forgiveness which you have appreciated so much and for so long. Those who help you, those who visit you, are the ones He wants you to help by telling them: His mighty action on the cross gives us His righteousness, the only way to reach heaven.

Some may not care to listen – but some of your next generations will be helped by the "rainbow" of your words of faith as they continue on their trails of life.

No matter my physical abilities, Lord, help me tell others about the faith I have in You as my Savior. Amen.

Christmas Is Coming!

"Comfort My people, comfort them," says your God. Talk to the heart of Jerusalem, and announce to her that her time of hard service is over, her wrong is paid for. Isaiah 40:1-2

One would have to be blind and deaf these days not to know that Christmas is coming. Christmas advertising makes sure of that. What kind of Christmas is being promoted, however? Buy, buy, buy – which appeals to our gimme-gimme natures.

But where is the actual meaning of Christmas? The message of "comfort" from God that our "wrong has been paid for" by the One Whose birth Christmas is supposed to celebrate? True, sometimes Baby Jesus is mentioned; yet how often is the purpose of why He came made clear? The unbelieving world around us wants nothing of that! Which is why Santa Claus is worshiped instead.

Increasingly our culture is like the time of the Roman Empire when December 25th was selected to observe Christ's birth. No one knew the actual date, but Christians then needed something to defend them against the temptations of Saturnalia, a pagan festival which celebrated the return of the sun after the winter solstice. So, December 25th was chosen to rejoice about Jesus' birth with Advent, a four-week period of preparation, before it.

We still need Christian preparation for Christmas. So in these December days we will think together about various Christmas customs which help keep us focused on Him, Whose birth is the true reason for this season.

O God, help me prepare all this month so I will not celebrate a holiday, but Jesus' birthday. Amen.

Advent Wreaths

A voice cries in the wilderness: "Prepare a way for the Lord; make a straight highway in the desert for our God. *Isaiah 40:3*

Many Christian families use an Advent wreath to remind themselves that Jesus' birthday is coming. An Advent wreath usually is a circle of four candles on a small wooden frame. One candle is lighted in family devotions on the last Sunday of November and lighted again each day in devotions that week. An additional candle is then lighted each Sunday for that week's devotions until Christmas comes. Purple or violet is the usual color of the candles.

The candles are often given names to emphasize a message for each week.   One family named the candles: NEED, PREPARE, MESSAGE, and REJOICE. In the first week they think especially how we need Jesus because of our sinning. The second week they remember how we need to prepare for His birthday in ways that please Him. The third week they remind themselves of His message: that He came as the only One Who can save us from our sins. The fourth week they already begin to rejoice because His birthday is only days away. They also sing an Advent hymn that fits the theme for each week.

So an Advent wreath can help us week by week to prepare for our Savior's birthday celebration.

Continually lead me, Lord, out of the wilderness of sin onto the highway of following You. Amen.

An Advent Calendar

Every valley must be raised; every mountain and hill be lowered.   The steep places must be made level; the impassable ridges be made a plain. *Isaiah 40:4*

Using an Advent wreath can help a family remember Jesus' birthday is coming.   But mere remembering in a formal way does not prepare us for Christmas unless the message affects our living day by day.   This is why many families also use an Advent calendar.

Advent calendars usually are made with a series of numbered flaps, one for each day of December until Christmas.   Daily a flap is lifted to reveal a suggested Bible verse and devotional thought or activity for that day. God the Holy Spirit can then work through these daily devotions to raise us from our sometimes valleys of discouragement, to cut down our mountains and hills of pride, to level off our jagged and rough words, and to plane off the barrier-producing sins which we so quickly inflict on others.

We never can become a perfectly prepared highway for God's glory.   But as we use His Word daily to be comforted that He keeps forgiving us because of Him Who came as our Savior, He can make "road improvements" which others might notice.

Holy Spirit, make Your Word more effective in me daily in these coming-to-Christmas weeks. Amen.

The Nativity Scene

Then the Lord will show His glory, and all people together will see it for the mouth of the Lord has said it. *Isaiah 40:5*

It is thought that St. Francis of Assisi set up the first nativity scene in 1223 to help his people better remember the birthday of Jesus. Now nativity scenes are a common Christmas custom.

Families may have one in the house with small figures kneeling around a tiny manger or larger statues outside as a Christmas yard decoration. Congregations may even have a living nativity scene with people and animals in place.

Some families do not wait until Christmas decorating time, however, to set out their in-house nativity scene, but use it in their Advent preparing. They add one or more figures to the scene each week until finally the figure of the Christ Child is placed in the manger the evening of Christmas Eve. In this way especially children, but also adults, are taught that the Lord's glory was *seen* when Jesus was born.

God's glory, we remember, is not primarily a brilliant light, but instead His love for all of us sinners. His love caused Jesus to come into our sinful world as a Baby, so He could live perfectly in our place, and finally suffer and die for our sins so we might in eternity joyfully see His complete glory.

Let my life today, Lord, show how I thank You for Your love to me and all people. Amen.

Christmas Cards

This is how Jesus Christ was born. His mother Mary had promised Joseph to be his wife. But before they came together, it was found that she was going to have a child – by the Holy Spirit. *Matthew 1:18*

If you haven't mailed your Christmas cards yet, warns the post office, maybe they won't get there before Christmas. Why? Because so many millions of cards are sent. Yet, this popular Christmas custom dates back only to the 1840s in England and to about 1875 in the United States. Sadly, most Christmas cards today are strictly secular.

Whom do you honor by the Christmas cards you send? Do your cards speak of Santa Claus or send only "Holiday Greetings", or do they witness to Jesus? Also, which Christmas postage stamps do you use? Do you take advantage of the Christ Child birthday stamps which the post office still issues?

What difference does it make, for who actually reads the cards or looks at the stamps? Maybe few do. But if we do not declare our faith in Him also in these little ways, even fewer people will pay any attention to His birthday at all. Since He came for all people, don't we want to use every opportunity we can to help all people at least think of Him? Your Christmas card witness could be used by the Holy Spirit to help a person at least begin to consider Who He really is.

O Lord, work through the message which my Christmas cards take to others. Amen.

Christmas Seals

Joseph, her husband, was a righteous man and didn't want to disgrace her. So he decided to divorce her secretly.
Matthew 1:19

The first known use of Christmas seals was in 1904 when a Danish mail worker sold 1¢ stamps to benefit the Copenhagen TB hospital. The custom spread to the United States in 1907, although charity stamps had been used in Civil War days, just not at Christmas time.

Christmas seals today still are a way of raising money for institutions which help people with special needs. If they portray a witness to Jesus' birthday, so much the better.

Many people give to help the needy during the Christmas season. The Salvation Army, Coats for Kids, Toys for Tots, Christmas dream trees, and Christmas baskets are examples of such helping.

But what about the rest of the year? Many charities need to receive much extra in December to make up for the lack of contributions during the other eleven months.

Because Jesus came to help us in our need for the forgiveness of our sins and because He came so we might have forgiveness all year long, shouldn't we for His sake try to help those who are in need every month, not just at Christmas time?

I know I can't help everyone, Lord, but work in me now and throughout the year to help at least some who are in need. Amen.

Christmas Concerts

After he thought about it, he saw an angel of the Lord in a dream, who said, "Joseph, son of David, don't be afraid to take your wife Mary home with you; her Child is from the Holy Spirit." *Matthew 1:20*

Music!   Glorious music!   To praise God!   For Jesus the Savior!

That's why for centuries stirring Christmas concerts have been presented in these weeks before Christmas. Bach's "Christmas Oratorio", written in 1734, still is often sung in orchestral Christmas concerts, while the Christmas half of Handel's "Messiah", written in a mere 24 days in 1742, is even more familiar.

Taking time to attend a Christmas concert with music that has thrilled Christians for hundreds of years or which has recently been written for church choirs today, can lift our hearts and minds above the Santa Claus songs so prevalent in our world so that we keep remembering *Who* Christmas is really all about: that Child Who was miraculously conceived by the Holy Spirit to be born of the Virgin Mary.

How thankful and thrilled I am, Lord, for the joyful Christmas concerts I have heard, whether presented by professional singers or by a local church choir. Amen.

December 8   Read: Matthew 8

Christmas Carols

She will have a Son, and you will call Him Jesus, because He will save His people from their sins. *Matthew 1:21*

Supposedly, Jacopone de Todi, a follower of St. Francis of Assisi, wrote the first true Christmas carol. To be sure, some of our carols date back into the early centuries of the Christian Church, but they were primarily church music. Jacopone wrote for ordinary people in their own language.

Since then, Christmas carols have become a regular part of Christmas concerts and the Christmas worship life of the church, but they really need to be part of our daily music in these days leading to Christmas. Why hum "Jingle Bells", when we could sing "Away in a Manger" or "Silent Night" or "Angels We Have Heard on High" or "Joy to the World"? Why save these for only Christmas Eve and Christmas Day, when we could be blessed by their message day by day until then?

But wouldn't we get tired of them, if we sang them every day? Not if we pay attention to their message: the message that the Child Whose birthday we will celebrate is named "Jesus, because He will save His people from their sins". Which He did, not just by being born, but by suffering and dying to make us sinners "His people" forever through faith.

Use the music and the message of Christmas carols, O Holy Spirit, to keep me thankful for Jesus, my Savior. Amen.

The Christmas Tree

All this happened so that what the Lord said through the prophet would come true: "The virgin will conceive and have a Son, and He will be called Immanuel", which means "God-with-us". *Matthew 1:22-23*

Some claim that Martin Luther in the early 1500s was the first person to bring an evergreen tree into his home as a Christmas tree. Certain pagan religions have worshiped particular trees, but for a Christian the evergreen tree at Christmas is only a symbol of Jesus.

Not a leaf-less tree, but a living evergreen gives its life to bring beauty to our eyes at Christmas. So Jesus, alive in a way no other human could ever be, since He was God come to earth, gave His perfect life into death on the cross to bring the beauty of eternal life to us sinners.

A Christmas tree lives for a few days after being cut down and then is dead forever. Jesus was physically dead for a few days, but then rose to life again. Because He lives, He still is Immanuel, God with us, forgiving, comforting, guiding, helping us through the power of His Word.

Lord Jesus, help me remember that You are alive and with me always, just as You have promised, to help and guide me daily. Amen.

Chrismons: Christ Ornaments For Christmas

When Joseph awoke, he did what the Lord's angel had ordered him to do. He took his wife home with him but didn't have relations with her until she had a son. And He called Him Jesus. *Matthew 1:24-25*

What is a Christmas tree without lights and ornaments and other decorations? But why use ornaments which say nothing about Him Whose birthday is being celebrated?

Therefore, many Christians use what are called "Chrismons", ornaments in the form of symbols which teach us about Jesus: Who He is, what He did when He was on earth, and why He did it. Some congregations make elaborate Chrismons with beads and pearls strung on wire into symbol form. Simpler Chrismons for the home can be made of Styrofoam and glitter. What materials are used is not as important as the symbol that is made: a manger, a star, a shepherd's staff, a cross – any symbol of the Christian faith.

Chrismons make a Christmas tree not only beautiful, but meaningful. We see and are reminded that Jesus, though born like an ordinary child, came in God's plan so we, who do not always do as the Lord has commanded, might have forgiveness of our sins and power to obey Him better.

Help me keep in mind, O Lord, that You do forgive me daily because of Jesus so I don't get discouraged over not being able to live for You more faithfully. Amen.

Christmas Tree Lights

Jesus was born in Bethlehem in Judea when Herod was king. Then wise men came from the east to Jerusalem. "Where is the Child Who was born King of the Jews?" they asked. "We saw His star in the east and have come to worship Him." *Matthew 2:1-2*

Originally, Christmas tree lights were burning candles. Especially when seen through strands of spun glass (called "angel hair"), their flickering glow looks like twinkling stars. For safety's sake candles aren't used any more; instead we use Christmas tree lights, invented and first used in New York City in 1882.

Why not, however, when we look at our specially lighted tree, remember that special starry light seen by Wise Men in the east, which drew them to search for the One "born King of the Jews"? We don't know exactly what they saw – we don't know how they knew it was a sign about Jesus; we only know they came searching.

How blessed we are to know that Jesus came, not as king for only one nation, but as Savior for all sinners, including us.

There still are people searching in life, searching for meaning and peace. How blessed they will be, if we help them see Jesus as the One Who will give them meaning and peace, not just for this life, but even forever.

Do any of the people you know show they are searching? How can you help them to see Jesus?

Somehow use me, Lord, even today in this Christmas season, if possible, to help someone come to You. Amen.

Luminarias To Light The Way

When King Herod heard about this, he became alarmed and all Jerusalem with him. He called together all of the people's ruling priests and Bible scholars and tried to find out from them where the Christ was to be born. "In Bethlehem, in Judea," they told him, "because the prophet has written: And you, Bethlehem, land of Judah ... from you will come a leader Who will be the Shepherd of My people Israel." *Matthew 2:3-6*

Especially in the southwest people set out luminaries (called "farolitos" by some) on Christmas Eve by their homes, on their streets, to their churches. The tradition of luminaries (small candles flickering inside paper sacks) was to symbolically light the way of the Christ Child to enter that home or that church. Now luminaries have usually become only a form of Christmas decoration.

But we want Jesus to enter our hearts and lives. He comes, however, not because of outward forms but through His Word. The Wise Men learned, when they searched for Jesus, that the directions they needed were available only in God's Word.

Christmas symbols of all kinds can be helpful; but the only way Jesus really comes to us is as we use God's Word – His Word about our sinning so that then we become thankful for His Word about our being forgiven through Him, Who didn't need guiding lights but only His love to bring Him to the manger and finally to His cross.

Thank You, O Holy Spirit, for having used Your Word to bring Jesus to me so that I can be sure of being forgiven also today. Amen.

This Is The Christmas Spirit?

Then Herod secretly called the wise men and found out from them the exact time the star had appeared. Then he sent them to Bethlehem. "Go and search carefully for the little Child," he said. "And when you find Him, report to me, so that I too may go and bow down before Him." *Matthew 2:7-8*

Sure, Herod! You want to worship the new-born king? But we know from what you did that it was really murder you had in mind. Such hypocrisy!

Yet isn't hypocrisy still a large part of the modern observance of Christmas? These days we hear much about "the Christmas spirit". True, sometimes it means: helping those less fortunate than you. But even that usually means: Buy them things – and say it came from Santa Claus! More things? And Santa Claus? This is "the Christmas spirit"?

Yet we also can get caught up in that "spirit", both in the wanting of things and in the thinking that things will really make Christmas happy for us and those we love. But how can soon-broken or quickly-forgotten things and how can a myth bring happiness? These haven't worked in past years; how can they work now?

Instead, our joy in life can only be based on having peace, peace with God. And our peace with God can only be based on the birthday Child of Christmas: Jesus, Who came not to give us things, but to take sins from us so God would accept us as His people. That is the Christmas spirit which gives us joy, whether we have many things or not.

Help me today, Lord, so I don't think so much about things, but have joy because of peace with You through Jesus. Amen.

Did Scrooge Find The Christmas Spirit?

In those days Caesar Augustus ordered a census taken of the whole world. This census took place while Quirinius was ruling Syria. *Luke 2:1-2*

We all know about Ebenezer Scrooge in Dickens' story, "A Christmas Carol". Like Caesar he wanted only money, more money! (Why else did Caesar want a census except to increase tax collections?) But after a terrifying dream Scrooge "found the Christmas spirit". Or did he?

According to many "the Christmas spirit" is charity, helping the needy. God does want us to help others, of course. But that is not "the Christmas spirit" for God's people. Instead "the Christmas spirit" actually is to be more consciously aware and thankful for the Savior – not just that He came, but that He did all He had to do throughout His entire life, especially by His death.

The most the unbelieving world might think about Jesus at Christmas is "that poor little baby". But we use our Christian Christmas customs to remind ourselves daily that His being a man on a cross was more important than His being just a baby in a manger, for that is how He is our Savior. That is the spirit which joyfully guides us to help others.

Help me, Holy Spirit, to be joyful when I help others by keeping me aware that I am doing it because of Jesus. Amen.

Christmas Yard Decorations

Everyone went to register, each to his own town. Joseph also went up from the town of Nazareth in Galilee to David's town, called Bethlehem, in Judea, because he was of the house and family of David. *Luke 2:3-4*

Do you decorate your yard at Christmas? Some families do, but why? Undoubtedly some enjoy the beauty they create, include a witness to the Savior's birth, and want to share this with others.

But just as undoubtedly some get carried away by human pride to put out gigantic displays which say in lights: Look at us! Look at us!

We who are God's people through faith in Jesus must constantly guard against inner pride which shows off outwardly. God calls us not just to stay away from sin, but to do as much good as we can as Christian citizens, as Christian neighbors, as helpers to others in their needs. But always our purpose must be not to attract attention to ourselves, but to encourage people to give attention to Jesus, Who came into the world also for them.

True, others will notice us in what we do in this Christmas season. But if we show in our decorations and say with our Christmas songs that Jesus is the One we care about more than anything else at Christmas, they might also be drawn toward following Him with us.

Lord Jesus, may others see You through what I do now in the Christmas season and all year long. Amen.

The Children's Christmas "Program"?

(Joseph went there) to register with Mary, his fiancee, who was going to have a child. *Luke 2:5*

Many churches in the Christmas season have a special service for the congregation with children reciting the Christmas Bible verses and singing carols – the "Children's Program" is what it usually is called.

"Program"? Is it intended to show off cute children or to honor the Child Whose birthday is being celebrated? Do we attend a "program" to see children now or to hear what they are saying about the Savior Who was born?

Truly it is heart-warming to listen as children and youth speak and sing the message of that holy night when God came to earth in a Baby's birth. But what is our attitude? To look at them or to have them help us worship Him? Is it a "program" to us or a worship service? Our attitude will greatly influence the children involved, either to perform for us or to help us praise Him by what they do.

Lord, help me be an influence on others, young and old, to keep worship of You uppermost in our minds and hearts all through these days of Christmas, for then everything else in this season will be both satisfying and strengthening. Amen.

Finding The Right Present

And while they were there, the time came for her to have her child. She had her first Son, and she wrapped Him in strips of cloth and laid Him in a manger. *Luke 2:6-7*

Only a few shopping days left! Have you found the right present for each one on your Christmas gift list yet? Is the "right present", however, what a person wants or what that person needs?

People usually just want things – that's what shopping ads are all about! But things never satisfy for very long. That's why people soon want more things, different things. We also are tempted to think exactly the same way.

God has given us all so many things as we live. But His "right present" for everyone on His list, that is, for everyone in the world, is what everyone needs most of all: forgiveness of sins so we can be His people on earth and into eternity. Therefore, He has given us that needed gift, wrapped up in the Baby Who became the Man Who hung on a cross. In Him we have joy no mater what other things we might receive at Christmas.

Thank You, O Lord, for giving me what I need most: forgiveness of sins through Jesus. Amen.

Who's Knocking There?

She wrapped Him in strips of cloth and laid Him in a manager because there was no room for them in the inn. *Luke 2:7*

A little-known German Christmas carol is called: "Who's Knocking There?" It portrays Joseph and Mary going from house to house, looking for a place to spend what became the first Christmas night. Tradition says they were turned away by many – God's Word says only that "there was no room for them in the inn" except for an animal's stall out in a cave-barn.

In this way God-come-to-earth began a life of humility which led to the humiliation of a cross-death. He accepted such rejection so that we who should be rejected by God forever because of our sinning might be accepted into eternal blessings instead.

Do we hear Him knocking, however, as He wants to enter every area of our lives to guide all we do and say? He does not bang on our hearts with great emotional feelings, but knocks quietly through His Word (even in this little devotion) to make us think of what He did for us and what thankfully we can do for Him, yes, even as we live this day.

Lord, help me so that You more fully enter and control all my deeds and words and thoughts today and daily. Amen.

Dreaming Of A White Christmas?

There were shepherds not far away, living in the field and taking turns watching their flock during the night. *Luke 2:8*

The traditional American Christmas scene has to include snow – unless you live where snow rarely falls. Was there snow when Jesus was born? Most likely not, for shepherds camping out in the pasture fields to watch their flocks through the night implies it was early spring, perhaps even lambing time, not the dead of winter. The fact is: we don't know for sure in which season Jesus was born.

Yet, snow at Christmas is a good symbol for why the Christ Child lived His life and died. Bare northern winter landscapes are ugly with frozen ground, dead weeds, and often dreary skies. What a difference a snowfall makes! Everywhere there is beauty as sunlight glistens off all those snowflakes!

Before God and even to our own consciences the landscapes of our lives are ugly with sin: cold hearts at times, deadly words, dreary attitudes, outright wrong actions. To which His Word promises: "Though your sins have become like scarlet cloth, they will turn white as snow" (*Isaiah 1:18*). In His plan the One born in an animal stall shed His red blood to cover over our sins so that, as we trust in Him to save us, God's "Son-light" makes us now in His sight as beautiful as a white Christmas.

Thank You, Lord, for bringing me to faith in Jesus so that You have covered up also my sins in Your sight through what He did by His birth and suffering and death. Amen.

Christmas Eve Candlelight Services

Then an angel of the Lord stood by them, and the Lord's glory shone around them. They were terrified. *Luke 2:9*

It must have been a moonless night, when Jesus was born. Why else would the light of the Lord's glory so terrify those shepherds? Then they made their way to a dark cave-barn, probably lighted only by a glowing lantern or two. No halo of glory was around the head of the Child there, just an ordinary-looking baby, though born in not so ordinary conditions.

On Christmas Eve we likely will make our way to a candlelight worship service. The darkened church, lighted only by flickering candles, reminds us of that animal stall with our Savior's first bed, a hay-filled feed trough. How could such a one in such a place be God? Where is His glory?

The shepherds teach us. Because they heard God's message, with eyes of faith they could see God's glory, His love, being revealed in that little One. Not the glow of candlelight, but God's message about that little One and what He would do is what makes a Christmas Eve candlelight service so special and meaningful for us. He was willing to come so humbly and then die so horribly for you and me? How glorious He is!

Let Your glory, Your love, Lord, shine also through me as I joyfully, but humbly praise You in these Christmas days. Amen.

Don't Be Afraid!

"Don't be afraid," the angel said to them. *Luke 2:10*

Fear! Fear of what might happen in our world! Fear of what might happen to us personally in our lives! Fear surely can plague us.

Yet the worst fear is fear of God because of what *He* might do to us! Even we who do believe the message that Jesus came to rescue us, even we can have this fear gnawing in the background of our feelings. Then in those times when God's Law forcefully gives us guilt over a particular sin, that fear becomes more vivid to make us wonder: can God really forgive me? when I've done that!

Such was the terror of those Christmas night shepherds, as they realized they were spotlighted in the shining glory of the holy God! Yet the angel of the Lord said: Do not be afraid! Fear not! Why? A hymn stanza has the answer:
> *What harm can sin and death then do?*
> *The true God now abides with you.*
> *Let hell and Satan rage and chafe,*
> *Christ is your Brother – ye are safe!*

Because He came, every sin, all our sins, are forgiven. So, though we never want to willingly sin, no matter that we do keep on sinning, we have peace, not fear, because of Jesus.

Thank You, Jesus that because of Your coming I don't have to fear, though I still sin. Amen.

Good News!

The angel said to them: "I have good news for you."
Luke 2:10

So much of the news these days is bad news! despairing news! fearful news! The violence and cruelty of criminals, the personal tragedy of accidents which kill or maim, the heartache of families torn by conflict, the destructiveness of catastrophes! Such is what usually fills the news broadcasts even in these Christmas season days. True, occasionally some good news events are mentioned; but those are so few and all the evil is so inundating that life can seem hopeless.

Yet the angel says: Good news! Good news can be reported in this sin-filled world! Not about peace on earth between warring nations, ethnic clans, or criminal gangs – not about the end of calamities and tragedies and conflicts and sinning – none of these will stop as long as this world exists.

Instead, we are given the good news of God's love for sinners: shown in the Baby become the Man on the cross, given to us now by God's forgiveness as we trust in that Savior, Who lived and died and rose to life again to rescue us.

This good news does not solve all our problems, but it gives us comfort and strength to go on with confidence in God in spite of all the bad news we hear each day.

Lord, help me daily to have hope and confidence because of Your love and power. Amen.

Great Joy!

"Don't be afraid," the angel said to them. "I have good news for you. A great joy will come to all the people. *Luke 2:10*

Christmas is the time for joy, isn't it? The point of all the gift-giving is to make others happy and to be happy yourself, isn't it? "Merry Christmas" is the usual greeting heard these days.

But did you notice how those words changed from "joy" to "happy" to "merry"? That's because the way of the world never brings joy, real joy, lasting joy. Things may make us happy for a while, Christmas activities may be merry while they are happening, and occasionally we do have joy in family love or friendships. But all these leave us empty sooner or later, even loving relationships. Why? Because sin always eventually ruins even the best of what we have and do. Sin and joy cannot co-exist.

So when the angel announced "great joy will come to all the people", forgiveness of sins is what was meant, forgiveness of sins through the Child born that night. Through Jesus God destroys the power and the punishment of sin so that even though sin remains in our lives here on earth, we are comforted to know it will not keep us from God and His eternal blessings. Therefore, we can sincerely sing at Christmas and be comforted all life long:

Joy to the world!
The Lord has come! Amen!

Savior! Christ! Lord!

"The Savior, Who is Christ the Lord, was born for you today in David's town. *Luke 2:11*

We've read and heard these words about Jesus so often that we perhaps think of them only as names for Him without grasping their meaning. Those terrified shepherds, however, knew!

"Savior" meant: the One Who would rescue them, not from occupation by an earthly power, but from the power of sin and death and the devil which threatened to destroy them forever.

"Christ" meant: the promised One of God, Who would do this work of rescuing them, the One Whom already Adam and Abraham and all the Old Testament people of God had trusted in without knowing His name but in response to God's promises.

"Lord" meant: "Immanuel", God with us, God come to earth so He would have the power to rescue them and all people.

What exciting news this was for them! At last God's promises were being fulfilled! No wonder they "hurried" (*v.16*) to see "what they had been told about this Child" (*v.17*)!

We cannot feel the emotional excitement those shepherds felt. But because we know Who He is and how He carried out His work as Savior for all, we make our way mentally to that manger bed this evening to give Him our praise.

O come, let us adore Him, Christ, the Lord! Amen!

Glory to God! Peace on Earth!

"Glory to God in the highest heavens, and on earth peace, among people who have His good will." *Luke 2:14*

How especially blessed those shepherds were! They were the only human audience for the most magnificent choir ever assembled, a heavenly host of angels come from eternity to give glory to God!

The angels' praise was not because they themselves benefited from what God had done; they already enjoy God's eternal blessings. Instead, they gave their praise, because they were awe-struck at God's good will toward us sinners!

For why should God care about us specks of life in His tremendous universe, especially since daily we fight against Him by our sinning?

Yet, instead of unleashing His destructive punishment upon us, He gives us peace through the gift of His Son, Who gave Himself not only into the poverty of His birthplace, but also into the agony of His deathplace. Jesus is God's good will to us.

So, in humility and joy our Christmas praise is:
> *Hark! The herald angels sing:*
> *"Glory to the new-born King;*
> *Peace on earth and mercy mild,*
> *God and sinners reconciled."*

To which we say:
> *Amen! Alleluia!*

Twelve Days Of Christmas?

The shepherds went back, glorifying and praising God for everything they had heard and seen. It was just as they had been told. *Luke 2:20*

You've probably heard the old English carol, "The Twelve Days of Christmas". Now it sounds like merely a generous love song; originally, however, each gift mentioned, some say, secretly symbolized a Christian teaching, one for each day after Christmas until Epiphany, which commemorates the coming of the Wise Men to the Christ Child.

But who continues Christmas for so long in our modern culture? Take down the tree, put away the decorations, clean up the clutter as soon as possible is the attitude of most.

Wouldn't we benefit, however, if we continued our Christmas celebration in the days after Christmas, especially in song? Think how the shepherds continued to "glorify and praise God" after they had worshiped the little One Whom God's angel had told them was "the Savior! Christ! the Lord!"

Perhaps you could begin your own tradition of singing a Christmas carol or other hymn each day after Christmas until January 6th, Epiphany. For that matter, since God's blessings through Jesus continue each day, why not sing a different hymn of praise to God each day of the entire year?

I praise You, O God, for Your blessings to me through Jesus not just at Christmas but every day of the year. Amen.

After-Christmas Let-Down

After the wise men left, Joseph saw an angel of the Lord in a dream, who said, "Get up, take the little Child and His mother, and flee to Egypt. Stay there until I tell you." *Matthew 2:13*

About now, two days after Christmas, you perhaps have felt an after-Christmas let-down: family visitors have gone home, decorations are put away, and gifts have lost at least some of their thrill. What's more, probably life has begun to get back into its old routine: get up, rush to work (if you are young enough) or just fill up the hours (if you are old enough or lonely), then to bed to start it all over again – at least that's how life sometimes can feel.

Don't be too surprised to especially suffer an emotional let-down after a holiday. It can happen to God's people, because we still have the sinful nature. Also, if we suffer from some real difficulties of life or pains of body, maybe we were able to set them aside somewhat in the excitement of Christmas, but now they take over our thoughts again.

Yet, God gives us guidance and strength to endure whatever each day holds. As we think again that the Baby of Christmas was not just a baby, but our Savior, Who had to endure danger and discomfort not too long after His birth as well as finally suffer for our sinning, we are comforted and strengthened to go on, no matter what He is allowing in our days.

Comfort me daily, Lord, but especially when life gets heavy for me. Amen.

To Go In Peace

Lord, now You are letting Your servant go in peace as You promised, because my eyes have seen Your salvation. *Luke 2:29-30*

Why do people die? Not really because of age nor illness nor accident, but because of sin; which is why also babies can and do die: not because of sin done to them, but because of sin done *by* them, for God's Word includes them also, when it flatly says: "Because all have sinned, death spread to all people" (*Romans 5:12*).

No one escapes sinning, and so no one can escape death (except those alive when Jesus returns on Judgment Day). The only difference in people dying is: do you die at peace with God or not?

No matter how much good we have done this past year, no matter how few sins we think we have done, there could be no peace for us by ourselves. Just three sins a day (and hasn't it been much more daily for each of us?) would total over a thousand for the past year – then multiply that by each year we have lived; what a record of peace-breaking on our part!

Our only peace is to "see Your salvation", the salvation belonging to God, which He gives us through Jesus and His work of making peace for us. That peace He personally gives to us through the message of His Word and Holy Communion.

As we "see" Jesus by faith, we have peace with God while we live now; and when we die, we also will go in peace.

Humbly I thank You, Lord, for having peace with You through Jesus in spite of all my sinning this past year. Amen.

Coming Toward The End?

So while we are in this tent, we sigh, feeling distressed because we don't want to put off this body but put on the other and have life swallow up our death. *2 Corinthians 5:4*

Especially as the years of life begin to pile up, coming to the end of a year can make you think more seriously about coming to the end of life. Even when younger, you may think back to remember those who died this past year. Then, if your body has more aches and pains than a year ago, you really can wonder about the length yet of your life on earth.

The strange thing is, however, although your body makes you feel that way, the "you" inside your body feels much the same as years ago. In fact, you may wonder why other people have gotten so old – until you happen to look at the family photo album and realize: I sure was young then!

The fact is that "you" never really get old, only your body does. Also, through faith in Jesus "you" are going to live forever! First without your body in God's presence after you die, and then in your resurrected body after Judgment Day.

When the end of your life or mine on earth will be, this year yet or next year or many years after, we cannot know. Because of Jesus, however, we are sure of where we are going, and that is enough.

Thank You, Jesus, for providing eternal life for me though I sure don't deserve it. Amen.

Finally at Home with Him

If the earthly tent we live in is torn down, we know we'll get one from God, not made by human hands but lasting forever in heaven. *2 Corinthians 5:1*

Have you had the experience of living in various parts of the country, but never feeling completely comfortable – until you moved to where you quickly felt "at home"? You had enjoyed other places, but something now satisfied a deep longing in you. You were "home"! Perhaps that is where you are now – perhaps you are still looking.

Unless this year has been filled with conflict, pain, financial stress, or loneliness, we most likely enjoy life here on earth, at least at times. We have seen beauty, felt loved, heard thrilling music, experienced satisfaction in helping others. Life has not been perfect, but it's at least been acceptable.

Yet we probably also feel an inner unsettled yearning from time to time. Perhaps how quickly a year goes by triggers it – perhaps a hollowness attaches itself to what we accomplish. Whatever it is, we don't feel totally content.

That's as it should be, if we are God's people. Because Jesus paid for us by His life and death, we belong to Him. We are no longer completely of this world – we have an eternal home.

We don't know if we will live through the entire coming year. If we do, we will be thankful for the blessings He gives us. But if we don't, we will finally be at home with Him.

Thank You, Lord, for life here and the eternal home You will give me because of Jesus, my Savior. Amen.

The Path Of Life

We go through life by faith, not by sight. *2 Corinthians 5:7*

As we come to the close of this year of devotions together, the following song might be helpful to you. It was composed while reflecting on how we need to follow God's guidance by faith even though we so often cannot see what His plan for us might be.

> *The path of life is never smooth;*
> *It has its joys but sad times, too.*
> *That's when we ask: Lord, must these be?*
> *Such burdens to bear when we're serving Thee.*
>
> *Our Savior came and brought God's grace.*
> *On Calvary's cross He took our place*
> *To die in pain that we might gain*
> *All sins forgiv'n and a home in heaven.*
>
> *So the children of God faithfully face*
> *The troubles of their time and place;*
> *For we are sure we will endure*
> *To finish our race by the power of His grace.*
>
> *Yes, the path of life may be hard and long,*
> *But in His hands it won't go wrong.*
> *He'll take us through all that will come*
> *Until we are safe in our heavenly home,*
> *Until we are safe in our heavenly home.*

May you also see God's love and guidance as you live with faith in Jesus no matter the "rattlesnakes" or the "rainbows" that come in the year or years still ahead of you on *The Path of Life.*

Written and music composed in September of 1989 while moving from Rathdrum, Idaho, to Truth or Consequences, New Mexico.